Stanislavsky on
The Art of the Stage

Konstantin Stanislavsky

STANISLAVSKY

ON

THE ART OF

THE STAGE

translated

with an Introductory Essay

on Stanislavsky's 'System'

by

DAVID

MAGARSHACK

Faber and Faber Limited

3 Queen Square

London

First published in 1950
by Faber and Faber Limited
3 Queen Square London W.C.1
First published in this edition 1967
Reprinted 1973 and 1977
Printed in Great Britain by
Alden & Mowbray Ltd, at the Alden Press, Oxford
All rights reserved

ISBN 0 571 08172 X (Faber Paperbacks)
ISBN 0 571 06935 5 (hard bound edition)

Contents

PREFACE TO SECOND EDITION

The Stanislavsky 'system' has been adapted in one form or another by many schools of acting, including the school of acting known as the Method, the chief practitioner and high priest of which is Mr. Lee Strasberg, the principal of the New York Actors' Studio. It was the Group Theatre, a shortlived theatrical venture started in New York by Mr. Harold Clurman and Mr. Lee Strasberg, that actively propagated the Stanislavsky 'system' in the United States, on which the Method is said to be based. The Method propagandists obtained their first notion of Stanislavsky's theories from Mrs. Hapgood's translation of Stanislavsky's works. These translations, however, fail to convey Stanislavsky's always hesitant approach to the art of acting. In his introduction to the first authoritative analysis of the Method* by Mr. Robert Lewis (another Method specialist), Mr. Clurman defines the Method as 'a codified formalization of the technique of acting', and in his account of the Group Theatre, published under the title of *The Fervent Years*,† Mr. Clurman defines the aim of the Stanislavsky system as 'a way of enabling the actor to use himself more consciously as an instrument for the attainment of truth on the stage'—definitions that Stanislavsky would have considered to be contrary to the whole spirit of his 'system'.

In a talk to the actors and producers of the Moscow Art Theatre two years before his death in 1938, Stanislavsky most emphatically repudiated any attempt to 'codify' his system. 'There can be no question', he declared, 'of "your" or "my" system. There is only one system—creative organic nature. There is no other system. And we must remember', he went on, 'that this so-called system (let us not talk of the system, but of the nature of creative art) does not remain stationary. It changes every day.'

---

* *Method—or Madness?*, Heinemann & Co., 1960.
† Hill & Wang, Inc., New York, 1957.

1

Preface to Second Edition

Having begun as a producer-autocrat, Stanislavksy ended by recognising the unique position of the actor on the stage, a position that must not be imperilled by the imposition of an extraneous interpretation of his part, as is generally the case with producers in England and the United States. Moreover, he came to the conclusion that an actor's training is only possible in the theatre. To Stanislavsky the very idea of an actor who does not form part of a permanent company is inconceivable. No less inconceivable to him is the idea that an actor could be trained in his or anyone else's system or method outside a theatre, which to him meant a permanent company of actors and actresses not worried by the problem of getting a job and not 'rested' as soon as the play in which they are acting comes to the end of its run. 'First of all,' he told the Moscow Art Theatre actors and producers, 'one has to create a company—it is only then that you will have both a play and a theatre.' The idea of an Actors' Studio divorced from a theatre would have appeared bizarre to Stanislavsky. However, considering the chaotic state of the theatre in England and the United States, any place where an actor can get some training is not to be dismissed out of hand, however exaggerated or even grotesque the claims of those who run such training centres may be. Anything is better than to let an actor eat his heart out in idleness. The danger is that the actor may become what Mr. Robert Lewis calls 'a true believer'. But no actor worth his salt would. A real artist creates his own individual art and is capable of digesting any 'method'. It is only the second-rate actor who becomes what is generally known in the profession as a 'Method actor'.

It was during the last years of his life that Stanislavsky began an experiment which the Method practitioners seem to have made into one of the chief elements of their instruction. Stanislavsky was concerned with what he called 'the logic and sequence of feelings' and he thought it might be achieved by giving the actor a general idea of his part and then making him improvise it with his own words. 'At first,' Stanislavsky explained, 'I am trying not to give the actor any words at all. All I want is the bare bones of action. When the actor has gone through it, he has gained a sort of inward line of action which he begins to under-

2

stand with his body and muscles. When this has been done, the actor begins to see what he has to aim at. A moment will come when he will have to act for a certain reason. It is at that point that he will begin his search. . . .' Stanislavsky had never really applied this purely theoretical idea to prove its efficacy in practice. The 'Method' practitioners were more enterprising in this respect. They appear to concentrate on improvisation in which actors are made to play scenes similar to those in the play but with their own dialogue. This is supposed to make the actor more aware of the meaning of each situation and lead to the achievement of the right mood through his own resources. The creation of a 'mood' by recalling an experience giving rise to a similar mood in the actor's private life is, of course, something that Stanislavsky and his followers have practised to a larger or smaller extent. But it may be well to remember that the achievement of a true emotional mood in this way very often merely becomes the achievement of a false emotion imposed on the actor by his producer or his 'Method' instructor. Megalomania is an endemic disease of the theatre. Stanislavsky's 'system', unlike the Method, is indeed chiefly concerned with the elimination of what Stanislavsky called 'the ignorant maniacs' of the theatre. 'The highest wisdom', Stanislavsky wrote, 'is the realisation of one's own ignorance. I have got as far as that and I freely admit that in the sphere of intuition and the subconscious I know nothing except that these secrets are known only to artist-nature.'

But there was something else Stanislavsky (as, indeed, most other producers) did not know because the subject has never really been studied—namely, the art of the dramatist. The facile assumption so prevalent among producers and actors that anything written in dialogue is *ipso facto* a play is to a large extent responsible for their inability to distinguish between the work of a dramatist and something written for the stage by a novelist or a poet. There is, of course, the further danger to the art of the dramatist that 'producers of genius', of whom there seems to be quite a big crop, do not hesitate to destroy the work of the dramatist for the sake of achieving some meretricious success by some theatrical trick or other. Stanislavsky was keenly aware of this danger. Indeed, he had the terrible example of Vsevolod

Meyerhold, the great assassin of the art of the dramatist, always before him. To Stanislavsky the dramatist was the only lawgiver on the stage. Unfortunately, he knew nothing of the laws of drama. To him *A Month in the Country* was a dramatic work no less than *The Cherry Orchard*. He never realised that Turgenev's 'play' was merely a short story in dialogue, whereas Chekhov's comedy was the work of a dramatist of genius. He thought that the best way of discovering the dramatist's intention was by finding the 'ruling idea' and the 'through-action' of his play. 'I work a great deal,' he wrote, 'and it is my considered opinion that there are only two things that count in the final analysis: the ruling idea and through-action—that is the main thing in the art of acting. . . . Why did audiences like us? Because we understood our ruling idea. And when we did not understand it we got nothing right.'

Here, however, Stanislavsky is doubly wrong: the fact that a play is a success does not mean that the producers and the actors have interpreted the author's intention and ideas rightly, and the best proof of that is the young Stanislavsky's production of *The Seagull*, which so outraged Chekhov that he declared that he would not let them perform the fourth act of the play because it was not his at all; secondly, it is quite possible to misinterpret the ruling idea of a play and still get it accepted and, as with *The Cherry Orchard*, impose this wrong interpretation not only on the Russian stage, but have it adopted by the rest of the world. Chekhov's comment on Stanislavsky's production of *The Cherry Orchard* as a tragedy was: 'Stanislavsky has ruined the play for me.' Now, it is a remarkable fact that 'the terrible scenes', as Chekhov's wife described them, between Chekhov and Stanislavsky and Nemirovich-Danchenko, the other director of the Moscow Art Theatre, have remained a complete blank in the history of the relationship between Chekhov and the Moscow Art Theatre. Stanislavsky has left his reminiscences of Chekhov and so have some of the actors of the Moscow Art Theatre, but no account is extant of what exactly happened during those preliminary discussions of the productions of Chekhov's plays. Why was Chekhov so furious? What was it that brought about this clash between him and Stanislavsky? *The Cherry Orchard*, as it is still produced by the Moscow Art Theatre, makes it abundantly clear that the chief reason for these rows was Stanislavsky's failure to understand Chekhov's art as a dramatist.

A small scene from the first act of *The Cherry Orchard* in the recent Moscow Art Theatre production in London will perhaps best illustrate this point. Varya and Anya are discussing the impending sale by public auction of the cherry orchard or, in other words, Mrs. Ranevsky's estate.

ANYA: Well, has the interest on the mortgage been paid?

VARYA: Good heavens, no.

ANYA: Oh dear, oh dear. . . .

LOPAKHIN (poking his head in at the door, bleats): Bah-h-h. . .

In the Moscow Art Theatre production Chekhov's stage direction is completely ignored. Instead of poking his head in at the door, Lopakhin for some extraordinary reason is sent out to fetch a huge trunk and comes in dragging it across the stage and, as he approaches the two girls, whose conversation he could not possibly have overheard, turns to them and bleats. The reason, of course, why any producer changes a playwright's stage directions is that he fails to understand their purport. To relegate Lopakhin to the position of a menial, however, is so much against the whole spirit of the play that it is clear that it is not only the particular stage direction the Moscow Art Theatre did not know what to make of, but that this misinterpretation of the scene is merely one tiny piece of evidence of its misinterpretation of the whole play.

The play opens with Lopakhin waiting for the arrival of Mrs. Ranevsky from abroad in the small hours of the morning. The question, surely, a producer of the play ought to ask himself is why does Chekhov open the play with Lopakhin. Or, to put it another way, why does Lopakhin, a man who is fully conscious of his position as a big business man, a tycoon who demands to be treated with respect, a man whose business interests are so vast that he cannot spare a moment for social calls, why does such a man spend a sleepless night, baring his soul to a maidservant, in expectation of the arrival of a woman he had not seen for years? What has brought him there? Could he not have come to pay his respects to Mrs. Ranevsky, who was the first human being to treat him decently and to whom he owed a debt of gratitude, at some more convenient time? The reason becomes clear before the end of the first act: Lopakhin has a plan for saving the cherry orchard and thus repaying the debt he owes to its owner. He has a plan! He is so full of it that he cannot suppress his excitement: he even blames himself for having fallen asleep. Unless his terrific excitement is shown from the very first appearance of Lopakhin on the stage, from the moment, in fact, the curtain goes up on the first act, and the growing tension round the theme of the cherry orchard clearly indicated, the whole play collapses—as indeed it does collapse into a sort of *inactive*, so-called Chekhovian, morass of mood and feeling, which so aroused Chekhov's disgust at its first performance. This mounting excitement of Lopakhin's Chekhov conveyed in the little scene between Lopakhin, Anya and Varya. Lopakhin is so obsessed with his plan (and, indeed, it is the only way to save the estate from bankruptcy) that he walks about restlessly all over the house and, hearing the two girls speaking, listens at the door and, unable to disguise his contempt for the feeble way in which they are trying to think of some way of preventing the sale of the cherry orchard, pokes his head in and bleats. Unless, therefore, this mounting excitement, so essential to the mounting tension of the play which finally explodes in the third act, is conveyed by the actor, this little scene becomes meaningless and the producer, who has failed to appreciate its importance to the development of the action, does not know what to do with it and, as is all too common with producers, does not hesitate to change the playwright's stage direction to cover up his ignorance. In the Moscow Art Theatre production of *The Cherry Orchard* this reduction of the ruling idea of the play to a *personal* level is the real reason of Stanislavsky's misinterpretation of Chekhov's masterpiece. It explains why he turned it into the familiar tear-jerker instead of what it really is—a high comedy where the fate of the characters is irrelevant in the light of the great brooding intelligence of its creator contemplating a world in transition and the folly of man with sympathy and understanding, but also with the quizzical eye of a born humorist.

'An analysis of the actor's basic creative processes,' as Mr. Lee

Preface to Second Edition

Strasberg puts it,* 'regardless of the material he is working on', seems in view of the foregoing argument to be a rather fruitless pursuit. A technique of emotional experience, which Mr. Strasberg regards as 'an essential of any acting theory or practice', cannot, in fact, be divorced from the material the actor is working on. Even Stanislavsky's two main essentials—the ruling idea and through-action—can only be useful to the actor if he first comprehends the art of the dramatist and this can be achieved only through a thorough study of the dramatist's technique. Such a study, however, is completely neglected by the various schools of acting and the various 'methods' of acting, and so long as this is so, no amount of technical training in the art of acting will be of any avail for the achievement of a right interpretation of a dramatic masterpiece.

D. M.
1960

* Introduction to *The Paradox of Acting* by Denis Diderot and *Masks or Faces?* by William Archer. Hill & Wang, Inc., New York, 1957.

Introduction

I

The theory of acting, as evolved by Stanislavsky in his famous 'system', is not based on reasoning, as many of his critics assert, so much as on experience. It is the result of a lifetime devoted to the art of the stage, of years of experiment as actor and producer, and of a feeling of dissatisfaction with what passes for 'success' both among actors and audiences. While certain general principles of acting had been laid down by a number of famous actors and playwrights, these, Stanislavsky found, had never been reduced to a system with the result that teachers of acting have nothing on which to base their teaching, since 'inspiration' on which the theoreticians of the stage put so much stress, cannot be taught, nor can it be expected to materialise itself just when the actor needs it. Neither can producers be relied on to assist the actor in capturing this elusive 'inspiration'. 'Producers,' Stanislavsky writes, 'explain very cleverly what sort of result they want to get; they are only interested in the final result. They criticise and tell the actor what he should *not* do, but they do not tell him *how* to achieve the required result. The producer,' Stanislavsky adds, 'can do a great deal, but he cannot do everything by any means. For the main thing is in the hands of the actor, who must be helped and instructed first of all'.

Stanislavsky, who was born in Moscow in 1863 (he also died there in 1938), began his career as producer, both in his first amateur company and at the Moscow Art Theatre, as the still all too common type of producer-autocrat. 'I treated my actors as mannequins,' he declares. 'I showed them what I saw in my imagination, and they copied me. Whenever I was successful in getting the right feeling, the play came to life, but where I did not go beyond external invention, it was dead. The merit of my work at that time consisted in my endeavours to be sincere and to search for truth. I hated all falsehood on the stage, especially theatrical falsehood. I began to hate the theatre in the theatre,

11

and I was beginning to look for genuine life in it, not ordinary life, of course, but artistic life. Perhaps at the time I was not able to distinguish between the one and the other. Besides, I understood them only externally. But even external truth helped me to create truthful and interesting mise-en-scenes, which set me on the road to truth; truth gave birth to feeling, and feeling aroused creative intuition.'

What led Stanislavsky to abandon the methods of producer-autocrat and go in search of 'the elementary psychophysical and psychological laws of acting' was his study of the methods of the great actors, and, above all, those of the famous Italian actor Tommaso Salvini (1828–1916). Those methods were so simple and yet so difficult to copy. They seemed, moreover, to possess certain qualities that were common to all great actors, and indeed, looking back on his own experience as an actor and analysing his own most famous parts, and particularly his part of Stockmann in Ibsen's *An Enemy of the People*, Stanislavsky found that he too possessed the identical qualities. But the difference between him and Salvini was that while the latter seemed to be able not only to re-create them at will, but also in a way that was unique for every performance of the same play, he himself could not do it. After his first foreign tour in Germany with the Moscow Art Theatre in 1906, Stanislavsky went for a holiday in Finland, during which for the first time he tried to analyse his experience as an actor and producer and discover the laws of the technique of acting.

At the time Stanislavsky already enjoyed a world reputation. The Moscow Art Theatre, which he had founded with Nemiro-vich-Danchenko in 1898, was firmly established. He had behind him thirty years of theatrical activity, first among his own amateur group of actors from 1877 to 1887, then as producer of the Society of Art and Literature, founded by him, from 1888 to 1898, and lastly as one who was chiefly responsible for the stage productions of the Moscow Art Theatre. During that time, and especially since the foundation of the Moscow Art Theatre, he had created a gallery of stage characters which put him in the forefront of the greatest actors in Russia. He did it all the hard way, and not all his parts were successful. To take one example, his part as Trigorin in *The Seagull*, the play that launched the Moscow Art Theatre on the road to international fame and laid the foundations of Chekhov's reputation as one of the greatest playwrights of modern times, did not please Chekhov. 'Your acting,' Chekhov told Stanislavsky, 'is excellent, only you are not playing my character. I never wrote that.' And in a letter to Gorky, Chekhov complained that 'Trigorin walked about and talked as though he were paralysed; he has "no will of his own," so the actor interpreted that in a way that made me sick to look at him.' Stanislavsky's failure in the part of Trigorin was later explained by him as due to the fact that Chekhov's art as playwright did not at first appeal to him, but as an examination of the photographs of Stanislavsky in the different parts of Chekhov's plays (reproduced in this volume) will show, he was at the time of the production of *The Seagull* still relying too much on the external rather than the internal conception of the character he represented. However that may be, the fact remains that in *The Seagull* Stanislavsky first displayed his genius as producer, and it was this that brought such great success to the play and gave Chekhov the necessary confidence to continue writing for the stage.

During these years, as Stanislavsky himself declares, he had learned a great deal, understood a great deal, and also discovered a great deal by accident. 'I was always looking for something new', Stanislavsky writes in *My Life in Art*,* 'both in the inner work of the actor, in the work of the producer, and in the principles of stage production. I rushed about a great deal, often forgetting the important discoveries I had made and mistakenly carried away by things that were of no intrinsic value. I had collected as the result of my artistic career a sackful of material of every possible sort on the technique of the art of the stage. But everything was thrown together indiscriminately, and in such a form it is impossible to make any use of one's artistic treasures. I had to bring everything in order. I had to analyse my accumulated experience. I had, as it were, to lay the materials out on

* All the quotations from *My Life in Art* in this volume are taken from the Russian edition, which Stanislavsky completely revised, recast and enlarged after the first publication of his autobiography in the United States, following his American tour in 1922. (D.M.).

the different shelves of my mind. What was still unhewn had to be made smooth and laid, like foundation stones, at the base of my art; what had become worn, had to be repaired. For without it, any further progress was impossible'.

It was during his Finnish holiday, therefore, that Stanislavsky for the first time undertook to supply a theoretical basis for the art of the stage. He was first of all worried by the fact that all his joy in creation had gone. In the old days he used to be bored when he was not playing, but now, on the contrary, he was glad when he was not required to play. He was told that that was something all professional actors experienced, but such an explanation did not satisfy him, for he could not help feeling that if that was true, then the professional actors seemed to have a very poor opinion of their art. But as a matter of fact, it was not true of the great actors like Duse, Yermolova and Salvini, who had played their chief parts many more times than Stanislavsky had played his and who, in spite of it, were able to improve on them, while he was getting staler and staler every time he had to play a part in which he had become famous. Step by step he went over his past, and it became more and more obvious to him that the inner content he had put into his parts when he had first created them and the external forms which these parts had assumed in the course of time, were 'poles apart'. At first the character of every part he created seemed to depend on the exciting inner truth that he had perceived in it, but later on all that remained was its empty shell which had nothing to do with genuine art. There was his part of Dr. Stockmann, for instance. Before, he remembered, he had found it so easy to assume the point of view of a man who only looked for what was good in the hearts of his fellow-men and who was blind to their evil passions. 'What interested me most in Ibsen's play and in my part', Stanislavsky writes in *My Life in Art*, 'was Stockmann's passion for truth which allowed nothing to stand in its way. In this part I found it easy to put on a pair of rose-coloured spectacles of naive faith in people, and look on everybody around me through them, believing in them and loving them sincerely. When gradually the rottenness in the souls of Stockmann's would-be friends came to light, I could easily feel the perplexity of the man I represented on the stage. And at the moment when at last he realised the truth, I did not seem to know whether I was sorry for Stockmann or for myself . . . From intuition I came instinctively to the inner image of my part, with all its idiosyncrasies. The short-sightedness which revealed so clearly Stockmann's inner blindness to human vices, his child-like nature, his youthful high spirits, his comradely attitude towards his wife and children, his gaiety, his love of a joke and games, his sociability, and his charm which made everyone who came in contact with him a purer and a better man. From intuition I came to Stockmann's outer image: it flowed naturally from his inner one. Stockmann's body blended with his soul naturally; the moment I thought of Dr. Stockmann's own thoughts and worries, the signs of his shortsightedness appeared by themselves as well as the forward inclination of his body and his hurried way of walking. His eyes peered trustingly into the soul of the man or woman with whom he spoke or had anything to do with on the stage; the second and third fingers of my hand were thrust forward so as to lend greater conviction to his words, as though I wished to ram my feelings, words and thoughts into the very soul of the person I was talking to. All these things and habits appeared instinctively and unconsciously'.

When going over this part again in his mind while meditating on top of a cliff in Finland, Stanislavsky tried to discover where he had got all those characteristic features of Stockmann's part from, and he came to the conclusion that the feelings he had put into it were taken from his own memory. 'Before my very eyes', Stanislavsky writes, 'a friend of mine, a man of sterling honesty, was hunted down like Stockmann because his inner conviction did not permit him to do what was demanded from him . . . A few years after creating this part,' he further remembered, 'I met a professor in Berlin I had known before in a Vienna sanatorium and I realised that I had got my fingers in the part of Stockmann from him. I must have acquired them unconsciously from that living model. And my manner of shifting from foot to foot a la Stockmann I had taken over from a well-known Russian musician and critic'.

This discovery was to play an important part in Stanislavsky's 'system', as well as his other discovery that 'even if I assumed Stockmann's external mannerism off stage, the feelings and sensations which had once given birth to them immediately arose in me. The image and the passions of the part became my own organic ones, or rather the reverse was true: my own feelings were transformed into Stockmann's, and in the process I experienced the greatest joy an actor can ever experience, namely, the ability of speaking the thoughts of another man on the stage, of putting yourself entirely at the service of someone else's passions, and of reproducing someone else's actions as if they were your own.'

However, Stanislavsky discovered to his dismay that in the course of time these living memories of his (he was later to call them 'emotional memories' in his 'system') which had been the motive forces of Stockmann's spiritual life and the *leit-motif* which went through the whole play, became fainter and fainter till they were entirely lost. And that was true of his other parts. 'During my last tour abroad', he writes, 'and before it in Moscow, I kept repeating mechanically those well-drilled and firmly established "tricks" of the part—the mechanical signs of an absence of genuine feeling. In some places I tried to be as nervous and excited as possible, and for that reason performed a series of quick movements; in others I tried to appear naive and technically reproduced childishly innocent eyes; in others still I forced myself to reproduce the gait and the typical gestures of the part— the external result of a feeling that was dead. I copied naivety, but I was not naive; I walked with quick, short steps, but I had no feeling of an inner hurry which produced such quick steps, and so on. I exaggerated more or less skilfully, I imitated the external manifestations of feelings and actions, but at the same time I did not experience any feelings or any real need for action. As the performances went on, I acquired the mechanical habit of going through the once and for all established gymnastic exercises, which were firmly fixed as my stage habits by my muscular memory, which is so strong with actors'.

In reviewing Stockmann and other parts, analysing his memories which contributed to their creation, and comparing them with the artificial methods he now resorted to in his acting of the same parts, Stanislavsky could not help coming to the conclusion that his bad theatrical habits had crippled his soul, his body and his roles themselves. The next thing he asked himself was how to save his parts from degeneration, from spiritual torpor, and from the despotism of acquired stage habits and external training. An actor, he thought, must have some sort of spiritual preparation before the beginning of a performance. Not only his body, but also his spirit must put on new clothes. Before beginning to act, every actor must know how to enter into that spiritual atmosphere in which alone 'the sacrament of creative art' was possible.

Like Dr. Stockmann, Stanislavsky during his Finnish holiday made a number of great discoveries, which were no less important because they were known before. His first discovery was that an actor's state of mind on the stage when facing a large audience was not only unnatural, but also constituted one of the greatest obstacles to real acting. For in such a state of mind, an actor could only mimic and 'act a part', pretend to enter into the feelings of the character in the play, but not live and give himself up entirely to his feelings. Stanislavsky had, of course, known it before, but now he understood it, and, as he writes, 'in our language to understand means to feel'. An actor, for instance, has to pretend to be violently in love in front of thousands of people, who have paid money for their tickets and who have a right to demand that they should be given what they had paid for. They therefore expect the actor to speak so that they can hear what he is saying, with the result that he has to shout words of endearment, which in real life a man would only whisper to a woman and that, too, when he was alone with her. He has, besides, to be seen and understood by everybody in the theatre, and that is why he has to make gestures and movements for the benefit of those who are sitting in the last row of the stalls. How, then, can he be expected to think of love, let alone experience the sensations of love, under such circumstances? All he can do is to put every ounce of energy he possesses into his acting and strain himself to the utmost just because the problem he has to solve is insoluble.

The theatre, however, has invented a whole assortment of signs, expressions of human passions, theatrical poses, voice inflexions, cadences, flourishes, stage tricks, and methods of acting which are supposed to convey feelings and thoughts of 'a lofty nature'. These signs and theatrical tricks, 'acquired in the mother's womb', become mechanical and unconscious, and are always at the service of the actor when he feels himself utterly helpless on the stage and stands there 'with an empty soul'.

'What can an actor do in such a state to appear to be desperately in love?' Stanislavsky writes. 'All he can do is roll his eyes, press his hand to his heart, raise his eyes to the skies, lift up his eyebrows with a martyred air, shout, wave his hands about, so as to prevent the spectator from getting bored, and above all, avoid pauses which are so desirable at times of real inspiration, when silence becomes more eloquent than words'.

The natural state of mind of the actor is, therefore, the state of mind of a man on the stage during which he has to show outwardly what he does not feel inwardly. It is that abnormal state of mind in which the actor's mind is preoccupied with his private worries, his petty resentments, his successes or failures, while his body is at the same time forced to express 'the most lofty impulses of heroic feelings and passions'. This spiritual and physical abnormality, Stanislavsky points out, actors experience most of their lives: in the daytime between twelve and half past four at rehearsals, and at night from eight till midnight at the performance. And in an attempt to find some solution of this insoluble problem, actors not only acquire false and artificial methods of acting but also become dependent on them.

'Ever after I realised the existence of this abnormality', Stanislavsky writes, 'the question "What is to be done?" had haunted me like a phantom'.

Having realised the harmfulness and anomaly of the actor's state of mind, Stanislavsky began to look for a different condition of an actor's mind and body on the stage, a condition that he calls a *creative* state of mind. Geniuses, he noticed, always seemed to possess such a creative state of mind on the stage. Less gifted people had it less often, only on Sundays, as it were. People who were even less gifted got it even more seldom, on Bank Holidays. And to third-raters it was only vouchsafed in exceptional cases. Nevertheless, all people who are engaged in the pursuit of the art of the stage, from the genius to the man of ordinary talent, seem capable to a greater or lesser degree of achieving in some mysterious, intuitive way this creative state of mind, except that it is not given to them to achieve it as and when they like. They receive it 'as a heavenly gift from Apollo', and, Stanislavsky adds, 'we cannot, it seems, evoke it by our human methods'.

All the same, Stanislavsky could not help asking himself whether there were not some technical ways of achieving the creative state of mind. That did not mean that he wanted to produce inspiration itself in some artificial way, for that he realised was impossible. What he wanted to find out was whether there was not some way of creating the conditions favourable to the emergence of inspiration; an atmosphere in which inspiration was more likely to come to the actor. For when an actor said, 'I'm in a good mood today!' or 'I'm in excellent form today!' or 'I seem to be able to enter into the feelings of my part today!' it simply meant that he had been successful in achieving the creative state of mind by accident. The question therefore was whether such a creative state of mind could be achieved by the actor not accidentally, but at his own pleasure, 'to order,' as it were. Moreover, if it could not be achieved at once, could it not be done in parts, by putting it together, as it were, from different elements, even if each of these elements had to be produced by the actor within himself by a series of systematic exercises. If a genius, Stanislavsky argued, had been granted the ability to achieve the creative state of mind in the fullest possible measure, could not ordinary actors achieve it to some extent after a long and painstaking course of training? Such people would not, of course, become geniuses because of it, but it might help them to come as close as possible to whatever it was that distinguished genius.

The question Stanislavsky next set himself to answer was therefore what were the constituent elements and he nature of the creative state of mind.

He had noticed that the great actors as well as the talented actors of the Moscow Art Theatre had something in common, something that only they seemed to possess, something that made them akin to each other and that reminded him of all the others. What kind of faculty was that? The question was a highly complex one, but Stanislavsky set himself to answer it by analysing this quality of greatness in the actor step by step. The first thing that struck him about this creative state of the actor was that it was invariably accompanied by a complete freedom of the body and a total relaxation of the muscles. The whole physical apparatus of the actor was, in fact, entirely at his beck and call. Thanks to this discipline, the creative work of the actor was excellently organised, and the actor could by his body freely express what his soul felt. And so excited was Stanislavsky by this discovery that he began to transform the performances in which he appeared into experimental tests. But what worried him was that apparently none of the actors or spectators noticed any change in his acting, so that 'apart from some complimentary remark about some pose, movement or action, noticed by the more attentive and sensitive of the spectators, this discovery alone did not seem to make much difference.'

It was then that, again by accident, Stanislavsky discovered another elementary truth. He realised that he felt so well on the stage because, in addition to the relaxation of his muscles, his public exercises riveted his attention on the sensations of his body and thereby distracted him from what was happening in the auditorium on the other side of that 'terrible black hole of the stage'. He noticed that it was at those moments that his state of mind became particularly pleasant.

'Soon', Stanislavsky writes, 'I obtained a confirmation or explanation of my observations. At a performance given in Moscow by a famous foreign actor, I became aware, while watching him intently, of the presence of the familiar creative state of mind in him. There was a complete relaxation of muscles coupled with a maximum of general concentration. I felt that all his attention was concentrated on his side of the footlights and not on ours, that he was occupied with what was happening on the stage and not in the auditorium, and that it was precisely this attention of his, concentrated on one point, that forced *me* to take an interest in his life on the stage and aroused *my* curiosity to find out what it was that interested him so much there. At that moment I realised that the more an actor tries to entertain the

20

spectator, the more will the spectator sit back like a lord and wait to be entertained without making the slightest effort to take part in the creative work that is taking place before him; but that as soon as the actor stops paying any attention to him, the spectator will begin to show an interest in him, especially if the actor himself is interested in something on the stage that the audience, too, finds important'.

Continuing his observation of himself and others, Stanislavsky realised that creative work on the stage was first of all the fullest possible concentration of the whole of the actor's spiritual and physical nature. Such a concentration, he discovered, extended not only to hearing and sight, but to all the other five senses of the actor, and in addition, took possession of his body, mind, memory and imagination. The conclusion Stanislavsky arrived at was that all the spiritual and physical nature of the actor must be centred on what is taking place in the soul of the person he is representing on the stage.

This second truth was again checked by Stanislavsky on the stage during his performances with the help of exercises he had devised for the purpose of the systematic development of his attention.

Another interesting observation Stanislavsky made relates to the attention that an audience can be expected to give to the actor's play on the stage when unaided by other actors. 'Experience has taught me', he writes, 'that an actor can hold the attention of an audience by himself in a highly dramatic scene for at most *seven minutes* (that is the absolute maximum!). In a quiet scene the maximum is *one minute* (this, too, is a lot!). After that the diversity of the actor's means of expression is not sufficient to hold the attention of the audience, and he is forced to repeat himself with the result that the attention of the audience slackens until the next climax which requires new methods of presentation. But please, note that this is true only in the cases of geniuses!'

The third discovery Stanislavsky made concerns the time of the arrival of the actor at the theatre. He happened one day to be at a Moscow theatre where the leading actor made a point of being late for every performance. 'A home-bred genius', Stanislavsky observes, 'will always arrive five minutes late and not, like Salvini, three hours before the beginning of the performance. Why? For the simple reason that to be able to prepare something in his mind for three hours, he has to have *something* to prepare. But a home-bred genius has nothing except his talent. He arrives at the theatre with his suit of clothes in his trunk, but without any spiritual luggage. What on earth is he to do in his dressing-room from five to eight? Smoke? Tell funny stories? He could do that much better in a restaurant'.

This applies not only to actors who are habitually late for a performance, but also to those who arrive just in time for its beginning. Even actors who come to the theatre in good time do so just because they are afraid to be late. They are in time to prepare their bodies, to make up their faces, Stanislavsky observes, but it never occurs to them that their souls too have to be dressed and made up. They do not care for the inner design of their parts. They hope that their parts will assume the exterior forms of a stage creation during the performance. Once this happens, they fix it in mechanical stage habits, but forgetting all about the spirit of the part, they let it wither away with time. 'An actor who disregards the wise creative feeling and is a slave of senseless stage habits,' Stanislavsky writes, 'is at the mercy of every chance, of the bad taste of the audience, of some clever stage trick, of cheap external success, of his vanity and, indeed, of anything that has nothing whatever to do with art'. No part, in fact, can be really successful unless the actor *believes* in it. The actor must believe in everything that is taking place on the stage and, above all, he must believe in himself. But he can only believe in what is true. He must, therefore, always be aware of truth and know how to find it, and to do that he must develop his artistic sensibility for truth. And Stanislavsky makes it clear that what he means by truth is the truth of the actor's feelings and sensations, the truth of the inner creative impulse which is striving to express itself. 'I am not interested in the truth outside me', he declares. 'What is important to me is the truth in me, the truth of my attitude towards one scene or another on the stage, towards the different things on the stage, the scenery, my partners, who are playing the other parts in the play, and their feelings and thoughts.

Introduction

'The real actor', Stanislavsky goes on, 'says to himself, I know that scenery, make-up, costumes, and the fact that I have to perform my work in public—is nothing but a barefaced lie. But I don't care, for things by themselves are of no importance to me . . . But—*if* everything round me on the stage were true, I should have done this, and I should have acted this or that scene in such and such a way'.

It was then that Stanislavsky realised that the work of the actor began from the moment when what he calls the 'magic', creative 'if' appeared in his soul and imagination. While tangible reality and tangible truth, in which man could not help believing, existed, the creative work of the actor could not be said to have begun. But when the creative 'if', that is, the would-be, imaginary truth made its appearance, the actor discovered that he was able to believe in it as sincerely, if not with even greater enthusiasm, as real truth. 'Just as a little girl believes in the existence of her doll', Stanislavsky writes, 'and in the life in and around her, so the actor, the moment the creative 'if' appears, is transported from the plane of real life to the plane of a different kind of life which he himself has created in his imagination. Once he believes in it, he is ready to start his creative work'.

The stage, therefore, was truth; it was what the actor sincerely believed in. In the theatre, Stanislavsky claims, even the most barefaced lie must become truth in order to be art. To make this possible, the actor must possess a highly developed imagination, a child-like naivety and trustfulness, and an artistic sensitiveness for truth and verisimilitude both in his body and soul. For all that helped him to transform the crude stage lie into the most delicate truth of the imagination. These qualities and abilities of the actor Stanislavsky calls *the feeling for truth*. 'In it', he observes, 'is contained the play of imagination and the formation of creative belief; in it is contained the best possible defence against stage falsehood, as well as the sense of proportion, the guarantee of a child-like naivety and the sincerity of artistic feeling'.

Stanislavsky soon discovered that the feeling for truth, like concentration and relaxation of muscles, was subject to development and could be acquired by exercises. 'This ability', he declares, 'must be brought to so high a state of development that nothing should take place or be said or perceived on the stage without having first gone through the filter of the artistic feeling for truth'.

As soon as he made this fourth discovery, Stanislavsky put all his stage exercises for the relaxation of muscles and concentration to the test of the feeling for truth, with the result that it was only then that he succeeded in obtaining a real, natural and not forced relaxation of muscles and concentration on the stage during a performance. Moreover, in making these investigations and accidental discoveries, he found that many more truths that had been known in life had also their application on the stage. All of them, taken together, contributed to the formation of the creative state of mind as distinguished from the theatrical state of mind, which Stanislavsky regards as the real enemy of the art of the stage.

Finally, the last discovery made by Stanislavsky, 'after months of torment and doubt', was that in the art of the stage everything had to become a *habit*, which transformed everything new into something organic, into the actor's second nature. Only after having acquired this habit, could the actor make use of something new on the stage without thinking of its mechanism. This discovery, too, had a direct bearing on the creative state of mind of the actor, which could only be of any use to him when it became his normal, natural, and only means of expression. Should this not happen, the actor, Stanislavsky points out, would merely copy the external forms of any new movement without justifying it from within.

II

Stanislavsky, however, arrived at the essentials of his theory of acting only after a prolonged application of the methods of trial and error. At first he thought that the actor must start from the outer characteristics of his part in order to come to the inner feeling. Such a method, he found, was possible, though it was not by any means the best method of creative achievement in stage art. 'It was all very well', he writes, 'if the characteristic features of a part came to me of themselves, for then I mastered my part without difficulty. But mostly I could not get hold of it at once, and then I was helpless. Where was I to get it? I thought and worked a great deal over this question, and that was very useful because in chasing after the characteristic features of a part, I began to look for them in actual life. I began, as the famous Russian actor, Shchepkin, taught, "to take my models from life", and transfer them from there on the stage, whereas before whenever I tried to discover the methods of acting a certain part I used to bury myself in the dusty archives of old, worn-out theatrical traditions and conventions. But in those airless and dead storehouses you can find neither the material you want, nor the *inspiration of sub-conscious creative work and artistic inspiration'*.

It is the way from the conscious to the sub-conscious that became the pivot of his 'system'. It solved the problem of realism on the stage and supplied a reliable foot-rule for theatrical convention. So far as realism is concerned, Stanislavsky points out that it becomes naturalism on the stage only when it is not justified by the actor from within. As soon as it is justified, it becomes either unnecessary or is not noticed at all owing to the fact that external life is filled with its internal meaning. 'Those theoreticians who do not know this from practical experience', Stanislavsky writes, 'I should advise to check the truth of my words on the stage'.

As for stage conventions, Stanislavsky maintains that a good stage convention is created by those conditions which are best adapted for stage representation; it is *scenic* in the best sense of the word. Scenic, in short, is everything that helps the actor's play and the performance as a whole. This help must consist, above all, in the attainment of the fundamental aim of the art of the stage. Hence only that convention can be said to be good and scenic on the stage which helps the actors and the performance to recreate *the life of the human spirit* in the play itself and in its different parts. This life must be convincing. It cannot possibly take place in conditions of barefaced lies and deceptions. A lie must become, or at any rate must seem to become, truth on the stage before it can be convincing. And truth on the stage is what the actor, the artist, and the spectator believe to be true. Therefore stage conventions, too, must bear a resemblance to truth, that is to say, be credible, and the actor himself and the spectators must believe in them. A good convention must be beautiful, but it must be remembered that it is not what from a theatrical point of view dazzles and stupefies the spectator that is beautiful. So far as the art of the theatre is concerned, that is beautiful which exalts the life of the human spirit on the stage and from the stage, that is, the thoughts and feelings of the actors and spectators. It does not matter, Stanislavsky observes, whether the production and the acting is realistic, conventional, right-wing or left-wing, impressionistic or futuristic so long as it is convincing, that is, truthful or credible, and beautiful, i.e., artistic, and lofty, and represents the genuine life of the human spirit without which there is no art. Any stage convention that does not answer those demands is, in Stanislavsky's opinion, a bad stage convention.

Among the bad stage conventions Stanislavsky includes everything that interferes with the creative work of the actor and transforms the Theatre with a capital T into a theatre with a small letter. 'Let the places of entertainment', he declares, 'be satisfied with the bad theatrical conventions; there is no place for them in a Theatre with a capital T'.

What Stanislavsky, therefore, set himself to do was to find the laws of the creative art of the stage that are common to all actors, great and small, and that could be perceived by their consciousness. The number of such laws, he found, was not great; neither were they of any primary importance since they did not possess the power of transforming a second-rate actor into a genius. They were nevertheless laws of nature and had, as such, to be thoroughly studied by every actor, for it was only through them that he could set in motion his subconscious creative powers, the true nature of which was apparently beyond human grasp. 'The greater the genius', Stanislavisky writes, 'the more mysterious does its mystery grow, and the more necessary do the technical methods of creative work become for since these methods are perceived by consciousness, he can use them to explore the hidden places of his subconsciousness, which is the seat of inspiration'.

These elementary 'psycho-physical and psychological' laws form what Stanislavsky calls the 'psycho-technique' of his system, and their purpose is to teach the actor how to arouse at will his unconscious creative nature in himself for subconscious and organic creative work. 'The basis for my system', Stanislavsky writes in *My Life in Art*, 'is formed by the laws of the organic nature of the actor which I have studied thoroughly in practice. Its chief merit is that there is nothing in it I myself invented or have not checked in practice. It is the natural result of my experiences of the stage over many years.

'My "system",' he goes on, 'is divided into two main parts: (1) the inner and the outer work of the actor on himself, and (2) the inner and the outer work of the actor on his part. The inner work on the actor himself is based on a psychic technique which enables him to evoke a creative state of mind during which inspiration descends on him more easily. The actor's external work on himself consists of the preparation of his bodily mechanism for the embodiment of his part and the exact presentation of its inner life. The work on the part consists of the study of the spiritual essence of a dramatic work, the germ from which it has emerged and which defines its meaning as well as the meaning of all its parts.

'The worst enemy of progress', Stanislavsky concludes, 'is prejudice, for it bars the way to development. In our art such a prejudice is the opinion which defends the actor's dilettante attitude towards his work. It is this prejudice that I want to fight. To do that only one thing is possible: I have to write an account of what I have learnt during my practice as actor and producer on the stage in the form of a kind of grammar with practical exercises. Let those exercises be done. The results, I am sure, will force those who are under the influence of this prejudice to admit that they are wrong. This work I hope to carry out in my next book'.

III

Stanislavsky's next book, *An Actor's Work On Himself** turned

* This book is published in an American translation under the title *The Actor Prepares*. The main fault of this American edition of Stanislavsky's great work is that it leaves out a great deal of the original book. (D.M.).

out to be much more than a grammar with practical exercises. It took the form of a course of study of the art of acting in which Stanislavsky, under the name of Tvortsov, a name that suggests 'creative artist', and a number of pupils (four men and two women) take part. The whole course is supposed to be taken down in shorthand by one of the pupils. In his introduction to the book, Stanislavsky disclaims any desire to be scientific. He points out that the terms he uses in his psycho-technique have been taken either from practice or suggested by his pupils themselves. The terms 'subconscious' and 'intuition', in particular, are used in a colloquial and not in a philosophic sense. The whole aim of the course is purely practical, and in it Stanislavsky conveys what his long experience as actor, producer and teacher has taught him. 'The work on the so-called "Stanislavsky system",' he writes, 'began a long time ago. At first I did not write down my notes for publication, but for my own use, as an aid to my investigations in the sphere of our art and its psycho-technique. Imperceptibly, year by year, there accumulated a huge mass of material on my "system".'

To begin with, Stanislavsky draws a clear distinction between the different types of actor to be found on the stage. There are, he maintains, broadly speaking three types of actor: the creative actor, the imitative actor, and the stage-hack, the last category including the lowest type of actor known, namely the ham-actor. So far as the creative actor is concerned his distinguishing characteristic is his ability to enter into the feelings of his part. Such an actor must be completely carried away by the play in which he is appearing, for it is only then that he can enter fully into the feelings of his part without being aware of his own feelings and without *thinking* what he is doing, everything happening by itself, that is, subconsciously. The trouble is that no actor can control his subconsciousness. What he can do, however, is to influence it indirectly, for certain parts of a man's mind can be controlled by his consciousness and will and these are capable of exerting an influence on his involuntary psychical processes. This involves very complicated work which is itself only partly amenable to the actor's control and to the direct influence on his consciousness. For the most part this work is unconscious and involuntary, and can be managed only 'by the most subtle and miracle-working artist—our organic nature herself'.

The creative artist must, therefore, know how to stimulate and direct nature, and, Stanislavsky insists, his special methods of psycho-technique exist for that very purpose and must, consequently, be learned very thoroughly by every actor who wants to become a creative actor. For the chief aim of these methods is to awaken the actor's creative subconsciousness by various indirect and conscious means.

Hence one of the main principles of the art of entering into the feelings of a part is 'the subconscious creative work of nature through the conscious psycho-technique of the actor (subconscious through conscious, involuntary through voluntary)'. The actor ought to leave the subconscious to 'magician-nature' and apply himself only to what is accessible to him, namely the conscious approach to his creative work through the conscious methods of psycho-technique, which will tell him first of all not to interfere with the subconscious when it begins to work.

The whole development of the subconscious powers of the actor therefore depends entirely on the conscious psycho-technique. It is only when the actor fully realises that his inner and outer life is developing naturally and normally according to the laws of human nature and in the conditions that he finds on the stage, that out of the innermost recesses of his subconscious mind feelings will emerge that he himself will not always be able to understand. These feelings will take possession of him for a long or short time and lead him where something inside him will tell them.

This mysterious force which seems to be beyond human powers of comprehension, Stanislavsky calls 'nature'. The moment that the actor's true organic life on the stage is interfered with, that is, the moment the actor stops representing life truthfully on the stage, his hypersensitive sub-conscious mind, shy of coercion, hides itself away in its inaccessible secret places. To prevent that from happening, the actor must first of all make sure that he does his work correctly. Thus, realism and even naturalism of his inner life is indispensable to the actor for stimulating the work of his subconsciousness and the impulses of his inspiration.

Introduction

However, since it is impossible always to depend on the subconscious and inspiration, the creative actor must prepare the ground for such subconscious work by seeing first of all that his conscious work is done correctly; for the conscious and correct creates truth, and truth begets belief, and if nature believes in what is taking place in the actor, she will herself take a hand in whatever the actor is doing on the stage, with the result that subconsciousness and even inspiration will be given a chance of asserting themselves.

But what does correct acting mean? It means, Stanislavsky maintains, that while on the stage the actor thinks and acts correctly, logically, consistently, and in accordance with the laws of human nature, as demanded by his part and in complete agreement with it. As soon as the actor succeeds in doing that, he will identify himself with the character of his part and begin to share his feelings, that is, he will enter into the feelings of his part. The process and its definition, Stanislavsky observes, occupy a foremost position in the art of the stage. For entering into the feelings of his part helps the actor to carry out the fundamental aim of the art of the stage, namely the creation of 'the life of the human spirit' of the part and the presentation of this life on the stage in an artistic form.

The main task of the creative actor, therefore, is not only to represent the life of his part in its external manifestations, but above all to re-create on the stage the inner life of the character he represents, adapting his own human feelings to this unfamiliar life and devoting to it all the organic elements of his own soul. It is the inner nature of his part, that is to say, its inner life, brought into being with the help of the process of entering into the feelings of his part, that is the main purpose of the actor's work on the stage and should also be his chief preoccupation. Moreover, the creative actor must enter into the feelings of his part, that is experience feelings that are absolutely identical with the feelings of the character he is representing on the stage, at every performance of the play.

'Every great actor', Stanislavsky quotes Tommaso Salvini, 'must, and in fact does, feel what he is representing. I should even go so far as to say that he ought not only to experience excitement once or twice while studying his part, but also to a larger or smaller degree every time he performs it, whether for the first or the thousandth time'.

The difference between the creative and the imitative actor is that the latter enters into the feelings of his part only during the preparatory stages of his work, while during the actual performance he does so only indirectly, that is to say, by imitating his former experience. Such acting, Stanislavsky points out, may be beautiful, but it is not deep; it is effective rather than powerful. In it the form is more interesting than the content. It creates a greater impression on the spectator's sight and hearing than on his spirit, and for that reason it thrills rather than moves him. The spectator, in short, admires rather than believes in such imitative acting. Its means are too superficial or too showy for the expression of great passions, for the subtleties and depths of human feeling defy all technical methods. They need the direct assistance of nature herself at the moment the actor enters into the feelings of his part and gives them an outward embodiment. But for all that the representation of a part which is only prompted by the process of genuine feeling must be recognised as an art.

As for the stage-hacks, they merely reproduce the text of their parts by means of once and for all worked out methods of stage acting, which, Stanislavsky observes, greatly simplifies their tasks. Unable to enter into the feelings of their parts, they never achieve even the external results of this creative process. All that remains for them to do, therefore, is to resort to overacting, for which there exists a large assortment of every kind of theatrical imitative method which is supposed to convey by external means all sorts of feelings one may encounter in the practice of the stage. These ready-made mechanical methods of acting, however, soon lose all resemblance to life and are transformed into mechanical stage tricks, devoid of all real feeling. The whole stage activity of this type of actor, in fact, consists of a clever selection of different theatrical clichés and their combination. Some of these clichés do not lack a certain beauty or appeal, and an inexperienced spectator might be even deceived into thinking that it was genuine art.

But it is only in theory, Stanislavsky is careful to point out, that one can divide actors into these three categories. In practice it will be found that they get all mixed up, a great actor sometimes descending to the position of a stage-hack, and a stage-hack occasionally rising to the heights of true art.

'Owing to the fact that it is a public institution and a place where people exhibit themselves in a play', Stanislavsky writes, 'the theatre is a double-edged weapon: on the one hand, it fulfils an important social mission; on the other, it encourages those who wish to exploit our art and make a career for themselves. These people make use of the lack of understanding of some or the perverted tastes of others, and they do not hesitate to pull strings, intrigue, and adopt all sorts of other methods which have nothing to do with the creative art of the stage. These exploiters of the theatre are its worst enemies. They must be fought ruthlessly, and if that should not prove sufficient, driven off the stage'.

Apart from the good or bad stage 'acting', therefore, there are two fundamental tendencies in the theatre: the art of direct experience, and the art of imitation. The actor who wants to become a creative artist can only avoid the dangers that lie in wait for him, Stanislavsky declares, 'by carrying out incessantly the fundamental aim of our art, which consists in the creation of 'the life of the human spirit' of his part and in the artistic embodiment of this life in a beautiful stage form'.

IV

Stanislavsky's 'system' is therefore an attempt to apply certain natural laws of acting for the purpose of bringing the actor's subconscious powers of expression into play. These laws, Stanislavsky claims, are sufficiently well-defined to be studied and put into practice with the help of psycho-technique, which consists of a large number of 'elements', ten of which—'if', given circumstances, imagination, attention, relaxation of muscles, pieces and problems, truth and belief, emotional memory, communication and extraneous aids—form the core of the famous 'system'.

Stanislavsky's genius as producer found expression at the very outset of his career in his realisation of the fundamental fact that dramatic art and the art of the actor are based on action. The great success of his production of Chekhov's plays is due solely to this. For while he had at first little sympathy with Chekhov as a dramatist and little understanding of the principles that governed Chekhov's plays of indirect action, his production of *The Seagull* and subsequently of the other plays of Chekhov showed that what he aimed at was to bring out their latent action. His methods of doing it may strike one as a little primitive, but they were effective none the less. As can be seen from the illustration of one of his sets of *Uncle Vanya* (facing page 34), he deliberately cluttered up the stage with all sorts of props so that the actors had to *do* something every time they moved. A study of Stanislavsky's mise-en-scenes of Chekhov's plays will confirm this characteristic feature of an early Stanislavsky production. To a great producer like Stanislavsky drama could only mean action, and not any kind of action, but purposeful and productive action. 'On the stage', he writes, 'the actor must act both externally and internally as well as purposefully and productively, and not just "in general". A stage action, that is, must be internally justified, logical, consistent and feasible in real life. An actor must not "play" passions and characters: he must act under the influence of the passions and in character.'

How is external and internal action created on the stage? It is created, Stanislavsky replies, through one of the most powerful elements of psycho-technique expressed in the monosyllable 'if'. That is to say, the only way in which an actor can give outer and inner expression to a stage action is by asking himself, What would I do, *if* certain circumstances were true? Stanislavsky usually describes this element as the *magic if*, for, as he points out, 'it transfers the actor from the world of reality to a world in which alone his creative work can be done'.

There are all sorts of 'ifs'. There are 'ifs' which fulfil themselves at once, and 'ifs' which merely supply the stimulus for the further logical development of action. There are one-storied and many-storied 'ifs'. The secret of the powerful influence of 'if' lies in the fact that it never deals with what actually exists, but only with what might have been—'if . . . .' It does not affirm anything; it merely assumes. It presents a problem that has to be solved, and it is the actor who has to supply the answer to it. Moreover, it arouses in the actor an inner and outer activity, and it does it naturally and without the slightest compulsion. The word 'if', in short, is an incentive and a stimulus to the actor's creative activity. It both begins the actor's work and provides the impetus towards the further development of the constructive process of his part.

The other element out of which stage action arises is 'the given circumstances'. It supplies the fable or plot of the play, its facts, events, period, time and place of action, the conditions of life, the actor's and producer's interpretation of the play, their additions to it, the mise-en-scenes, the production, the scenery and costumes of the stage designer, the properties, the sound effects, and so on. It includes everything, in fact, the actor is asked to take into consideration in his work on the stage.

Like 'if' itself, the given circumstances are a figment of the imagination, a mere conjecture. Both 'if' and the given circumstances are of the same origin: one is an assumption ('if') and the other an addition to it ('the given circumstances'). 'If' always starts the actor's creative work, while 'the given circumstances' develop it. Their functions, however, differ somewhat: 'if' supplies the impetus to the slumbering imagination, while 'the given circumstances' provide the justification for the existence of 'if'.

'In practice', Stanislavsky writes, 'the actor will first of all have to imagine in his own way all "the given circumstances" as found in the play itself, then the producer's plan of production, and, finally, his own artistic ideas. The whole of this material will create in his mind a general idea of the character he is to represent on the stage as well as the conditions among which he lives. It is the duty of the actor to believe sincerely in the possibility of such a life in actual fact; he has to get so used to it that it should become familiar to him. If he is successful, the truth of the passions and the verisimilitude of the feelings will arise in him automatically. The whole attention of the actor, in fact, must be concentrated on the given circumstances; let him live with them in good earnest, and "the truth of the passions" will be born in him of itself'

Introduction

So far as the nature of internal and external action is concerned, Stanislavsky points out that the art of the theatre is based on activity which finds its expression in the action on the stage. The spirit of the play is also conveyed in action. The actor's inner experience and the inner world of the play must therefore be shown in action.

An actor may attempt to present a part he does not feel inwardly as externally effective for the sake of applause. A serious actor, however, would never tolerate any interruption of a passage in which the most intimate feelings are expressed. An actor who does not mind sacrificing them to get some cheap applause merely shows that the words he utters have no meaning for him, and empty words can hardly be expected to excite serious attention. The actor wants them just as sounds to display his voice, diction and technique of speech, and his actor's temperament. As for the thought and feelings, they can only be conveyed 'in general' sorrowfully, 'in general' joyously, 'in general' tragically, and so on. Such a performance, however, is dead, formal and inartistic.

The same applies to external action. When an actor does not mind what he does on the stage, when his part and his art are not devoted to what they should serve, then his actions are empty, not inwardly felt, and consequently, they have nothing of importance to convey. In such a case, all that is left for the actor to do is to act 'in general'. When an actor suffers in order to suffer, when he loves in order to love, when he is jealous and asks for forgiveness in order to be jealous and ask for forgiveness, when all this is done merely because it is in the play and not because the actor has experienced it inwardly and created the life of his part on the stage, then he will find himself in a hopeless fix, and to act 'in general' is the only solution for him.

Real art and acting 'in general' are, in fact, incompatible. The one destroys the other. Art loves order and harmony, while 'in general' is chaos and disorder.

How is the actor to save himself from his mortal enemy 'in general'? To deal with it effectively he must introduce into his purposeless 'in general' acting something that is incompatible with it and that will be sure to destroy it. 'In general' being superficial and thoughtless, the actor must introduce into his play some plan and a serious attitude towards what is happening on the stage, which will destroy superficiality and thoughtlessness. 'In general' being chaotic and absurd, the actor must introduce logic and consistency into his part, which will eliminate these bad qualities. 'In general' always starting something and never finishing it, the actor must take care that his acting is characterised by finish and completeness. As a result, there will be real, purposeful and productive human action on the stage.

'Why am I so bitterly opposed to doing things "in general" on the stage?' Stanislavsky asks, and he replies, 'Because tens of thousands of performances are given daily all over the world according to this principle, while there are only a dozen or so performances that can be regarded as really artistic. Hundreds of thousands of actors, therefore, are thrown out of gear inwardly every day by systematically adopting incorrect and harmful stage habits. This is all the more deplorable since, on the one hand, the theatre itself and the conditions of its work force the actor to acquire these dangerous habits, while on the other, the actor himself, seeking the line of least resistance, is only too glad to avail himself of the inartistic 'in general".'

To be successful in this unequal fight, the actor, Stanislavsky insists, must first of all have the courage to admit that for all sorts of reasons he loses the sense of real life when he steps on to the stage. He forgets how he acts internally and externally in real life, and he has to learn it afresh just as a child has to learn to walk, talk, look and listen. His first duty, therefore, is to learn how to act on the stage like a normal human being, simply, naturally, organically correct, and without constraint. Not as required by the conventions of the theatre, but by the laws of living, organic nature. He must, in short, learn 'how to get rid of the theatre (with a small letter) in the Theatre (with a capital T)'.

'If', 'the given circumstances', and the internal and external action that arises from them are not the only important factors in an actor's work. He requires many more special abilities, qualities, and gifts such as imagination, attention, the feeling for truth, etc. The art of controlling all these 'elements' of psycho-technique demands much practice and experience.

36

V

In discussing the next element of imagination, Stanislavsky first of all stresses the fact that there is no real life on the stage. Real life, he declares emphatically, is not art, a statement that ought to dispose of many of his critics who accuse him of wishing to introduce a slavish imitation of life on the stage. The nature of art, he points out, demands fiction, which is in the first place provided by the work of the author. The problem of the actor and his creative technique is, therefore, how to transform the fiction of the play into artistic stage reality. To do that the actor needs imagination.

The playwright, Stanislavsky goes on to point out, does not give the actor everything he has to know about the play, and indeed it is hardly to be expected that an author could reveal the life of all the *dramatis personæ* in a hundred or so pages. The playwright's stage-directions are, besides, too laconic and insufficient to create the whole outward image of the characters, not to mention their manners, gaits and habits. And what about the dialogue? Is it just to be learnt by heart? There are, moreover, the producer's mise-en-scenes, and the production of the play as a whole. Could an actor possibly memorise it all and reproduce it formally on the stage? Does all this really depict the character of the person in the play and define every shade of his thoughts, feelings, impulses, and actions? According to Stanislavsky—and here one cannot help feeling that he goes perhaps a little too far and, being himself a producer of genius, is rather apt to dispose of the author in too cavalier a fashion—it is the actor himself who has to add to it all and expand it. Only if he does that will everything the author and the other artists of the theatre have given him come to life and stimulate the different dormant feelings in his soul and the soul of the spectator. Only then will the actor himself be able to give expression to the inner life of the person he represents on the stage and act as the author, the producer, and his own genuine feelings tell him.

In this work the actor's best friend is his imagination with its magic 'if' and 'the given circumstances'. For it not only adds to what the author, producers and others have omitted, but makes it all come to life. An actor must, therefore, possess a strong and vivid imagination, which he must use at every moment of his life and work on the stage, both when he is studying and when he is performing his part.

An actor who has no imagination, Stanislavsky declares, has either to develop it or leave the stage, for otherwise he will be entirely in the hands of the producers who will foist their own imaginations on him, which would be tantamount to his giving up his own creative work and becoming a mere puppet.

The actor's imagination must be active and not passive. It must also be remembered that an actor's work does not consist of the inner work of his imagination alone, but also of the outer embodiment of his creative dreams, which must always be logical and consistent. These creative dreams of the actor's imagination Stanislavsky calls the visual images of his inner eye.

The actor needs first of all an uninterrupted sequence of 'given circumstances' and, secondly, an uninterrupted series of visual images which have some connection with the given circumstances. He needs, in short, an uninterrupted line not of plain but of illustrated given circumstances. Indeed, at every moment of his presence on the stage and at every moment of the outer and inner development of the play, the actor must be aware either of what is taking place outside him on the stage (i.e. the external given circumstances created by the producer, stage-designer, and the other artists) or of what is taking place inside him, in his own imagination, that is, those visual images which illustrate the given circumstances of the life of his part. Out of all these things there is formed, sometimes outside and sometimes inside him, an uninterrupted and endless series of inner and outer visual images, or a kind of film. While his work goes on, this film is unwinding itself endlessly, reflecting on the screen of his inner vision the illustrated given circumstances of his part, among which he lives on the stage.

These visual images create in him a corresponding mood which will influence his spirit and arouse in him a corresponding inner feeling.

An actor needs his imagination not only in order to create, but also in order to infuse new life into what he has created and what is in danger of wearing thin. Every invention of the actor's imagination must, besides, be fully justified and firmly fixed. The questions who, when, where, why and how, which the actor puts to himself to set his imagination working, should help him to create more and more definite pictures of non-existent, imaginary life. There will be times, no doubt, when they will come by themselves without the aid of his conscious mental activity and without any promptings from his reason. But it is impossible to rely on the activity of the imagination left to its own devices, and to dream 'in general' without any definite and clearly defined theme is a waste of time.

Every movement and every word on the stage must be the result of the correct life of the imagination. If an actor utters a word or does something on the stage in a mechanical way, without knowing who he is, where he comes from, why he is where he is, what he wants, where he will go to and what he will do there, he is acting without imagination, and that fraction of time he spends on the stage, whether short or long, is not truth so far as he is concerned, for he has been acting like some wound-up mechanism, like an automaton. Not a single step must be taken on the stage mechanically and without some inner justification for it, that is, without the work of the imagination. To be equal to every task, an actor's imagination, in fact, must be lively, active, responsive, and sufficiently developed.

VI

To make the best use of his imagination, an actor must be able to control it. This he can only do by a well-trained attention. Hence attention is the next important 'element' of the psycho-technique of Stanislavsky's 'system'.

Like action, attention may be either internal, in which case its main function is to supply the actor with the creative material for his imagination, or external, which is no less important since it helps to concentrate the actor's mind on what is taking place on the stage and so distracts it from the terrifying black hole of the proscenium.

It is absolutely essential, Stanislavsky insists, that the actor should learn by a series of exercises how to keep his attention fixed on the stage so as to prevent it from straying into the auditorium. He must acquire a special technique that will help him to concentrate his attention so firmly on some object on the stage that the object itself should distract him from anything outside it. The actor, in short, has to learn how to look and see on the stage. For the eye of the actor who knows how to look and see attracts the attention of the spectators, concentrating it on the object they too have to look at. The empty gaze of an actor, on the other hand, merely diverts the attention of the spectators from the stage.

Attention concentrated on some object on the stage will, in addition, evoke a natural desire to do something with it, and action will still more concentrate the actor's attention on the object. Thus attention, fusing with the object, will create the strongest possible connection with it.

To assist the actor to concentrate his attention on the stage, Stanislavsky propounds the theory of the circle of attention. He points out that in such a narrow circle, as in a circle of light, it is easy to examine the smallest details of the objects within its circumference, live with the most intimate feelings and desires, carry out the most complicated actions, solve the most difficult problems, and analyse one's feelings and thoughts. In addition, it is possible in such a circle to establish close communication with another person in it, confide to him one's most intimate thoughts, recall the past and dream of the future.

The actor's state of mind in such an imaginary circle of attention, Stanislavsky describes as 'public solitude'. It is public, he points out, because the whole audience is with the actor all the time, and it is solitude because he is separated from it by his small circle of attention. During a performance the actor can always withdraw himself to his small circle of attention and, as it were, retire into his solitude, like a snail into its shell.

With the widening of the circle of attention, the area of the actor's attention is also widened. This, however, can go on only as long as the actor can keep his attention fixed within the imaginary circle. The moment the circumference of the circle becomes blurred, the actor must narrow the circle to the limits of his visual attention. The actor has to acquire an unconscious, mechanical habit of transferring his attention from the smaller to the larger circle without breaking it. In the terrible moment of panic the actor must remember that the larger and emptier the large circle, the more compact must the middle and small circle be inside it, and the more solitary must his solitude be.

In addition to the external attention, that is, the attention directed to the objects on the stage, there is the actor's inner attention, which is also constantly diverted by the actor's memories of his private life. In the sphere of inner attention, too, there is therefore a continuous conflict in the actor's mind between the attention which is correct and useful for his part and the attention which is incorrect and harmful. Attention which is harmful draws the actor away from the problems of his part to the other side of the footlights or even beyond the walls of the theatre.

Inner attention is so important to the actor because the greater part of his life on the stage takes place on the plane of creative invention and fictitious 'given circumstances'. Hence all that resides in the actor's soul is accessible to his inner attention only. Another important quality of inner attention is that it enables the actor to transform its object from a cold, intellectual and rational one into a warm, emotional and sensuous one.

To develop his inner attention the actor must learn how to be attentive in life as well as on the stage. Stanislavsky is particularly anxious to drive home the fact that it is a great mistake to think that the actor can withdraw himself from life and take an interest only in his work on the stage. He had been accused by his critics of wishing to make the actor into a recluse, an anchorite. Nothing could be further from the truth. Again and again Stanislavsky insists that the true actor cannot tear himself away from life. He cannot stand aside from contemporary events. Indeed, so far as the development of his inner attention is concerned, it is outside the theatre that he must learn how to look and see, hear and listen. He must train himself to discern not only what is bad in life, a thing that comes easily to any man, but also what is good and beautiful. For the good and the beautiful, Stanislavsky points out, exalts the mind and evokes a man's best feelings, leaving indelible traces on his emotional and other memories. Nature being the most beautiful thing of all, it behoves the actor to study it most. 'To begin with', Stanislavsky advises the actor, 'take a flower, or a leaf, or a spider's web, or the traceries wrought by the frost on a window pane, and so on. These are all the works of art of the greatest artist we know— nature. Try to express in words what you feel about them. This will force your attention to dig deep into the observed object, and obtain a deeper understanding of its nature. And even here do not forget that all negative phenomena always have positive ones hidden in them, that there is beauty in ugliness, as there is ugliness in beauty. But the truly beautiful does not mind ugliness, for ugliness quite often brings out the beautiful.'

The actor must, therefore, examine both the beautiful and the ugly. He must try to put them into words and learn to see them. For without it, his idea of the beautiful will become one-sided, sugary, pretty, sentimental, and nothing could be more dangerous to art than that.

The actor must furthermore give the same kind of attention to works of art, such as literature, music, paintings and so on, for this will help him to acquire good taste and a love of the beautiful. He must be careful, however, not to attempt to train his sense of the beautiful analytically, with a notebook in his hand, as it were. 'A true artist', Stanislavsky writes, 'is inspired by everything that takes place around him; life excites him and becomes the object of his study and his passion; he eagerly observes all he sees and tries to imprint it on his memory not as a statistician, but as an artist, not only in his notebook, but also in his heart. It is, in short, impossible to work in art in a detached way. We must possess a certain degree of inner warmth; we must have sensuous attention. That does not mean, however, that we must renounce our reason, for it is possible to reason warmly, and not coldly'.

Since not every actor possesses the inner urge to study life in all its manifestations of good and evil, certain technical methods are necessary to arouse the actor's attention to what is happening around him in life. Stanislavsky advises such actors to use the same methods for arousing their attention as for awakening their imaginations. Let them put to themselves these questions and try to answer them honestly and sincerely: who, what, when, where, how and why is whatever they are observing taking place. Let them put into words what strikes them as beautiful or typical about a house, a room, the furniture in it or the people who own it. Let them find out the real purpose of a room or an object, why, for instance, the furniture is arranged in one way and not another, and what are the habits of their owners as indicated by the various things in a room.

Having learned how to examine everything around them and how to find their creative material in life, the actors must turn to the study of the material they require most for their creative work on the stage, namely, those emotions they receive from their personal and direct communication with people. This emotional material is so valuable because out of it the actors compose 'the life of the human spirit' of their parts, the creation of which forms the basic aim of their art. This material is so difficult to obtain because it is invisible, elusive, indefinite and only inwardly perceptible.

It is true that many invisible emotional experiences are reflected in facial expressions, in the eye, voice, speech, movements and the entire physical mechanism of man. That may make the task of the observer easier, but it is not so easy to understand the real motives of people, because they rarely open up their hearts to strangers and show themselves as they really are. As a rule, they conceal their true feelings, with the result that their external looks deceive rather than enlighten the observer.

Stanislavsky admits that his psycho-technique has not yet discovered the methods of solving all these difficulties, and all he can do is to give just a few hints to the actor which he may find useful in certain cases. 'When the inner world of the man the actor is observing', he writes, 'is revealed in his actions, thoughts, or impulses, the actor should devote all his attention to the study of those actions. He should ask himself, "Why did this man act thus and not thus? What was he thinking of?" and draw his own conclusions, define his attitude to the observed object, and try to understand the character of the man. When after a prolonged and penetrating process of observation and investigation he is successful in this task, he will obtain valuable creative material for his work on the stage. It often happens, however, that the inner life of the man the actor is observing is not accessible to his reason, but only to his intuition. In that case, he should try to find a way into the innermost recesses of the man's mind and look there for the material of his creative work with the help of as it were, "the antennae of his own feelings". This process requires very delicate powers of observation of the actor's own subconscious mind; for his ordinary attention is not sufficiently penetrating for probing into the living human soul in search of his material. In this complex process of looking for the most delicate emotional creative material, which cannot be perceived by his consciousness, the actor must rely on his common sense, experience of life, sensibility and intuition. While waiting for science to discover the practical approaches towards an understanding of a man's soul, the actor must do his best to learn how to discern the logic and consistency of its feelings and workings. This may help him to discover the best methods of finding the subconscious creative material in the external as well as the internal life of man.'

VII

Having dealt with the rather intangible, though not on that account less important, aspects of psycho-technique, Stanislavsky turns to its more tractable elements. The first of these is relaxation of muscles. Muscular tension, Stanislavsky observes, interferes with the actor's inner work and, particularly, with his attempts to enter into the feelings of his part. Indeed, while physical tension exists, it is a waste of time talking of correct and delicate feeling or of any normal psychical life of the part. Before beginning his work, the actor must, therefore, see that his muscles are sufficiently relaxed so as not to impede his freedom of movement. It is not, however, muscular spasms alone that interfere with the actor's work on the stage. The faintest strain anywhere can paralyse the actor's work, if not immediately discovered and dealt with.

An actor, being human, will always suffer from nervous strain during a public performance. If he relaxes it in his neck, it will appear in his diaphragm. He must, therefore, always fight this bodily defect of his, which it is impossible to overcome altogether. It can be fought successfully, however, if the actor evolves in his mind a special controller or observer for that purpose. The role of such a controller is rather a difficult one, since it must be constantly on the look-out for any nervous strain both in life and on the stage. If any unnecessary strain appears anywhere, the controller must remove it at once. This process of self-analysis and removal of tension must be so developed that it becomes automatic and unconscious. It must, in fact, be transformed into a normal habit, a natural necessity not only in the quiet places of the part, but above all in the moments of the greatest nervous and physical excitement. For at such moments it is natural for the actor to intensify his muscular tension. That is why an actor must take care that his muscles are completely free from any strain whenever his part demands particularly strong emotional action from him.

The habit of relaxing the muscles must be acquired by daily systematic exercises on and off the stage. The muscle-controller must become part of the actor's own mind, his second nature.

Each pose on the stage, however, must not only be checked by the actor's muscle-controller to make sure that it is free from all strain, but must also be justified by the invention of his imagination, the given circumstances, and 'if'. When this is done, the pose ceases to be a pose and becomes action. For, Stanislavsky insists, the stage is no place for any pose that cannot be justified. There is no room for artificial theatrical conventions either in the actor's creative work or in serious art. Should a conventional attitude for some reason become necessary, it must be the result of the inner feeling of the character, and not because it may be externally pretty.

The actor must never forget that nature exercises greater control over the human organism than consciousness or the so highly praised actor's technique. Each pose or position of the body on the stage, Stanislavsky points out, has three phases: (1) unnecessary tension which is unavoidable in every new pose because of the actor's state of agitation at a public performance; (2) the mechanical process of the relaxation of tension with the help of the controller; and (3) the justification of the pose in the case when the actor himself does not believe in it. *Tension, relaxation, justification.*

A living pose and real action (real, that is, in the imaginary life which is justified by the given circumstances in which the actor himself believes) will force nature to take a hand in the actor's work; for it is only nature that can fully control the muscles and bring them to a state of correct tension and relaxation.

It is obvious that the more delicate the feeling, the greater must be the precision, accuracy, and plasticity of its physical embodiment. This can be achieved only if the demands of the art of the stage are adapted to the demands of nature, for art lives in harmony with nature. On the other hand, nature is distorted by life and the bad habits that life engenders. The shortcomings which pass unnoticed in life become unbearable in the strong light of the stage. For in the theatre human life is shown in the narrow space of the frame of the stage, and people look at this life through binoculars; it is examined, like a miniature, through a magnifying glass. The actor, in fact, must always remember that the minutest strain in his acting will not escape the attention of the spectators.

VIII

The next element of psycho-technique which has a direct bearing on the methods the actor must apply to the handling of his part and which, incidentally, has provoked more criticism than any other element in the 'system' is that of 'pieces and problems'.

The division of a part into pieces is, according to Stanislavsky, necessary not only because this facilitates its analysis and study, but also because each piece contains its own creative problem, which either begets or is begotten by each piece.

Both the problems and the pieces must arise out of each other logically and consistently. There are large, not so large, and small pieces and problems which, if necessary, can coalesce. Both form the basic stages of a part which the actor must take into account during a performance.

There are many varieties of stage problems of any part in a

play, and not all of them are necessary or useful. The actor must, therefore, be able to differentiate between those which are useful to him and those which are not. To the former category belong: (1) problems dealing with the actor's side of the footlights, with the stage, that is, and not with the auditorium; (2) problems of the actor himself as a human being, which are analogous with the problems of his part; (3) creative and artistic problems, that is, those which contribute to the realisation of the basic aim of the art of the stage, namely the creation of 'the life of the human spirit of the part' and its artistic communication; (4) real, living and active human problems, which keep the part in a state of continuous motion, as opposed to artificial, dead, theatrical ones, which have no relation to the character represented by the actor, and are merely introduced for the entertainment of the spectators; (5) problems in which the actor himself, his partner, and the spectator can believe; (6) interesting and exciting problems which are capable of stimulating the process of entering into the feelings of the part; (7) problems which are typical of the part and which are not approximately but definitely connected with the main idea of the dramatic work; and (8) problems that correspond with the inner nature of the part and are not only superficially in accord with it.

All these are physical and psychological problems as well as problems 'elementarily psychological', or mechanical. The borderline between physical and psychological problems is not always easy to determine, but that, Stanislavsky observes, should not worry the actor. On the contrary, he should make the best use he can of this fact, always emphasising the physical side of it.

But however correct a problem may be, its chief and most important quality is the strong fascination it exerts on the actor himself. For it is very important that the problem should appeal to the actor and that he should want to carry it out, since such a problem possesses a magnetic force that attracts the creative will of the actor.

These problems Stanislavsky calls *creative problems*, and each of them, he points out, must be within the capacity of the actor to carry out.

As for the method of extracting these problems from the pieces into which the play has been divided, the actor, Stanislavsky advises, should invent corresponding names for each piece, for this will reveal the problem inherent in it. The problems—and this is rather an important point—must moreover be defined by a verb, for a verb always implies action, and the best verb for that purpose is 'I want to'. In fact, 'I want to' acquires almost the same magic quality in Stanislavsky's system as 'if'.

IX

The element of the 'pieces' into which a part is divided and the 'creative problems' of each piece expressed by 'I want to' depend for their effectiveness on the ability of the actor to represent them truthfully on the stage, which he can do only if he himself believes in them. Hence the actor's sense of truth and his belief form the next indispensable 'element' in Stanislavsky's system.

On the stage, Stanislavsky points out, truth and belief demand preliminary preparation, which consists in truth and belief arising first of all on the plane of imaginary life or artistic fiction and then being transferred to the stage. In life truth is what exists in reality and what every man knows for certain; on the stage truth is what does not exist in reality, but what could have happened 'if' the given circumstances of the play had really happened. Truth on the stage is, therefore, what the actor believes to exist in himself and in the minds and hearts of the other members of the cast. Truth and belief cannot exist without each other, and without them there can be no creative work on the stage.

But it would be a mistake to exaggerate the demands for truth or the significance of falsehood on the stage. The representation of truth for the sake of truth must needs lead to exaggeration which is the worst of all falsehoods. Fear of falsehood, on the other hand, will create an unnatural carefulness which is also one of the worst stage falsehoods. The actor must remember that truth is only necessary on the stage in so far as it helps to convince him and his partners and enables them to carry out correctly the creative problems inherent in their parts. As for falsehood, it too can be helpful to the actor inasmuch as it shows him the limits beyond which he cannot go.

The best way an actor can evoke a feeling of truth and belief in what he is doing on the stage is to concentrate on the simplest physical actions. What matters is not the physical actions themselves, but the feeling of truth and belief they help the actor to evoke in himself. If an actor finds it difficult to grasp at once the large truth of some big action, he should divide it, like his part itself, into smaller pieces, and try to believe in the smallest of them. Quite often by the realisation of one little truth and one moment of belief in the genuineness of his action, an actor will gain an insight into the whole of his part and will be able to believe in the great truth of the play.

Small physical actions, small physical truths and the moments of belief in them, Stanislavsky points out, acquire a great significance on the stage particularly in the climaxes of a tragedy. Actors ought therefore to make every possible use of the fact that small physical actions, occurring in the midst of important given circumstances, possess tremendous force. For it is in such conditions that the interaction between body and soul is created, as a result of which the external helps the internal, and the internal evokes the external. Another more practical reason why the truth of physical actions is so important during a tragic climax is that in a great tragedy an actor has to attain the highest degree of creative tension, so that to avoid overacting he must lay hold of something that is tangible and real. It is at such a moment, therefore, that what he needs most is a clear-cut, precise, exciting, and easily executed action, which will guide him along the right path naturally and mechanically, and will prevent him from being led astray. And the simpler such actions are, the quicker can he make use of them at a difficult moment of his part.

Tragic moments must consequently be approached without an undue sense of their importance and without any strain or nervousness. Nor should they be tackled all at once, as is the custom of most actors, but step by step and logically. For the actor has to *feel* each small or large truth of the physical actions and believe in it implicitly. This technique of the approach to feeling will produce a correct attitude towards tragic and dramatic climaxes in a play, and the actor will no longer be frightened by them.

Big and little physical actions are so valuable to the actor because of their clearly perceptible truth. They create the life of the actor's body, which is half the life of his part. They are also valuable because it is through them that the actor can enter into the life of his part and into its feelings easily and almost imperceptibly, and because they help to keep his attention concentrated on the stage, the play and his part.

Another important quality of physical actions is their strict logic, which introduces order, harmony and meaning into them and helps to create real and purposeful action.

In real life a man's subconsciousness generally ensures the logic and consistency of his actions, but on the stage neither the organic necessity of physical action nor its 'mechanical' logic and consistency exist, so that in place of the mechanical nature of such actions in real life, a conscious, logical and consistent stock-taking of every moment of the physical action must be introduced. As a result of frequent repetitions this process will grow into a habit.

But even logical and consistent physical actions on the stage will become artificial, that is, beget falsehood if they lack a sense of truth and if the actor does not believe in them.

'A formal approach to our complicated creative work and a narrow elementary understanding of it', Stanislavsky writes, 'is the greatest danger to my method, my whole system, and its psycho-technique. To learn how to divide up large physical actions into their component parts, to establish formally their logic and their sequence, to invent corresponding exercises for them and go through them with your students without taking into account the most important thing of all, namely the necessity of infusing a sense of truth and belief into the physical actions, is not so difficult and may be made into quite a profitable business. What a temptation to the exploiters of my system! But there is nothing more harmful or more stupid so far as art is concerned than a system for the sake of a system. You cannot make it an aim in itself; you cannot transform a means into an end. That would be the greatest lie of all!'

Introduction

A sense of truth and belief is even more necessary in a pause of 'tragic inaction', a very complex psychological state, and the problem of infusing life into it, that is, the logic and sequence of elusive, invisible and unstable inner feelings, is one of great importance. The actor has to ask himself what he would have done in real life if he had fallen into a state of tragic inaction. In life a man is active inwardly in his imagination before he takes any decision; he sees with his inner eye what is going to happen and how it is going to happen, and he carries out the indicated action in his mind. An actor, in addition, feels his thoughts physically, and can hardly restrain his inner calls to action, which crave to give an outward form to inner life. For this reason, an actor will find that his mental ideas about action will help him to evoke his inner activity. This process, moreover, is always taking place in the sphere of his normal and natural activity. For an actor's whole work takes place not in actual but in imaginary and non-existent life, a life which might have existed. This life the actors have a right to regard as real, and their physical actions on the stage as genuine physical acts. So far as the actor is concerned, the method of perception of the logic and sequence of feelings through the logic and sequence of physical actions is, therefore, entirely justified.

What the actor has to do in such cases, Stanislavsky advises, is to leave the complex psychological problem alone, since he could not possibly analyse it himself, and transfer his attention to an entirely different sphere, namely the logic of actions, where the problem can be solved in a purely practical and not scientific way with the help of his human nature, his experience of life, his instinct, sensibility, logic and the subconsciousness itself.

'By creating a logical and consecutive external line of physical actions', Stanislavsky writes, 'we *ipso facto* realise, if we pay proper attention to what we are doing, that parallel with this line there is created another line inside us—the line of the logical sequence of our feelings and sensations. This is obvious: for these inner feelings, unbeknown to us, beget actions and are inseparably linked with the life of these actions'.

The logical sequence of the physical actions and feelings will lead the actor to truth, and truth will evoke belief, and together

51

they will create what Stanislavsky calls 'I am', which means 'I exist, I live, I feel, and I think in the same way as the character I am representing on the stage does'. In other words, 'I am' evokes emotion and feeling and enables the actor to enter into the feelings of his part. 'I am' is, according to Stanislavsky, the condensed and almost absolute truth on the stage. 'I am' is the result of the desire for truth, and where there is truth, belief, and 'I am', there is inevitably also true human (not theatrical) experience. One of the consequences of this is that the spectator too is drawn into the action as an involuntary participant; he is drawn into the very midst of the life that is taking place on the stage, which he accepts as truth.

Truth on the stage, however, must be not only realistic, but also artistic. The actor, though, must remember that it is impossible to create artistic truth all at once, but that it is created in the course of the whole process of the gestation and growth of his part. In concentrating on the main inner features of his part, investing them with a correspondingly beautiful stage form and expression, and getting rid of anything that is superfluous, the actor, guided by his subconsciousness, his artistic flair, his talent, sensibility and taste, makes his part poetic, beautiful and harmonious, comprehensible and simple, and ennobling and purifying to all those who watch him. All these qualities help the stage creation to be not only right and truthful, but also artistic. These highly important feelings of the beautiful and the artistic cannot be defined in a formula. They demand feeling, practice, experience and time.

The actor must, therefore, avoid everything that is not in his powers to express and is contrary to his nature, logic, and common sense. For all that leads to distortion, violence, overacting and falsehood. The more frequently these appear on the stage, the worse for the actor's sense of truth, which becomes demoralised and perverted by untruth. The actor must fear the habits of deceit and falsehood on the stage. He must not let those evil seeds take root in him, for otherwise they will spread like weeds and smother the tender shoots of truth.

X

The basic principle of Stanislavsky's 'system' being, as stated earlier, the subconscious through the conscious, it is not surprising that he should include among the elements of psychotechnique one whose main function it is to arouse inspiration. This element is emotional memory, that is, the memory that resides in the actor's feelings and is brought to the surface of his consciousness by his five senses, though mostly by sight and hearing.

Stanislavsky illustrates the meaning of emotional memory by asking the actor to imagine a large number of houses, a large number of rooms in each house, a large number of cupboards in each room, drawers in each cupboard, large and small boxes in each drawer, and among the boxes one that is very small and is filled with beads. It is easy to find the house, the room, the cupboard, the drawer, and the boxes, and even the smallest box of all, but it will take a very sharp eye to find a tiny bead that fell out of the little box and, flashing for a moment, has gone for good. If it is found, it is by sheer accident. The same thing is true of the storehouse of an actor's memory. It too has its cupboards, drawers, and large and small boxes. Some of them are more and others less accessible. But, Stanislavsky asks, how is the actor to find one of the 'beads' of his emotional memory, which flashed across his mind once and then vanished for ever? When they occasionally appear the actor ought to be grateful to Apollo for having sent him those visual images, but he need not expect to be able to recover a feeling that has gone for good. He must be content with the things of today and not wait for something he had the day before to come to him again. He must never attempt to hunt after the old bead that is irretrievably lost, but every time do his best to achieve a new and fresher inspiration, even if it is weaker than that of the day before. The important thing is that it should be natural and come by itself out of the innermost recesses of his mind. Every new flash of inspiration is beautiful in its own way just because it is inspiration.

Feelings the actor has never before experienced on the stage are desirable because they are spontaneous, strong and vivid, though they only appear in brief flashes and are introduced into the part in separate episodes. The surprise hidden in these feelings contains an irresistibly stimulating force. But the trouble is that the actor cannot control these feelings, but is controlled by them. The whole thing, therefore, must be left to nature in the hope that when these flashes of inspiration do occur, they will do so when the actor wants them and will not be contrary to the play or the part. Unexpected and unconscious 'inspiration' is, of course, very welcome, but that does not in any way minimise the importance of the conscious and repetitive memories that are also a result of the actor's emotional memory, because it is through them that he can to a certain extent influence inspiration. Such conscious memories should be particularly dear to an actor because they are woven out of the carefully chosen material of his emotional memory.

'It must be remembered', Stanislavsky writes, 'that an actor always remains himself whatever his real or imaginary experiences may be. He must, therefore, never lose sight of himself on the stage. If he tried to run away from himself and renounce his own ego, he would cut the ground from under his feet, and no greater calamity could befall him. For the moment an actor loses sight of himself on the stage, his ability to enter into the feelings of his character goes overboard and overacting begins. In whatever part the actor may appear, therefore, he must always and without exception make use of his own feelings. The violation of this law', Stanislavsky declares emphatically, 'is tantamount to the murder of the character the actor is representing on the stage, for it means depriving it of his own living soul which alone can breathe life into a dead part'.

An actor, according to Stanislavsky, cannot help playing himself all his life, but he has to do it in different combinations and permutations of problems and given circumstances, which he himself conceives for his part and melts in the furnace of his own emotional memories, which are the best materials for his inner creative work. Hence the actor must always make use of them and never rely on what he may get from others.

Stanislavsky points out that the germs of all the human vices and virtues are to be found in the actor himself, who must use his art and technique for the discovery in a natural way of all those germs of human passions and then developing them for any of his parts. The 'soul' of the character represented on the stage is in this way composed of the living human elements of the actor's own 'soul', of his own emotional memories, etc. What the actor must do first of all is to find the methods of extracting this emotional material from his own soul and, secondly, the methods of creating out of them endless combinations of the human souls of his parts.

Since the stage sets and the mood they evoke in the actor stimulate his feelings, he must learn how to look, see and absorb everything that surrounds him on the stage so as to submit himself to the mood created by the stage illusion. But unfortunately not all good scenery stimulates an actor's emotional memory because producers and stage designers do not always realise that the sets, lighting, sound and other stage effects are much more important to the actor than to the audience, for it helps him to concentrate his entire attention on the stage, and distracts it from anything outside it. If the mood created on the stage by these effects is in harmony with the spirit of the play, an atmosphere will be created which will be favourable to the actor's work, rouse his emotional memory, and help him to enter into the feelings of his part. That is why an actor must learn how to look and see on the stage, and how to respond to his surroundings. He must, in short, know how to use all the stimuli of the stage.

Occasionally, however, the actor may find it necessary to reverse the process and, instead of going from stimulus to feeling, go from feeling to stimulus, especially if he wants to fix an inner experience that came to him by chance.

Stanislavsky illustrates this by an interesting experience of his own when playing the part of Satin (see illustration on page 56) in Gorky's *Lower Depths*.

The part as a whole, he writes, he found easy, but the monologue 'About Man' in the last act, which contains the key to the whole play, made him 'jib like a horse dragging a heavily laden cart up a steep hill' because of its great social, and indeed almost universal, significance. 'This "hill" in my part', Stanislavsky declares, 'destroyed all the joy I took in my work. It made me feel like a singer who had missed a high note'. But at the third or fourth performance something happened to remove that 'hill'. To find out the reason of his unexpected success, Stanislavsky went over the events of that day in his mind. He had received a large bill from his tailor which had made a terrible hole in his banking account, and that put him in a bad mood. He had lost the key from his writing desk, which made him feel worse. Then he had picked up a newspaper and read a notice of the play in which the weak points in his performance were praised and the good points criticised. That had further depressed him. He had gone over his part for the hundredth time, analysing it and trying to find the most significant thing about it. So absorbed had he been in this that during the performance itself he no longer worried about his part and did not think of the audience, being completely indifferent to his own acting and to the success of the performance as a whole. 'I did not even act that evening', Stanislavsky writes, 'but just carried out the tasks of my part logically and consistently in words and action. Logic and consistency led me along the right road, and the part acted itself and I never noticed its weak points. As a result my performance became of great importance to the play, though I never even thought of it'.

What happened was that all the events of that day had put Stanislavsky in a mood in which the newspaper notice had made a greater impression on him than it would have done otherwise. It undermined his accepted views of the general plan of the part and forced him to re-examine it afresh, with the result that his success was due to this re-examination. An experienced actor and good psychologist whom Stanislavsky approached with the request to tell him how to fix that stage experience, said to him, 'To attempt to repeat a feeling an actor accidentally experiences on the stage is like trying to revive a faded flower. Why not try growing a new one instead? How are you to do it? To begin with, forget all about the flower itself, but water its roots or plant a new seed, and a new flower will grow from this seed'.

The actor, Stanislavsky sums up his experience, must never think about the feeling itself, but try to find out what has caused it. It is the conditions that have produced the experience that matter. For these conditions are the soil, which after having been watered and manured, produce the feeling. When this happens, nature herself will as a rule produce a new feeling analogous to the feeling experienced by the actor before.

As for the character and quality of emotional memory, there is all the difference in the world, Stanislavsky points out, between an experience an actor has lived through himself and one which he has only heard of or read about. The actor has to transform the second type of emotional memory from sympathy into feeling. This will sometimes happen automatically. The actor enters into the position of the character he is representing on the stage so completely that he feels himself to be in his place, in which case sympathy will automatically be transformed into feeling. But if this does not happen, the actor has to call to his aid the magic 'if', the given circumstances, and all the other stimuli which will strike a responsive chord in his emotional memory.

'When we read a play for the first time,' Stanislavsky writes, 'we usually get a feeling of sympathy for the characters in it. This feeling of sympathy the actor must transform in the process of his preliminary work into his own genuine feeling of man-part'.

The actor, that is, must be able to call to his aid all the different inner and outer stimuli that arouse the right feeling in him. He must know how to find the stimuli for each feeling and he must be able to determine which stimulus produces which feeling.

The actor, however, can never rely on observation alone to replenish the storehouses of his emotional memory. It is not enough to widen the circle of attention by including in it different spheres of life; he must also understand the meaning of the facts he observes and be able to digest inwardly the received impressions of his emotional memory. For his acting to become creative and to represent 'the life of the human spirit', the actor must not only study this life, but take an active part in all its manifestations, wherever and whenever possible. Without it his art will dry up and become artificial. 'An actor who observes life from a distance', Stanislavsky writes, 'or experiences its joys and sorrows without trying to understand their complex causes, simply does not exist so far as true art is concerned. To live for

art he must at all costs grasp the meaning of the life that surrounds him, use his brains, widen his knowledge and constantly
re-examine his own opinions. An actor whose views on his art
are those of a philistine will merely succeed in destroying it. For
a philistine cannot be an artist worthy of the name. And the
great majority of actors are nothing but philistines who are using
the stage as a career for themselves'.

If an actor, therefore, is to fulfil what is expected of a real
artist, he must lead 'a full, interesting, beautiful, varied, exciting and exalted life'. He must possess 'an infinitely wide horizon,'
for he will be called upon to present 'the life of the human
spirit' of all the peoples of the world, present, past and future.

'The ideal of our creative work at all times has been and will
be what is eternal in art', Stanislavsky writes, 'what never grows
old and dies, and what is always young and dear to people. The
actor takes from real or imaginary life all it can give to man.
But he transforms all the impressions, passions and joys of life
into the material for his creative work. Out of what is transitory
and personal he creates a whole world of poetic images and ideas
which will live for ever'.

XI

Stanislavsky's theory of acting is quite properly mainly concerned with elucidating the problems which bear directly on
the ways in which an actor can enter into the feelings of his part.
But since drama is an art in which several persons are engaged
in re-creating 'the life of the human spirit' on the stage, it is no
less important that the actor should be able to communicate the
feelings of the character he is representing. He must, besides, be
able to understand what is passing in the minds of the other
characters in the play when they say something. Thought transmission, therefore, plays an essential role in the actor's technique,
all the more so as the audience too must be able to gain an
understanding of what is passing in the minds of the characters
in the play both when they say something and when they are
silent. Hence communication forms an important element of the
actor's psycho-technique.

Introduction

Indeed, as Stanislavsky points out, if a correct and an uninterrupted process of communication is necessary in life, then it is ten times more necessary on the stage. Such a process of stage communication, however, is only possible if the actor succeeds in banishing all his own personal thoughts and feelings during the performance. Since in most cases the private life of the actor does not cease when he comes on the stage, the line of the life of his part and his communication of it is interrupted by interpolations from the actor's private life which have nothing to do with the character he is representing. This is the first difficulty an actor must learn to overcome, for the nature of the theatre and its art are based on uninterrupted communication between the different members of the cast among themselves and each individual member with himself. Indeed, the spectators can understand and take part indirectly in the action only when the process of communication between the actors on the stage occurs. If, therefore, actors want to hold the attention of the audience they must take care that they communicate their thoughts, feelings and actions to their partners without interruption.

In soliloquies the process of self-communication can only be justified, Stanislavsky maintains, if it has a definite object of concentration. Stanislavsky himself always found that concentrating on his solar plexus solved this difficulty for him by helping him to stabilise his creative state of mind not only during pauses, but also during soliloquies. Similar difficulties exist in establishing mutual communication between the actor and his partner, and Stanislavsky advises the actor who experiences such difficulties to choose some particular point on his partner through which to communicate with him.

An actor, besides, must not only learn to convey his thoughts and feelings to his partner, but must make sure that they have reached his partner's mind and heart. To achieve this a short pause is necessary, for during this pause the actor can communicate with his eyes what his words cannot express. In his turn, the actor must know how to absorb the words and thoughts of his partner each time differently.

As for establishing communication with imaginary and non-existing objects (such as the ghost of Hamlet's father), it is a mistake, Stanislavsky thinks, for the actor to imagine its presence on the stage. Experienced actors know that what matters is not 'the ghost' but their own inner attitude towards it, and that is why they put in the place of the imaginary object (the ghost), their magic 'if' and try to find an honest answer to the question how they would have acted if there had been a ghost in the empty space before them.

So far as the audience is concerned, the actor must never try to communicate with it directly, but always indirectly. The peculiar difficulty of stage communication is that it takes place simultaneously between the actor, his partner, and the audience. However, there is this difference that between the actor and his partner on the stage the communication is always direct and conscious, while between the actor and the audience it is always indirect and unconscious. The remarkable thing is that in either case the communication is reciprocal.

Many people are of the opinion', Stanislavsky writes, 'that the external movements of hands, feet and trunk, which are visible to the eye, are an expression of activity, while the inner actions of spiritual communication, which are invisible to the eye, are inactive. This is a mistake, and all the more annoying since in our art, which creates the life of the human spirit of the part, every expression of inner action is highly important and valuable'.

Inner communication, therefore, is one of the most important active actions on the stage, which is indispensable to the process of the creation and transmission of 'the life of the human spirit' of the part.

As usual, Stanislavsky invents an utterly unscientific term for the definition of this inner and invisible communication. He calls it *ray-emission and ray-absorption*, or *irradiation* and *absorption*. In a calm state of mind, he explains, a person's ray-emissions and ray-absorptions are almost imperceptible, but in moments of emotional stress, esctasy, or heightened feelings, the ray-emissions and ray-absorptions grow more definite and perceptible both to those who are emitting them and those who are absorbing them. 'It is as though the inner feelings and desires,' he writes, 'emitted rays which, issuing through the eyes and body, poured in a stream over other people'.

Introduction

If the actor makes full use of the long series of logically and consistently interwoven experiences and feelings, the connection between them will grow stronger till, finally, they assume the form of reciprocal communication which Stanislavsky defines as *grip*, and which will invariably make the processes of ray-emission and ray-absorption stronger. On the stage there must be a grip in everything—in the eyes, hearing and all the rest of the five senses. 'If an actor listens,' Stanislavsky writes, 'he must both listen and hear. If he smells, he must inhale. If he looks, he must look and see, and not just glance at an object without hanging on to it as it were, with his teeth, which', Stanislavsky is careful to observe, 'does not mean at all that he should strain himself unnecessarily'. On the stage and particularly in tragedy, such a grip is absolutely necessary. To represent passions which impinge violently upon life, the actor must possess both an inward and an outward grip, either of which will result in ray-emission. As for the method of mastering this process, Stanislavsky again points out that if the actor finds it impossible to go from the inner to the outer, he has to go from the outer to the inner. He suggests two exercises to facilitate ray-emission and ray-absorption. In the first the actor arouses in himself any kind of emotion he likes with the aid of the different elements of psycho-technique and tries to convey it to another person. In the same way he can accustom himself to the sensation of ray-absorption, evoking it naturally and noticing it when in communication with other people. The second exercise consists in attempting to evoke only the physical sensation of ray-emission or ray-absorption without any accompanying emotional experience. Here the actor will require great attention, for otherwise he will be liable to mistake a simple muscular tension for the sensation of ray-emission or ray-absorption. When the physical process is ready, the actor should obtain from within himself any kind of feeling for its emission or absorption. He must remember, though, that ray-emissions and absorptions are produced freely, easily and naturally, without any expenditure of physical energy. This method should also help the actor to fix his attention on an object and keep it there, for without a focus point there can be no ray-emission.

Introduction

There are all sorts of ways in which actors can bring out some hidden nuance of a feeling to attract attention to their particular state of mind at some moment in the performance. What matters about these aids which actors use when communicating with each other on the stage is their vividness, subtlety, refinement and taste. There are two things an actor has to consider when inventing these aids, namely the way in which to choose them and the way in which to carry them out. The most effective of these aids to communication are subconscious. They appear in moments of genuine inspiration, and their main strength lies in their surprise, daring and boldness. Conscious aids suggested by the producer or fellow-actors must never be accepted by the actor as given. He must always adapt them and make them his own.

An actor, moreover, must never use his aids for the entertainment of the audience, however great the temptation may be to gain easy success, for they will inevitably lead to overacting and the disappearance of real human feeling and genuine action.

There is no direct way of evoking subconscious aids and the best thing is to leave everything to nature. As for the half-conscious aids, that is, aids which are only to a certain extent subconscious, something may be achieved there with the help of psycho-technique, but not very much, since the technique of originating aids is not very prolific. The actor must remember, however, always to introduce a new nuance into the aids he has already used and justify the change, and then his acting will gain a new freshness.

XII

Having mustered all the main elements through which the actor can re-create 'the life of the human spirit' of his part, the question that still remains unanswered is what it is that puts them all into motion. In other words, if an actor is given the script of a play in which he is to act one of the characters, what is it that rouses the elements into activity so as to assure a good performance of his part? First his reason enables him to understand the text of the play. Secondly, his will infuses the necessary courage in him to proceed with his work. Thirdly, his feeling enables him to transform mere sympathy for his character into experience. Reason, will and feeling are, therefore, what Stanislavsky calls the motive forces of the actor's inner life.

Reason (intellect), Stanislavsky points out, has two main functions, namely, the moment of its first impact which leads to the emergence of the idea, and the one originating from it, leading to the emergence of judgment. Reason, will, and feeling always act together, simultaneously, and in close dependence on one another (reason-will-feeling, feeling-will-reason or will-feeling-reason). Will and feeling are automatically included in the actor's creative work once he begins to use his reason, or, to put it another way, an idea about something naturally evokes judgment about it. The interdependence and close connection between one creative force and the rest is very important, and it would be a mistake not to make use of them for the actor's practical purposes. The technique of this mental process consists in rousing to action every member of the triumvirate, as well as all the elements of the actor's creative mechanism, naturally and organically, by the interaction of all its members. Sometimes the motive forces of inner life start working at one and the same time, in which case the actor must submit himself entirely to the ensuing natural creative tendencies of these forces. But when reason, will and feeling remain unresponsive to the actor's creative appeal he has to make use of the stimuli or baits, which not only each of the elements, but also each motive force, possesses. The actor must be careful, however, not to arouse them all at once. He should start with one, preferably reason, which is more accommodating than the other two. In such a case, the actor gets a corresponding idea from the formal thought of the text and begins to see what the words mean. The idea, in turn, evokes the corresponding judgment, and the thought, no longer formal and dry but animated by ideas, naturally arouses will and feeling.

It is quite possible that if the actor approaches the play or his part by taking feeling, and not intellect, for his starting point, all the other motive forces of inner life will be brought into action at once; but if not, he will have again to use some bait, which in this case will be rhythm. Will, on the other hand, can be indirectly roused by a problem.

Introduction

The correctness of the statement that the motive forces of inner life are reason, will and feeling is confirmed, Stanislavsky maintains, by nature herself in the existence of actors in whose characters emotion, reason or will prevail. The actors in whom feeling predominates over reason will, in playing Romeo or Othello, emphasise the emotional side of these parts. Actors in whose creative work will predominates over reason and feeling will, in playing Macbeth or Brand, emphasise their ambition or religious proclivities. While actors in whose creative nature reason predominates over will and feeling will, when playing Hamlet, involuntarily give an intellectual tinge to their part.

The predominance of one or another of the motive forces of inner life must, however, never be strong enough to suppress the others. There must, Stanislavsky insists, be a harmonious correlation between all the motive forces.

The direction taken by the motive forces of inner life, Stanislavsky maintains, must form one unbroken line. It is very rarely that the actor's reason, will and feeling grasp the chief meaning of a new play, are inspired by it creatively, and produce the inner state of mind which is necessary for his work. More often the text of the play is assimilated only to a certain extent by reason, only partially encompassed by feeling, and only arouses indefinite, scrappy impulses of will. During the first period of his acquaintance with the playwright's work, therefore, the actor only gets a vague idea of it, and his judgment of it cannot but be superficial. His will and feeling also react rather hesitatingly to his first impressions, and he only gets a 'general' perception of the life of his part.

This is only what can be expected, since in the majority of cases a great deal of work is required before the actor can grasp the inner meaning of a play. It may also happen sometimes that the actor finds it impossible to make head or tail of the text of a play at the first reading, his will and feeling remain passive, and he can form no idea or judgment of the work. This is often the case with symbolic or impressionistic plays. He has, therefore, to rely on someone else's opinions and judgment, and try to understand the text of the play with their help. After a great deal of hard work he will at last get a vague idea of what it all means, but he will still have no independent opinions about it, for these emerge only gradually. When they do, the actor will in the end succeed one way or another in getting all the motive forces of his inner life to take a hand in his work.

At first, while the aim is still obscure, the invisible currents of direction of the motive forces are in an embryonic stage. Only single moments of the life of the part, perceived by the actor when he made his first acquaintance with the play, have aroused the motive forces of inner life strongly enough to move in a certain direction. Thoughts and desires appear in spurts. They emerge, come to a halt, reappear and again vanish. If these lines, issuing from the motive forces of inner life, were to be represented graphically, one would get a large number of short jerky lines going in all directions. But the more familiar the actor gets with his part and the deeper his understanding of its chief aim, the straighter do these lines of direction become. It is then that the first stage of the actor's creative work arises.

The art of the stage, like any other art, must have an unbroken line, and the moment the different lines of direction of the motive forces straighten out, that is become one unbroken line, the creative work of the actor can be said to start. The actor, though, must have many such unbroken lines, that is to say, lines of the inventions of his imagination, attention, objects, logic and consistency, pieces and problems, inclinations and actions, uninterrupted moments of truth and belief, emotional memories, communication, extraneous aids and other elements that are necessary in his work.

If, for instance, the line of action is broken on the stage, then it means that the part, the play, and the performance have come to a standstill. If the same should happen with the line of the motive forces of inner life, say with thought (reason), then the actor will be unable to form any idea or judgment of the meaning of the words of his text, which means that he will not understand what he is doing or saying in his part on the stage. If, on the other hand, the line of feeling and will should come to a sudden stop, the actor and his part will cease desiring or experiencing anything.

The man who is the actor and the man who is the part have to live with all these lines on the stage almost without interruption. These lines impart life and movement to the character the actor is representing. The moment they come to a stop, the life of the part comes to an end and paralysis or death sets in. But such an alternation of death and revival is abnormal, for the part demands continuous life and an almost unbroken line.

In each part and play, moreover, the larger lines are composed of a large number of small lines, and on the stage they can encompass different intervals of time, days, weeks, months, years and so on. The author who creates the line of life of the play, however, does not indicate the whole line, but only parts of it, leaving intervals between each part. He does not describe many things that happen off stage, and the actor has often to use his imagination to fill in the gaps in the play left by the author. For without it, it is impossible to present on the stage the entire 'life of the human spirit' of the actor in his part, but only separate bits of it. To enter into the feelings of his character, however, the actor must have a relatively unbroken line of the life of his part and the play.

Gaps and breaks in the line of the part are inadmissible not only on the stage itself, but also behind the scenes. For they tear apart the life of the represented character, and leave dead, empty spaces in its place, which are filled by thoughts and feelings of the actor that have no relation to what he is playing. This drives him into the wrong direction, into the sphere of his private life. But many actors do not know how to carry on playing their parts off stage. In that case, it is enough if they only imagine what they would have done if they had found themselves in the same conditions as the person they are representing on the stage. Every actor must find his own answer to this question as well as to other questions relating to his part at every single performance. For otherwise there is no reason why the actor should arrive at the theatre and appear in front of a crowd of spectators. Indeed, an actor who leaves the theatre without having solved this question, has not carried out his duties.

It is important to realise that the life of a part is one unbroken sequence of objects and circles of attention on the plane of imagined reality, on the plane of memories of the past, or on the plane of dreams of the future. The fact that the line is unbroken is of great importance to the actor, and he must train himself to keep it unbroken, and always fixed on the stage, never for a moment letting it stray into the auditorium. If the attention of the actor is constantly moving from one object to another, then this constant change of the objects of his attention creates the unbroken line. Should the actor concentrate his attention only on one object, keeping it fixed on it during the whole of the act or during the whole of the play, there would be no line of movement, and even if one had been formed, it would have been the line of a madman, an *idée fixe*.

What direction do the lines of the motive forces of the actor's inner life take? They move in the direction of those inner creative powers in the actor which they influence, that is in the direction of his inner and physical nature, and in the direction of his inner elements. Reason, will and feeling raise the alarm, and with the strength, temperament and persuasion peculiar to them mobilise all the actor's inner creative powers. 'The endless inventions of the imagination, the objects of attention, the elements of communication, problems, desires and actions, truth and belief and the emotional memories', Stanislavsky writes, 'form long lines, and the motive forces of inner life pass along them in review, arousing the elements to action and as a result of it becoming themselves even more powerfully infected with creative enthusiasm. Moreover, they absorb from the elements particles of their natural qualities, and grow more active in consequence'.

The motive forces of inner life, in short, absorb all the tones, colours, nuances and moods of the elements and become impregnated with their inner content; in turn, they infect the elements with their energy, strength, will, emotion and thought, and imbue them with those particles of the part and the play with which they are associated and which are charged with their own creative impulses. It is out of these tender shoots of the soul of the part grafted on the elements that the feelings of the character in the play first arise in the soul of the actor. They are all set in motion under the guidance of the motive forces of inner life, making for what is credible on the stage and in the play, that is, artistic truth. And the further these elements go, the closer do the different movements of their lines become, and in the end they all coalesce. This merging of all the elements of the actor-part in their general movement towards artistic truth creates the important inner condition which Stanislavsky calls the inner creative state of mind of the actor on the stage, which is both worse and better than the normal state of mind: worse because it contains a bit of the theatre and the stage with its self-exhibiting impulses, and better because it contains the feeling of public solitude which is unknown in normal life.

All the actor's artistic abilities and natural qualities as well as some of the methods of psycho-technique, which Stanislavsky has called 'elements' are, in fact, elements of the inner creative state of the actor on the stage. When an actor comes out on the stage and faces a large audience, he is apt to lose his self-control from stage-fright, or from a sense of responsibility or from a realisation of the difficulties of his part. At such a moment the elements of his creative state tend to disintegrate and live apart from each other: attention for the sake of attention, objects for the sake of objects, the feeling of truth for the sake of truth, extraneous aids for the sake of extraneous aids, and so on. This is abnormal; for the elements which create his inner state of mind should, as in life, be inseparable. In fact, owing to the abnormal conditions of stage work, the actor's creative state of mind is intrinsically unstable, and he tends to act just for the sake of 'acting', and to communicate with the spectators rather than with his partners. What the actor must do, therefore, is to see that his creative state of mind on the stage approaches the natural state of mind that he normally experiences in real life. He must do his best to induce such a normal state of mnid artificially with the help of inner technique.

All actors make up and dress for their parts before the beginning of a performance, but what most of them forget is that it is no less important to make up and dress their souls for the creation of 'the life of the human spirit' of their parts. How are they to do it? First of all, they must arrive at the theatre in good time, that is at least two hours before the beginning of the performance in the case of a leading part. They must then 'tune their inner strings', check the different elements and 'baits' which help to bring their creative mechanism into action. They ought to start with the relaxation of their muscles, for without that no creative work is possible on the stage. 'And then?' Stanislavsky writes, 'Why, take any object. It is a picture. What does it represent? What is its size? Its colours? Take some remote object! The small circle—not farther than your feet or just up to your chest. Think of a physical problem! Justify it and bring it to life, first with one, then with another, invention of your imagination ! Bring your action to the point of truth and belief. Think of the magic 'if', the given circumstances, etc. After having brought all the elements into play, choose any element you like to start your work with, and the rest will come as a result of the natural inclination for team-work of the motive forces of inner life and the elements. And the same applies to the actor's creative state of mind.

'What nature hath joined together, let no actor put asunder', Stanislavsky goes on, adapting the ceremonial words to suit his own argument. 'For nature has its own laws and conditions which can be violated by the actor only at his own peril, and which every actor must thoroughly study, understand, and preserve. That is why he must repeat all his exercises at the beginning of every performance'.

These preliminary exercises before the performances are merely a 'check-up' of the actor's expressive apparatus, 'the tuning of his inner creative instrument'. If the actor's part has reached the stage where he can start his work, this preliminary process of self-adjustment will be easy and comparatively quick. If not, it will be more difficult, but not less necessary. At the rehearsals too and during his work at home, the actor must try to achieve the right creative state of mind, which usually suffers most from instability at the very beginning, when he has not yet come to grips with his part, and at the end when his part shows signs of wear and tear. The correct inner creative state of mind is always in a state of disequilibrium and demands constant adjustment, which in the course of time becomes automatic. An actor must always possess sufficient self-control to enable him to carry on with his acting and at the same time correct any inner element that has gone awry.

'An actor', Stanislavsky quotes Salvini again, 'lives, weeps and laughs on the stage, and while weeping or laughing, he observes his laughter and tears. And it is in this dualism, in this equilibrium between life and acting, that art finds its true expression'.

The inner state of mind of the actor depends on the nature of each problem and action. Hence the quality, strength, stability, firmness, depth, duration, sincerity and composition of the inner creative state are infinitely various. If in addition one takes into consideration the fact that in each of these aspects of the creative state a certain element, or one of the motive forces of inner life, or some natural idiosyncrasy of the actor usually predominates, then their diversity seems truly limitless. Occasionally the creative state will be reached accidentally and it will itself look for the theme of inner action. More often, however, it will be some interesting problem, or part, or play that will impel the actor to engage in his creative work and arouse in him the right creative state of mind.

XIII

If all the elements of the actor's creative state form one unbroken line, then what is the direction in which this line is moving? Or, in other words, what is the whole purpose of the performance? Its purpose, surely, is to provide a scenic embodiment of the playwright's ruling idea. Hence the unbroken lines formed by the elements of the creative states of all the actors taking part in the performance must all be moving in the direction of the play's ruling idea.

It is, therefore, the duty of the actor to grasp the meaning of the ruling idea for the sake of which the author wrote his play. In addition he must make sure that the ruling idea appeals to him—both intellectually and emotionally. For the playwright's intentions will never be fully expressed by the actor if the ruling idea of the play does not strike a chord in the heart of the actor himself. It will be found, as a rule, that the same ruling idea will strike a different chord in the heart of each actor playing the same part; for if each performer does not reveal his individuality in his part, his creation is dead. The actor, in short, must know how to make every ruling idea his own, that is, 'find in it an inner meaning which is akin to his soul'.

The process of finding the ruling idea will be facilitated if the actor defines it by a phrase, for this will impart a meaning and a direction to his work on the play. 'Very often', Stanislavsky writes, 'the ruling idea is discovered only after the performance of the play, and sometimes the spectators themselves help the actor to find the right name for it'. If the ruling idea enters firmly into the actor's imagination, thoughts, feelings and all the elements of his creative state; if it reminds him constantly of the inner life of his part and of the aim of his work; and if it helps him to keep his sensory attention in the sphere of the life of his part, then the process of entering into the feelings of his character will take its normal course. If, on the other hand, there should be a conflict between the inner aim of the play and the actor's own aims, his part will be a failure, and the whole play may suffer disastrous distortion.

This active inner movement of the motive forces of the inner life of the actor-part through the play forms what Stanislavsky calls the 'through-action' of the actor-part. But for the through-action all the pieces and problems, the given circumstances, communication, extraneous aids, moments of truth and belief, etc., would have remained quiescent, separated from each other, and without hope of coming to life. But the line of through-action welds them together, threading all the elements like beads on one string and directing them towards the ruling idea. If an actor acts his part without taking through-action into account, he is not acting on the stage in the given circumstances and with the magic 'if', nor is he drawing nature herself with her sub-consciousness into his work, nor is he creating 'the life of the human spirit' of his part. Indeed, everything in Stanislavsky's 'system' exists for the sake of through-action and the ruling idea. The graph of through-action represents a straight line made up of the different lines of the actor's part, some short and some long, but all moving in one direction, thus:

 *ruling idea*

These short lines of the life of the part are inter-connected and form one long line of through-action, which passes through the whole of the play. But if the actor lacks a ruling idea, each of the lines of the life of his part will be moving in different directions thus:

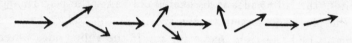

Under such conditions the through-action is destroyed, the whole play is torn into bits and pieces, moving in different directions, and each part of it has to exist by itself. But however beautiful each of these parts may be when considered separately, it is by itself quite useless so far as the play as a whole is concerned.

The task of defining the ruling idea of a play and so making sure that the through-action follows the course the author had intended for it, becomes even more tricky than it is if the producer wishes to introduce some tendentious interpretation into it. Stanislavsky is very outspoken about the dangers of tendentiousness in general. 'Tendentiousness and art', he writes in *My Life in Art*, 'are incompatible: the one excludes the other. As soon as one approaches the art of the stage with tendentious, utilitarian, or any other non-artistic idea, it withers away. It is impossible to accept a sermon or a propaganda piece as true art.' If, therefore, a tendentious idea having nothing to do with the play's ruling idea is introduced into a play, some parts of the play will be torn out of the straight line of the through-action and diverted from the ruling idea, thus:

ruling idea

tendency

If, on the other hand, the tendentious idea corresponds to the ruling idea, then the creative process will take its normal course, thus:

ruling idea

tendency

This is particularly true if the producer of a classical play tries to graft 'new' ideas on it in order to 'bring it up-to-date'. In such a case the 'new' ideas will ruin the old masterpiece if they are forcibly imposed on the old play for the sake of topical interest; if, however, the modern tendencies, as sometimes happens, agree with the ruling idea of the old play, they will cease to exist independently and merge with the ruling idea.

XIV

What makes every performance of a play, no matter how many times it may be repeated, always fresh, sincere, truthful, and above all, quite surprisingly different? It is not the actor's technique, nor the producer's ingenuity, nor even the playwright's genius. It is only, Stanislavsky suggests, the actor's subconscious and intuitive creative ability which can infuse a different sort of life into every performance of the same play. The actor who repeats himself is lost; for there is nothing more unendurable than a well-drilled performance in which everything has been thought out beforehand. It is the actor who can invest his 'now' with ever new and ever fascinating properties who is the creative actor *par excellence*.

What, however, must the actor do to evoke the subconscious powers of creative art? First of all, he must get rid of all muscular and inner strains. But even if he achieves a complete relaxation of outer and inner tension, it is only very seldom that he will obtain a complete illusion of reality on the stage. He will mostly find in the imagined life of his part truth alternating with verisimilitude and belief with probability. It is all the more necessary, therefore, that he should make friends with his subconscious mind, so active in real life but so rarely met with on the stage. Without the subconscious work of his inner organic nature, his performance is false as well as rational, lifeless as well as conventional, uninspired as well as formal. The actor must consequently give his creative subconsciousness a free pass to the stage. He must eliminate everything that interferes with it, and strengthen everything that helps to evoke it. It is the basic task of psycho-technique, therefore, so to mould the actor's mind as to awaken in him the subconscious processes of organic nature.

But how is the actor to approach consciously something that is unamenable to consciousness? This serious objection to his 'system' Stanislavsky meets by pointing out that fortunately there is no sharp division between conscious and subconscious experience. Besides, consciousness quite often indicates the direction in which subconsciousness is moving when carrying out its creative work. This fact is very widely used by psycho-technique, that is, by the methods of Stanislavsky's system whose aim it is to stimulate the actor's subconscious creative powers through his conscious inner technique.

The process has already been discussed. The actor must see that the activities of all the elements of his inner creative state as well as the motive forces of his inner life (reason, will, feeling) and through-action become indistinguishable from normal human activities, for it is only then that he will experience the inner life of his organic nature in his part and will find in himself the real truth of the life of the person he is representing on the stage. Since it is impossible not to believe in truth, the 'I am' of the part will be created by itself.

In fact, every time truth and belief are born in the actor involuntarily, organic nature with her subconsciousness will take a hand in his work. It is thus that through the conscious psycho-technique of the actor, carried to its fullest extent, the ground is prepared by nature herself for the creative sub-conscious process. The important thing is that the actor must carry out the methods of psycho-technique to their fullest extent, for only then can he hope for assistance from his subconsciousness. And he must further realise that it is a mistake to think that every moment of creative work on the stage must needs be some-thing great, complicated and exalted. The opposite is true: the most insignificant action and the most unimportant technical device can become of vital importance if they are carried out to their fullest extent, for it is there that truth, belief, and 'I am' arise. When that happens, the actor's inner and physical mechan-ism is working normally on the stage, just as in life, in spite of the abnormal conditions of work in front of an audience. What comes about normally in life, is brought about on the stage by psycho-technique.

The actor must therefore never forget that the most in-significant physical and inner action, if driven to the absolute limit of 'I am', is capable of drawing his inner organic nature with its subconsciousness into his work.

As for the psycho-technical methods of bringing it about, Stanislavsky points out that in chemistry when two solutions produce too weak a reaction, a minute quantity of a third acts as a catalytic agent which at once brings the reaction to the required strength. The actor, too, must introduce such a catalytic agent into his work in the form of some impromptu action or some small detail of truth, as soon as he has been successful in achieving the correct inner creative state, and as soon as he feels that with the aid of psycho-technique everything in him is only waiting for a push for nature to start her work. Such catalytic agents must be sought everywhere—in the performances, the visual images, feelings, desires, in the small details of the inventions of the imagination, in an object with which the actor is in communication, in the hardly perceptible details of the stage setting, or mise-en-scene. There are hundreds of ways in which the actor can discover some tiny grain of human truth which will evoke belief and create the conditon of 'I am'. As a result of these few moments of unexpected and complete fusion between the life of the character in the play and the life of the actor on the stage, the actor will feel the presence of bits of himself in his part and bits of his part in himself, after which truth, belief in it, and 'I am' will deliver him into the hands of organic nature and her subconsciousness.

Another method of inducing subconsciousness to take over more and more of the actor's conscious work, is for him to concentrate on his big problems, which will automatically leave the small problems to his subconsciousness. The big problems of his part are, therefore, his best psycho-technical methods for exerting an indirect influence on his subconscious nature. The same thing happens to the big problems the moment the actor's mind is beginning to be preoccupied with the ruling idea of the play. They too are then to a large extent carried out subconsciously. Since, moreover, through-action consists of a long line of big problems, each of which contains an enormous number of small problems which are carried out subconsciously, the total number of moments of subconscious creative work concealed in the through-action, pervading the whole play from beginning to end will also be enormous. Through-action is consequently the most powerful method for influencing subconsciousness the actor can possibly find.

Through-action, however, does not arise by itself. Its creative impetus is directly dependent on the interest which the ruling idea can arouse. Hence, through-action and the ruling idea, which also contains many properties capable of giving rise to subconscious creative moments, are the most powerful 'baits' for stimulating the subconscious creative work or organic nature. It must therefore be the chief aim of every actor to be fully aware of all their manifold implications, for then he can safely leave the rest to be carried out subconsciously by 'the supreme magician—nature'.

Since conscious psycho-technique helps to create the methods and the favourable conditions for the creative work of nature with her subconsciousness, the actor ought always to think of the things which stimulate the action of the motive forces of his inner life and which help him to achieve his inner creative state. He must also always keep in mind the ruling idea and through-action, and indeed everything that is accessible to his consciousness, with whose help he must learn to prepare the ground for the subconscious work of his artistic nature. What he ought never to do is to try to achieve inspiration in a direct way, just for the sake of inspiration. Stanislavsky's 'system' does not manufacture inspiration; it merely prepares the ground for its manifestation in a natural way. That does not mean, however, that Stanislavsky is against the actor's making use of 'happy accidents', that is to say, accidents which, though unforeseen by the producer or actor, give a touch of truth to a certain scene. On the contrary, Stanislavsky strongly advises the actor to use such accidents as a 'tuning fork' which will give him the right note of life among the conventional lies of the stage and make everybody feel and believe in 'I am'. It may, accidentally, also help the actor to find a subconscious approach to his part. Coincidences and accidents on the stage, however, must be used wisely: the actor must never overlook them, but he must not rely on them either.

The fundamental principle of Stanislavsky's theory of acting is, as we see, that the actor's work is not a technical conjuring trick or a game of 'let's pretend'; it is, on the contrary, in every way a natural process, a natural creative act, resembling, Stanislavsky suggests, the birth of a human being, in this particular case, the man-part.

Every artistic stage character is a unique individual creation, like everything else in nature. In the process of its creation, there is a 'he', that is, 'the husband', namely the author of the play, and a 'she', that is 'the wife', namely the actor or actress, big with the part conceived from the author and the seed of his creation. There is 'the child'—the created part. There are in this process, besides, the moments of the first acquaintance between 'him' and 'her', their first friendship, their falling in love, their quarrels and differences, their reconciliations, and their union, followed by conception and pregnancy. During these periods the producer, Stanislavsky points out, helps the process of the birth of the man-part by playing the role of matchmaker. As in pregnancy, there are different states in the creative process which exert a good or bad influence on the actor's life. For instance, a woman gets all sorts of strange notions during her pregnancy, and the same thing happens to an actor. The different periods of the conception and the ripening of the part influence, each in its own way, the character of the actor and his state of mind in private life. The organic growing into a part, Stanislavsky estimates, takes a considerably longer time than the bearing of a child. In other words, an actor, according to Stanislavsky, ought to devote more than nine months to the study of his part. During this period the producer changes his role of matchmaker to that of midwife. 'In the normal course of pregnancy and delivery', Stanislavsky concludes his comparison, 'the inner creation of the actor assumes a physical form naturally, and is then nursed and brought up by his "mother"—the actor. But there are also in our business premature births, miscarriages, and abortions. It is then that unfinished and malformed monsters make their appearance on the footboards'.

The analysis of this process, Stanislavsky observes, convinces him that organic nature always acts according to certain well-established laws whenever it is creating something new in the world, whether it is something biological or something created by the imagination of man. In short, the creation of a living human being on the stage (or a part) is a natural act of the organic creative nature of the actor.

XV

In *An Actor's Work on Himself* Stanislavsky deliberately applies the *magic if* of his 'system' to make his book, above all, a practical rather than theoretical exposition of his ideas of acting. He assumes the fiction of a school of acting in which he is the teacher. He explains the psycho-technique of his system by examples of dramatic scenes which he either himself invents or takes from famous plays and which he lets his pupils act again and again in order to demonstrate his theories. The same method is applied in *The System and Methods of Creative Art* with the difference that the fiction of his first book becomes reality in this posthumous collection of lectures taken down in shorthand by one of the actors. These 'discourses' of Stanislavsky were given in the 'studio' of the Moscow Bolshoy Theatre, the famous Moscow opera house, between 1918 and 1922. In *My Life in Art* Stanislavsky gives a detailed account of his work at the studio of the Moscow Bolshoy Theatre. A 'studio', by the way, Stanislavsky defines as 'neither a theatre nor a dramatic school for beginners, but a laboratory for the experiments of more or less trained actors'.

In 1918 it was decided to raise the level of acting of the opera singers of the Moscow Bolshoy Theatre, and Stanislavsky was invited to do it. He had had experience of opera work at the very beginning of his career in the *Alexeyev Circle* (Stanislavsky's real name was Alexeyev and he adopted the stage name of Stanislavsky to keep his family name out of his first stage experiments in French musical comedy, in which he appeared in parts that did not exactly shed a lustre on the social position of his father who was a rich Moscow business man). When in his twenties he was appointed a director of the Moscow Conservatoire and the Russian Musical Society, he came in close touch with opera. After a short period of enthusiasm for the ballet, he thought for a time of becoming an opera singer himself and took lessons in singing from the famous tenor Theodor Kommissarzhevsky, father of the Russian producer Theodor Kommissarzhevsky and the famous Russian actress Vera Kommissarzhevskaya. However, he soon realised that he was not cut out for opera, and devoted himself entirely to drama. About thirty years later, he was again active in opera, but this time as a teacher of acting.

At the time his 'system' was ready, though not as yet published. In his work with the members of the Moscow Bolshoy Theatre, he applied it to opera.

The importance of these 'discourses' lies in the fact that in them we see Stanislavsky's methods of putting into practice his long experience as actor and producer. They include a great deal of material that forms a valuable addition to his famous 'system', especially so far as its philosophic background is concerned. Such, for instance, is Stanislavsky's new treatment of attention and rhythm, and his formulation of the fundamental principles of acting in his Seven Steps of Perfection, namely concentration, mental alertness, courage, self-composure, heroic tension, nobility of mind, and gladness, to which he devotes six chapters (XV to XX). But perhaps the real value of these 'discourses' lies in their bringing the reader in close contact with Stanislavsky's personality, with his infectious enthusiasm for the art of the stage, his great love of man, and his infinite patience with an actor's shortcomings.

These 'discourses' were never prepared, and therein probably lies their great charm. Stanislavsky did not believe in 'lecturing'. He always accompanied his theoretical work with practical examples, and was never afraid of repeating himself. He welcomed difficulties because they merely gave him another chance of demonstrating that in art nothing is impossible, provided the artist does not violate the laws of nature but applies them logically to his art.

The transcripts of five rehearsals of Massenet's opera *Werther*, reproduced at the end of this volume, give us for the first time an insight into Stanislavsky's manner as producer. Again there is no formal approach based on 'rules', all his efforts being directed, as one of the opera singers who took part in the rehearsals put it, 'towards the creation of an atmosphere that would facilitate the work of the actors, make it easier for them to achieve the creative state, and enter more intimately into the artistic life of each little scene'. In these rehearsals we can see the great difference between the Stanislavsky of the early days of the Moscow Art Theatre, when he was the typical producer-autocrat who treated his actors 'as though they were mannequins', and his later period when his famous saying, 'In art one can only inspire people, but never order them about', was applied by him in practice.

In *The System and Methods of Creative Art* Stanislavsky gives a much more detailed analysis of the actor's work before the beginning of each performance. He once more quotes the example of Tommaso Salvini, whose methods had impressed themselves vividly on his imagination. And he again repeats his statement that his theory of acting was not invented by him, and that in fact every great actor is a most faithful practitioner of it. The truth of this statement will appear more convincingly perhaps than in any example Stanislavsky himself brings in his books, in this short extract from the 'Remarks on the Character of LadyMacbeth', by Sarah Siddons which Stanislavsky did not seem to know, but which illustrates his points very aptly:—

'Being only twenty years of age," Sarah Siddons writes, 'I believed, as many others do believe, that little more was necessary than to get the words (of LadyMacbeth) into my head; for the necessity of discrimination and the development of character, at that time of my life, had scarcely entered my head.

'About six years after I was called upon to act the same character in London. By this time I had perceived the difficulty of assuming a personage with whom no one feeling of common general nature was congenial or assistant. One's own heart could prompt one to express with some degree of truth the sentiments of a mother, a daughter, a wife, a sister, etc., but to *adopt* this character must be an effort of judgment alone. Therefore, it was with the greatest diffidence, nay, terror, that I undertook it, and with the additional fear of Mrs. Prichard's reputation in it before my eyes. The dreaded first night at length arrived, when just as I had finished my toilette and was pondering with fearfulness my first appearance in the grand, fiendish part, comes Mr. Sheridan, knocking at my door, and insisting, in spite of all my entreaties not to be interrupted at this to me tremendous moment, to be admitted. He would not be denied admittance, for he protested he must speak to me on a circumstance which so deeply concerned my own interest that it was of the most serious nature. Well, after much squabbling, I was compelled to admit him, that I might dismiss him the sooner, and compose myself before the play began. But, what was my distress and astonishment when I found that he wanted me, even at this moment of anxiety and terror, to adopt another mode of acting the sleeping scene. He told me he had heard with the greatest surprise that I meant to act it without holding the candle in my hand; and, when I urged the impracticability of washing out that "damned spot" with the vehemence that was certainly implied by both her own words and by those of her gentlewoman, he insisted that if I did put the candle out of my hand, it would be thought a presumptuous innovation, as Mrs. Prichard had always retained it in hers. My mind, however, was made up, and it was then too late to make me alter it; for I was too agitated to adopt another method. My deference to Mr. Sheridan's taste and judgment was, however, so great that had he proposed the alteration whilst it was possible for me to change my own plan, I should have yielded to his suggestion; though even then it would have been against my own opinion and my observation of the accuracy with which somnambulists perform all the acts of waking persons. The scene, of course, was acted as I had myself conceived it, and the innovation, as Mr. Sheridan called it, was received with approbation. Mr. Sheridan himself came to me, after the play, and most ingenuously congratulated me on my obstinacy. When he was gone out of the room, I began to undress; and while standing before the glass, and taking off my mantle, a diverting circumstance occurred to chase away the feelings of this anxious night; for while I was repeating, and endeavouring to call to mind the appropriate *tone and action* to the following words, 'Here's the smell of blood still!' my dresser innocently exclaimed, 'Dear me, ma'am, how very hysterical you are tonight; I protest and vow, ma'am, it was not blood, but rose pink and water; for I saw the property man mix it up, with my own eyes'.

The remarkable thing about this description is that it contains all the esentials of Stanislavsky's system, beginning with the circle of public solitude, which when Sheridan tried to break it, provoked such a violent protest from Mrs. Siddons, to Stanislavsky's injunction to the actor that he must live his part not only on the stage, but also behind the scenes and in his private life. Mrs. Siddons, after her great triumph on the first night in Lady Macbeth's 'fiendish part', was not in a hurry, it seems, to leave the theatre to enjoy her triumph among her friends, but was still lingering in her dressing-room 'trying to call to mind the appropriate tone and action' of a line in her part! No less amazing is Mrs. Siddons' remark about her own observation of the behaviour of somnambulists which, surely proves that she must have taken great care to observe *in life* the facts she wanted for her play and then transmute them into her *plan* of the part. In fact, she too believed in Stanislavsky's great precept—from the conscious to the subconscious, though she would hardly have put it in those words.

The chief criticism of Stanislavsky's 'system' came from people who argued that the demands made by it on the actors were not only impracticable, but also unnecessary, because the great majority of actors, including some of the greatest, never made such demands on themselves, which did not prevent them, however, from displaying their talents on the stage. As for what they did off stage, that was their own affair. Stanislavsky never admitted the truth of such criticism. He pointed out that every artist expressed only himself in his art, and that this was particularly true of the actor who could not dissociate himself bodily from his art as all other artists can and do. As for the actors who do not live their parts outside the walls of the theatre, his reply was that if they had not forgotten their art in their private lives, their art on the stage would have been a hundred times more successful, and they would besides have raised the prestige of the theatre to a height it never enjoyed in the past. Stanislavsky shared the view of the great German actor Iffland who used to say that if an actor wanted to appear noble on the stage, he had to be noble in his private life too.

But Stanislavsky did not shut his eyes to the painful fact that

his 'system' required so great a devotion to the art of the stage
that only a few actors could be equal to it. 'I have had too many
disappointments', he writes. 'I have been working for a great
many years in the theatre and hundreds of actors have passed
through my hands, but I can regard as my true followers only
a few of them, because only a few possessed sufficient will-power
and perseverance to reach the stage of real art. It is not enough
to know my system. One must also know how to apply it, and one
must be able to put it into practice. This, however, requires
constant daily training throughout the whole of the actor's
career on the stage'.

A more outspoken and reasoned criticism of Stanislavsky's
system came from the Russian producer Theodor Kommissarzhevsky in his little book *The Actor's Creative Work and
Stanislavsky's System.*

Kommissarzhevsky finds that Stanislavsky's reason is always
at loggerheads with his intuition. Stanislavsky's great talent,
he claims, was very often either distorted or wrongly interpreted
by his reason. His system, he declares, is based on rational errors
with regard to the inner abilities of man, on a one-sided understanding of psychology, and on an unfounded desire to transform
the theatre into life, while in fact the theatre is theatre and life
is life, and a copy of life is unnecessary because life exists anyhow.
Kommissarzhevsky criticises Stanislavsky for alleging that an
actor can convey the playwright's ideas on the stage only with
the help of the memories of his own experiences in life, reproducing these experiences with the help of his 'affective memory'.

'Stanislavsky', Kommissarzhevsky writes, 'divides a play up
into small pieces, each of which contains some feeling. He then
finds among those pieces some which are similar in their feelings
and unites them under one general feeling. This work he
carries on until he reduces the whole play to two, three, or four
definite feelings, which he further reduces to one basic feeling,
which is known, according to Stanislavsky's terminology, as
'through-action'. All this is perfectly all right so far as it is
necessary for Stanislavsky's own work as an actor and producer,
or for the work of other actors so far as it corresponds to their
manner of acting. Every actor acts in his own way. But as a

method of teaching and as a method compulsory for every actor, such a manner of studying a play and a part appears to me deadly and certain to paralyse the actor's spontaneous feeling and creative work'.

However, Kommissarzhevsky is ready to admit that 'if the principles of Stanislavsky's system are not taken too seriously and if his conclusions based on his feelings are distinguished from those based on his reason', then his system undoubtedly represents a valuable source of study. For 'whatever the errors Stanislavsky was led into by his theories, he has nevertheless by his system laid the foundation stone for the construction in future of a theory of a true inner expression of the art of the stage, and has erected certain signposts which every genuine actor has to follow, if he does not want to be a mere grimacing clown'.

Kommissarzhevsky, moreover, does not under-estimate Stanislavsky's achievement in being the first in Russia to establish a theory of acting based on psychological data. Stanislavsky, too, was the first, according to Kommissarzhevsky, to point out to the actor the necessity of entering into the feelings of his part and to formulate the corresponding methods for it. 'These methods may be erroneous', he writes, 'but a number of the fundamental theses of his theory are profoundly true, and they open up new vistas before the old theatre, and in them we see formulated the principles on the basis of which all great actors have always played. It is the method of the formulation of an inner ensemble, based on *inner* communication, that was Stanislavsky's greatest discovery, and in the Moscow Art Theatre we saw and felt such an ensemble for the first time'.

It is, of course, quite true that Stanislavsky was often led astray by his reason. There are many examples from his productions, especially during his first period as producer of the Moscow Art Theatre, which show that he misinterpreted the ruling idea of a play and, as a result, distorted its meaning. Chekhov, who could never forgive Stanislavsky his misinterpretation of the ruling idea of *The Seagull*, and particularly of the part of Trigorin, could not rid himself of his mistrust of Stanislavsky's methods of production. During the production of *The Three Sisters*, for instance, he was very anxious to get to Moscow to be present at

the rehearsals of the play because, as he stated in a letter, he
could not trust Stanislavsky with three heroines. He was ap-
palled at Stanislavsky's interpretation of *The Cherry Orchard*
as showing the sombre side of Russian life, while he had
written it as a light comedy. Speaking to a Russian writer who
told him that he could not help crying at his plays, Chekhov
said, 'You say you can't help crying at my plays. Well, you are
not the only one. But that is not my fault. I did not write my
plays for that. It is Alexeyev who made my characters into cry-
babies. That was not what I wanted'.

It must, of course, be remembered that Chekhov's strictures
referred to Stanislavsky during the first period of his career as
producer. Chekhov did not know the mature Stanislavsky. On
the other hand, it is quite true that Stanislavsky's attitude to his
authors was an attitude that is unfortunately too typical of a
producer, that is to say, he did not seem to have ever regarded a
playwright as an artist of the theatre in his own right. It never
occurred to him that the problem of 'the bare stage floor', which
had worried him for years, was not perhaps such a terrible problem after all, since the playwright naturally takes it into
consideration as indeed he takes into consideration all the other
problems of stage production, if, that is, he is a playwright and
not a literary gentleman who decides to try his hand at writing
plays. It never occurred to him that the great difficulties he had
experienced in producing Turgenev's *A Month in the Country*
were chiefly due to the fact that Turgenev was not a born playwright, while Chekhov was. Again in the first Moscow Art
Theatre production of Shakespeare it never occurred either to
him or to Nemirovich-Danchenko that the problem of a Shakes-
pearian production was closely connected with the problem of
adapting Shakespeare's apron stage to the quite different stage
of the Moscow Art Theatre. Instead, before putting on *Julius
Caesar*, the Moscow Art Theatre sent out an expedition, headed
by Nemirovich-Danchenko himself, to Rome so as to reproduce
on a modern stage as faithful a replica of ancient Rome as the
materials gathered on the spot allowed, a thing that never
occurred to Shakespeare himself. When acting Othello, Stanislavsky tried to reproduce the living image of a modern Arab

(this is still being done on the Russian stage), although Shakespeare could hardly have been expected to have had an Arab in mind when writing *Othello*. It never occurred to Stanislavsky to study the original texts of Shakespeare's plays (a fault remedied in Russia today), so that when Gordon Craig came to Moscow to produce *Hamlet*, he discovered (according to Stanislavsky himself) that the Russians had quite wrong ideas about a number of important passages in the play owing to their bad translation. All these faults were due chiefly to the fact that Stanislavsky was not able to rise above the all too prevalent attitude of a producer who is rather apt to treat the playwright as an interloper in his own sphere instead of as an artist of the theatre. But all this does not affect the correctness of the general conclusions of Stanislavsky's system. To claim, as Kommissarzhevsky does, that Stanislavsky demands that the actor should imitate himself on the stage does not seem to be altogether fair, since Stanislavsky himself points out again and again the need for the subconscious promptings of an actor's mind for the achievement of the complete fusion of the actor and his part. The whole idea of Stanislavsky's advice to the actor to cultivate his emotional or 'affective' memory is that it is the *only* way in which the actor can influence his subconscious mind. Stanislavsky was always scornful of 'intuition' as a blind force on which the actor has to rely entirely. For, as he pointed out over and over again, it is only the genius who seems to possess the ability to control his intuition, and even he does not do it haphazardly, but by methods similar to those Stanislavsky evolved after years of experience. Indeed, as has already been observed, Stanislavsky always claimed that his system was based on his observations of the methods of great actors.

The chief error of Stanislavsky's critics is to ascribe to him a rigidity of method he himself denounced. This is mainly due to Stanislavsky's followers who, in teaching his system, cannot see the wood for the trees. But it is unjust to saddle Stanislavsky with the mistakes of his followers whom he himself repeatedly condemned. For Stanislavsky had a horror of text-books. 'The book of creative art is man himself', he declared.

The only thing one can justly object to in his system is that it demands too much of the actor, but then it is the actor who is a true artist Stanislavsky had in mind. And one can never demand too much from an artist.

D. M.

1950

The System and Methods
of Creative Art

—

CHAPTER I

It is not accident that brings people together in art. They come together because some of them are anxious to share their experiences with their fellow artists, while others, finding it impossible to stand still, want to move forward because their inner powers grow stronger and develop, and search for new ways in which to express themselves in creative action.

It is this that has brought us together now: I want to share my experience and try to apply it to opera, while you, I am sure, are all inspired by the wish to move forward. If, therefore, there are still people among the actors of your theatre who wish to share their views and experience with me so that we may mutually assist each other in attaining perfection in our art—mutually, because in the theatre both those who give their work freely and those who accept it can be said to move forward together at the same time—then we can start our work of studying the principles of our art without further delay. I may add that it is my firm conviction that it is impossible today for anyone to become an actor worthy of the time in which he is living, an actor on whom such great demands are made, without going through a course of study in a studio.

Now, it is necessary to rid oneself of the prejudice that it is possible to teach people 'to act' certain feelings. It can, I think, be stated quite definitely that no one can be taught to act.

From the great examples provided by the actors of genius we can clearly see how all the conventional principles of the stage of their day are flung to the winds; indeed, they stand out from among all the rest of the actors in the play by the special rhythmic harmony of every part they perform and by the amazing freedom of all their physical and psychological actions. They break through the walls of the stage conventions, annihilate the distance that separates them from the auditorium, and find their way straight to the hearts of the audience, carrying the spectator along with them right into the life of each instant of time during

91

which they are creatively active on the stage, just because they have grasped the true nature of the passions they are portraying; they do it because they have succeeded, by means of the action of their artistic intuition which is so indivisibly linked with their genius, in bringing out the true value of each word, which they never fling at the spectator unless it is simultaneously expressed in true and correct physical action.

It is this work—the work of grasping the true nature of each emotion through one's own powers of observation, of developing one's attention for such a task, and of consciously mastering the art of entering the creative circle—that I find absolutely essential for anyone who wants to become a true actor worthy of the times in which he is living.

If the whole object of the theatre had been to provide entertainment, it would perhaps not have been worth while devoting so much labour to it. The theatre, however, is the art of reflecting life. 'The theatre', as Nero expressed it, 'is a sea of human forces', and this thought, in spite of the centuries that have elapsed since Nero's time, is still true today.

The theatre, to be sure, is created by human forces and reflects human forces through itself. Every talent is not a miracle that has suddenly appeared out of the blue, but the fruit of the development of the human force in each actor and the attention devoted by every actor to the forces which are found in the seething sea of human lives all around us. The fleeting moments of the life on the stage, that is to say, those unique moments in an actor's work when he has to infuse the truth of the passions into the given circumstances, are not by any means moments of accidental flashes of inspiration; they are rather the fruits of hard inner training, and of the study of the nature of the passions; and the main idea of this hard training and study is to bring about true inspiration and to make sure that no obstacles in him or around him should break his attention or his concentration on his work.

Work in a studio must bring about such a development of the actor's own powers as to enable his imagination, controlled by self-discipline, to direct all his powers along one route only, namely, the one that is determined by his part. But how is one to reach that point of perfection in the creative art of the stage where 'I am impersonating someone' ends, and 'if I am such and such a character, what is the true nature of my feelings and what are the correct physical movements for me now?' begins. Years of work devoted to exercises and problems are necessary to achieve this. It is impossible to put it into words. One can say that the genius of Pushkin who defined dramatic art as the power of transmitting the truth of the passions in given circumstances has not been excelled even today. One can also say that in our studio work we shall follow just that path and engage in the study of the nature of human passions and emotions and the correct physical action corresponding to them.

The object of our first researches in psychological problems, however, must be the ordinary, everyday life that is lived by people all over the world. People, and consequently also the stage as a reflection of life, are engaged in the pursuit of the most ordinary occupations and not in the performance of deeds that could be performed only by heroes. But that, surely, does not mean that the average man is not capable of an heroic effort on any ordinary day. It is, therefore, all these steps of the ladder leading from a very ordinary and simple movement across a room to the highest efforts of self-sacrifice in the case of a man who gives his life for his country, or for his friend, or for a great cause, that we must learn not only to understand, but also to transmute into living images, and reflect in truthful and correct physical action.

But how are we to observe and reflect all this in all the moments of our life? What is it without which we shall never convince the spectator that our art is both intelligible and necessary? If we do not realise that the foundation of the whole of a man's life, the rhythm given to him by nature, namely respiration, is also the foundation of the whole of our art, we shall never be able to find the one and only rhythm for an entire performance and, in subordinating to it everybody who takes part in the performance, create one harmonious whole. The rhythm, which every man has to express in life, originates from his breathing and, consequently from his entire organism, from his first need, without which life is impossible. And so in art, too, the reason why it is impossible to imitate anyone is due to the fact that in his creative work every man is a unique individuality, an individual rhythmic entity.

But does this mean that no one needs to learn anything but can, having once defined and established his rhythm, rely entirely on his inspiration? The adherents of the so-called school of 'inspiration' sought first of all to stimulate and arouse all their instincts and because of that very often, instead of giving us the results of the highest and inwardly purified powers of true intuitive inspiration, gave us only exaggeration, false pathos, overacting, which came straight from the instincts and out of which arose the artificial stage situation of 'such and such a feeling must be acted in such and such a way'. All this can be made clear only in the course of a long and absorbing study in a studio by those who do not love and admire only themselves in art, but look upon art as their chosen career in life, as something without which life to them is not worth living.

There may still be another question that requires an answer: if art is an individual and unique form of expression for every man engaged in it, how is it at all possible to create a studio where many people study together? Perhaps every man ought to have his own studio? Well, we shall see in the course of our work that although each man carries all his creative abilities within himself, and although one man's creative genius cannot possibly develop along the same lines as another man's, there are many steps and problems of a general nature that apply equally to all creative artists and in which every one can look for one and the same thing, namely, the nature of the powers he carries within him. And how he will find and discover them, by means of which aids he will develop and purify them so as to become an actor who finds in beauty a common denominator for himself and the spectator—that too forms the common work of student and teacher, their common road leading to perfection. Each of them must find his own rhythm of creative work, while the teacher must, in addition, include the rhythms of all his pupils in his own creative circle.

CHAPTER II

Do not imagine that I am going to expound to you some boring art system of mine, which, if you learnt it by heart, would enable you to become an actor. I am even less inclined to impose any undue strain on your memory. All I want to do is simply to share my views on art with you. Not, mind you, on the sort of art which may appear enchanting at a distance, which one can only dream about, and which would enable you to win over the hearts of men without any work, but on the art which makes up the sum total of man's life and work.

But what does the phrase 'to live in art' really mean? Does it not mean that we can truly claim to live in art only when we no longer regard ourselves as a unit of one or another kind of art, but instead think of art, as a whole, as a pantheon comprising in itself and uniting in itself the lives of all the people on earth? But, I am afraid, that is philosophy, and I do not propose to stray into it but merely to examine the nature of life in art which, in spite of all its complexities, ought to be easily understood by everyone.

'Simpler, easier, higher, gayer'—those are the words which ought to be inscribed on the front of every theatre—the temple of art, if theatres had been such temples. Only love of art and everything sublime and beautiful that lives in the heart of every man, only that should be brought into a theatre by everyone entering it and poured out from every man as from a pail of pure water, a thousand of which will today wash off the dirt from the whole building, if it had yesterday been contaminated by the passions and intrigues of men.

Those who found a studio or a theatre ought first of all to pay the greatest possible attention to the atmosphere that prevails in it. Great care must particularly be taken to make sure that fear in whatever shape or form does not find its way into a studio and dominate the minds of those who either run it or study in it, and that the hearts of everybody there should be inspired and united only by beauty. Without the idea of union in beauty no true theatre can exist, nor indeed would such a theatre serve any purpose. If, moreover, there is no initial understanding of oneself and the whole complexity of one's powers as happy servants of one's country, then such a theatre is of no use either, for it will never become one of the creative units among all the creative forces of the country. All this ought to make us realise what a tremendously important thing the selection of a permanent company of a theatre is, always the weakest and the sorest spot of the theatrical business. Everything that leads to the choice of actors not according to ability or character, but according to whether one actor or another possesses influential friends among the people who are in charge of the theatre; or, in the case of a studio, everything that leads to the enrolment of students of the drama as a result of somebody knowing somebody or recommending somebody; in short any pulling of strings or backstage entry into a theatre lowers its prestige as well as the prestige of the performance and the rehearsals; it also tends to foster the spirit of boredom in it, with the result that the creative efforts of all the participants will in all such cases be characterised by a simulated affection for art and not by a genuine love of it which alone should inspire all those who come to study dramatic art.

The rules of a theatre in which the rehearsals are conducted simultaneously with several groups of actors, only some of whom are taking an active part in them and are working together, while the rest are sitting about without taking any part in the solution of the problems and without making any attempt to attune their spirits to the creative work that is taking place there, but, on the contrary, filling the atmosphere with envy and captious criticism, are inadmissible in a studio where all are equal in creative work. In a studio everyone knows that if not today, then tomorrow, his turn will come, and everyone understands that in order to follow the work of his colleagues intelligently, one has to devote all one's attention to the problem that forms the subject of discussion. A state of affairs where no respect for those who take their orders from the actors exists, and where there is no real understanding of the meaning of civility, creates an atmosphere of degeneration. The chaos that is born of rudeness and that permits the raised voice will never lead to the creation of that atmosphere of gladness and ease in which alone the high culture of spirit and thought can thrive. Only in a simple and easy atmosphere can the word find expression as a full-blooded reflection of those passions whose nobility and high value the theatre has to reflect.

The hours an actor spends in a theatre at rehearsals must gradually lead to his transformation into a full man—a man who is a creator in art, the sort of fighter for beauty and love who would be able to tranfuse into the hearts of his listeners the whole meaning of each word and sound he utters on the stage. If after a rehearsal the actors go away without feeling that they have become better men in feeling and thought, if their inner illumination is only on a fractional scale, if the actor says to himself, 'While I was rehearsing I was carried away by everything and there was a feeling of great serenity in my heart', but no sooner does he leave than he relapses once more into self-conceit and vulgarity, saying to himself, 'I am an actor, I am an important person', then this can only mean that those who are responsible for the rehearsal possess little genuine love of art and little ability to fire the imagination of the actor.

Indeed, the very conception of 'responsibility' for a performance as understood by producers and all sorts of 'maestros' and as expressed in the outward clockwork precision of a production, is one of the worst possible illusions. Let us take a simple example from the life of the theatre. It happens again and again that a producer of straight plays turns to the production of operas. But what is it that he mostly produces? First of all, he produces 'himself'. He has scraped some kind of acquaintance with the music, he has made some kind of arrangement with the stage designer, and he has begun his rehearsals with the actors, either by selecting those of the opera singers whose appearance he liked, or by reluctantly accepting those who have been palmed off on him, without bothering to get to know the people and their idiosyncrasies thoroughly. The living treasures—the hearts of men—do not exist for him; the harmony of each of them separately, the individual creative uniqueness of each one of them, is something he does not notice; he does not see them because he has no conception of the meaning of harmony in himself, having never troubled his head about it when applying himself to his creative work. In one way or another he has 'tipped off' the actors about what he wishes them to do; somehow or other the actors succeed in picking up a few crumbs of another man's spirit and will, having in the process successfully barred all the roads to their own intuition and their own creative work.

What the 'creative' achievement of the actors amounts to is either a poor or rich reflection of the personality of the producer in accordance with his or their talents. The producer next turns his attention to the orchestra, and here too there is a new drama, a new war of personalities, if, that is, the conductor like the producer is a man who has a poor conception of his responsibilities in the theatre and does not try to find the right way of transfusing the dramatic action into the rhythm and harmony of the music.

It is indeed scarcely possible to convey the whole chaos and all the constant defects and corrections hourly introduced into a performance not because of any organic necessity, but solely because some actor or some stage effect did not meet with the approval of someone or other. But what matters is not the actors or the stage effects but the most important principle of the creative art of the theatre, namely, the necessity of teaching the actor to search in himself for the right understanding of the value of words, of teaching him to develop his attention and to concentrate it introspectively on the organic qualities of his part and on the nature of human emotions and not to judge from outside the effectiveness of one kind of action or another in the belief that it is possible to learn how to act one kind of feeling or another. What needs to be done is to introduce the living heart of the living actor into the chain of inward and outward actions which in life always run parallel to each other; what needs to be done is to help the actor by a whole series of devices to free his body and his inward world of every sort of tension so as to enable him to reflect the life of the play in which he is appearing. His powers of attention must be brought to such a pitch of alertness as to make quite sure that the conventional and the external do not interfere with his understanding of the organic nature of human passions.

System and Methods of Creative Art

These are the problems that the studio must do its best to solve. This is the only way in which every actor can and must develop the grain of talent that lies buried in him and transform it into a force which acts as beauty. It must be remembered, however, that in art it is only possible to inspire and to love. Orders are out of place in art.

CHAPTER III

What is a 'studio' or a practice theatre attached to a theatre? Let me discuss this question with you today and together with you try to think it over myself once more. Now, it is clear, I think, that a dramatic school, if I may put it that way, corresponds to the demands of our time, for an enormous number of such schools of every kind, type and variety has recently sprung up all over the country. But the longer you live and the more thoroughly you free your mind of all superficial and generally accepted preconceptions, the more clearly you realise your own and other people's shortcomings in creative work.

The studio is the first halting place for people who have fully grasped the idea that a man's whole life consists of his own creative work, that so far as he is concerned this creative work exists only in the theatre, and that it is in the theatre alone that his life finds its full expression. An actor must realise that there are no causes acting from without and influencing creative art and that there exists only one impulse of creative art, namely, the creative powers each one of us carries within himself. The foundation of the studios has thrown a light into that chaotic darkness of ignorance which was so characteristic of the theatres of the old days in which people only pretended to come together for creative work, while in reality they were there for their own self-glorification, to earn easy fame, lead an easy dissipated life, and for the exercise of their so-called 'inspiration'.

Every aspect of a studio's work must be carefully organised; the relationship between all its members and between its members and the people around them must be governed by the utmost respect for one another; the fundamental basis of the spiritual resources of those who wish to learn the art of drama in a studio must be the development of unbroken attention. The studio must teach the actor the art of concentration, and for that purpose it must discover all sorts of interesting and pleasing auxiliary aids for the development of the inner powers of the actor in an atmosphere of gladness, ease, and enthusiasm, and not look upon these as hateful, though unavoidable tasks. The misfortune of our modern actor in general is his habit of looking outside himself for the causes that stimulate his creative work. The actor seems to be always under the impression that it is extraneous facts that supply the impulse to his creative work and are, indeed, the main cause of it. It seems to him that the real causes of his success on the stage are all extraneous facts, including patronage and *claques*. His failures on the stage are of course due to his enemies and ill-wishers who never give him a chance to show what he can do or to rise to the full glory of his genius. The first thing, therefore, a studio has to teach the actor is that he will find everything—all the creative powers—in himself. An introspective outlook on things and affairs and the search within himself for the powers, causes and effects of his creative work, must become the main object of tuition. For what is creative work? Every student must learn to understand that, generally speaking, there is no life that does not contain in itself some element of creative work. The personal instincts, the personal passions, in which the life of the actor is spent, if they destroy his love for the theatre, create a morbid susceptibility of the nervous system, a hysterical propensity that finds expression in external exaggeration which the actor tries to explain away by the peculiarity of his talent and which he likes to call his 'inspiration'. But everything that comes from external causes can arouse in life only the activity of the instincts and cannot awaken the subconsciousness in which true intuition and temperament reside. A man who moves about on the stage under the pressure of his instincts and without having formed an exact plan of action, is so far as incentives are concerned indistinguishable from the animals—a dog at a shoot stealing up to a bird, or a cat stalking a mouse.

The difference will become apparent only when the passions, that is, the instincts, are purified by thought, that is to say, by man's consciousness, and are ennobled by alert attention. Then whatever is temporary, ephemeral, conditional, unimportant, and ugly in every passion will be discovered, and attention will not be concentrated and fixed on it but on whatever is organic and inseparable from intuition and what exists everywhere and at all times and in all passions and is common to every human heart and mind. There is no royal road to art. It is impossible to fasten on Mary and John the same external methods and the same external aids of the mise-en-scene; what is possible is to disclose to all Marys and Johns the great value of their inspiration and of their own spiritual powers, and to show them where to look for it and how to develop it in themselves. Nothing can be more harmful to student-actors than to transfer them constantly from one task to another, or to give them a great number of exacting tasks at one and the same time, or to fill their heads with new subjects of study which have only recently emerged and whose achievements have still to be put to the test of practical work in the theatre. Do not therefore attempt to begin your education as student-actors by trying to do too many things at once, or to find your special aptitudes for playing certain parts because of some external traits, but give yourselves ample time to change your habits of mind which force you to live and act by relying on external influences. Conceive of your creative life as a melting pot in which your inner and outer life become merged, and start on your exercises with a gay heart and without forcing yourself in any way. A studio is the place where a man should learn to observe his own character and his inner powers; it is a place where he must cultivate the habit of looking on himself not as a man who just allows the current of life to sweep him along with it, but as one who loves art and who wants by his creative work, through and out of himself, to fill every man's day with the joy and happiness of his art. The studio is no place for anyone who does not know how to laugh, who is always grumbling, who is always depressed, who easily takes offence and is, generally, a wet blanket. The studio is, as it were, the portals of the temple of art. Here there should be inscribed for each of us in fiery letters the notice, 'Learn to overcome all obstacles by loving art and rejoicing in it'. If one were to admit to the studio a lot of badly educated people with no special abilities just because they happen to be tall and handsome, or just because they are clever and possess good voices, one would only turn out hundreds more failures with whom the actors' market is already overcrowded. And instead of happy workers who are devoted to art because they love it, our studio would turn out people who are well versed in intrigues of all sorts, who have no desire to use their creative work for entering the social life of their country as her faithful servants, but who merely want to become the masters whom their country should serve with all the wealth of her natural resources.

Nor is there any justification for those people who put the reputation of their studio above everything else and pay little regard to those ardent hearts for whose benefit each studio exists. He who teaches in a studio must always bear in mind that he is not only a principal or a teacher, but also a friend and a colleague. He must remember that he is, as it were, the happy journeyman in whom his own love of art becomes united with the love of those who have come to be taught by him. It is only on this basis and not on that of personal choice that the teacher must guide them to achieve a sense of harmony with themselves, with their fellow students, and with all their teachers. Only then will the studio become that initial group of people in which a feeling of goodwill towards one another becomes the generally accepted rule of conduct, and where in due course a harmonious production of a play, that is, one that corresponds to the demands of our time, will be achieved.

CHAPTER IV

If one were to imagine an ideal state of the world in which art, owing to the high demands made on it by mankind, would provide a ready answer to all the questions which the mind, the heart, and the spirit of man might care to ask, then art itself would, I think, be the book of life. But that period in man's evolution is, I am afraid, still far off. However, it can already be stated that the difference between the present and the past is that our 'today' is looking to art for the master-key to life, while our 'yesterday' was looking to it only for entertainment.

What, therefore, ought our modern theatre to give us in life? To begin with, it should not on any account give us the bare reflection of life itself; it must rather reflect everything that exists in life in all its hidden heroic tension; in a simple form of what seems to be everyday life, but actually in precise and luminous images in which all the passions are ennobled and alive. The worst thing that can happen to a theatre is to produce a play in which tendentiousness is over-emphasised, and in which ideas are thrust on the characters who are not even living people but puppets invented at the producer's table without love, without ardent love for the human hearts such as the playwright wished to depict in his play.

If the ultimate value of man's whole life on the stage is determined by his creative work, that is to say, by the harmonious blending of his heart, mind, and physical actions with every word he utters, then it can be said that the ultimate value of a play is directly proportionate to its author's love for the hearts of his *dramatis personae*.

In a play by a great dramatist it is extremely difficult to decide which of his characters he loves best. Everything in it expresses the eager throbbing of his heart, everything in it—heroes and villains—has taken shape in his imagination not when his mind was active while his heart was acting the part of a silent observer, of a man in grey standing aloof; in him both mind and heart

104

were consuming themselves, and it was in himself that he felt all the greatness and all the horror of the ways of men. And it was only then that there flowed from his pen both the high and the low, but always the living, and it is this living thing that every true theatre—not the theatre that only admires itself, but the theatre that works for its generation—can transmute into the outward actions of the characters of the play.

What is it therefore that we, student-actors, should be guided by when choosing a play? If your heart is full of understanding of the great value of your creative work, it must also be full of man's first love—love for your country. And, in choosing a play, you must make sure that the characters depicted by your author are rounded and not one-sided human figures. You must make sure that the play is not a deplorable imitation of some classical master-piece, but that it reflects life faithfully; for then you too will be able to reflect it through yourself on the stage as a slice of life. It does not matter if the name of the author is unknown so long as the people depicted in his play are not copies of some conventional stage figures but living people; for in them you will be able to discover the whole range of man's emotions and powers, beginning with weakness and ending with heroism. The only thing you must be careful about is that they should not represent some hackneyed ideals which one is, it seems, supposed to worship just because they have been 'acted' in this or that way for generations!

Always think of yourself as some character in the play. If you *are* that man or woman in the play, what ought your organic feelings to be?

Let us assume you have found the play which reflects a certain phase of life. What sort of work must the theatre concentrate on once the new play has been chosen? It must not dwell on its stage effects or tendencies; you will never attract spectators by the one or the other, nor will you fire them with courage, or an heroic thought, or honour, or even beauty. At best you will get a successful propaganda play; but that is not the task of a serious theatre, for that only means the inclusion of the theatre in the utilitarian needs of the hour.

Only that which remains in the play as the grain of eternally pure human feelings and thoughts, only that which does not depend on the mounting of the play and is understood by everybody in every age and in every language, only that which unites the Turk and the Russian, the Persian and the Frenchman, only that which can never under any circumstances lose its sense of beauty, such as, for instance, Tatyana's pure and radiant love— it is that, and only that, which a theatre must look for in a play. Then there is no need to fear that the theatre may lose its way. It cannot lose its way because it has not embarked on the search of 'itself', its own fame and aims, but instead seeks, as it were, to be a magic lantern which reflects life—vibrant and happy. It has undertaken the task of facilitating the perception of beauty by those people who can perceive it more easily in themselves and themselves in it through the medium of the theatre; those who, living their ordinary lives, are capable of perceiving themselves as a creative part of life with the help of the ideas that come across to them from the other side of the footlights.

The beginning of the work on a play is its most important moment. For it is here that the whole significance of the play for those who will one day come to the theatre to see it begins to emerge; it is here that the foundation stone is laid on which the gifted theatrical people are to build the magic fairy-tale of love for the people who, though also gifted, are engaged in a different sort of work.

How is one to create this enchanting magic carpet of life's truth on the stage? If the first conditions for it are lacking, if, that is, there is no love among those who begin the work on the play, if there is no courage among its future performers and producers, no energy, no mutual respect, and no unity of purpose, then you will never succeed in raising the play above the stereotyped level of 'a good play'. Nor will you do it, if the actors are not unanimous in their desire to convey the highest, the purest, and the most beautiful ideas of the play so as to become the conductors of energy and beauty to all those who come to the theatre as spectators. Once you have chosen the path of creative stage work, you can obtain results only if you become one happy family. The way of those who choose a theatrical career is quite unlike the way of life chosen by other people. Those to whom beauty as expressed in the art of the stage means nothing are bound to lead a double life. They may have their own private life which has nothing to do with their life on the stage, and indeed they may have a score of other interests in which their family may share to a larger or smaller extent. But the true artist is the man to whom the theatre is the be-all and end-all of his entire life. His affairs are part of the business of the theatre. The stage is his only way of serving his country. All his love and the unquenchable fire of his art are devoted solely to his parts. The stage is his country, his inspiration, his source of eternal courage.

One must never think of the theatre as a place for some special sect of dedicated people. One must never look upon it as a place which is divorced from life. All the roads of creative human endeavour lead to a manifestation of life as 'all roads lead to Rome'. And the Rome of every man is one and the same: every man carries his entire creative genius within him, and he pours everything out of himself into the broad stream of life. One must therefore never create external sects out of theatres.

Indeed, it is only those theatres in which the inner consciousness of the grain of genius that is to be found in every man is dead, that concentrate on external clowning and external mannerisms. They are either searching for a stage without a curtain, or mass uniformity in action, or topsy-turvy stage designs, or false rhythms of actions, and they invariably make a terrible hash of things, for they lack a common and generally comprehensible incentive.

Rhythm is a great thing, but to build up the whole of the production of a play entirely upon rhythm one must first understand why it is so important and what its real meaning is.

No doubt different theatres, in so far as their policies are determined by their directors, can and must go their different ways. But their policies, whatever they may be, must be based on considerations that arise out of the artistic consciousness of the directors and are not due to all sorts of external aids. External aids must be the result of inner thought and take this or that form strictly in accordance with the underlying idea of creative art as understood by the actors and directors of the theatre.

The directors of a theatre may believe that they know where they want it to go, but if they do not move along in rhythm with contemporary life, if they refuse to introduce any changes in their external aids, holding fast only to the unchangeable, though also eternally moving core of life, i.e. love of man, they will never be able to create a theatre which is the servant of their country, a theatre of world importance, a theatre that expresses all the aspirations of their own time and takes an active part in the building of contemporary life.

I have often been told that certain people reproach me for asking too much from the actor; they accuse me of demanding that an actor should become almost an anchorite and devote himself entirely to the theatre and his art. Now, the first mistake they make who accuse me of seeing in the actor an anchorite is to fail to perceive what is meant by the word 'actor'.

An actor, like any other artist, is endowed with talent. He is already marked out by a heightened sensibility and he has already brought with him the grain of genius, though at his arrival in the helpless, poor, and naked condition in which we all arrive on the earth, no one as yet suspects the riches hidden within him.

A man who possesses talent is already doomed to the heroism of creative work. In him the flame is burning which will make him carry on with his creative work to his last breath. It is this creative force which holds man in its embrace and tells him, 'You are mine!' that is so important in the life of all those who are endowed with talent. For here all are alike: actors, singers, painters, sculptors, poets, musicians. Here there are no demarcation lines between one art and another. The demarcation lines make their appearance with the gradual development of man's consciousness, his will-power, the high or low level of his moral principles, his tastes, the breadth of his understanding of contemporary life and of the general culture and the civilisations of different peoples. Differences in artists develop in the same way as organic and unique individual idiosyncrasies develop in men. It is on and around these individual idiosyncrasies that the rings of the current conditions are deposited, the generally accepted accessory circumstances which we in a stage part call 'the given circumstances'.

There can be no doubt that anyone who has brought talent into the world with him lives under its influence. All the activities of a man are conditioned by his talent, and true talent forces its way through to creative work in absolutely all 'given circumstances'. Never believe a man who tells you that hard life has ruined his talent. Talent is a burning flame and it is impossible to put it out, not because there are not enough fire-extinguishers, but because talent is the very substance of the man himself, the very core of his being, his life force. It follows, therefore, that it is possible to crush a man but not his talent. And here, too, as in all other branches of creative work, talent will be a burden to some people, and man will become its slave. To others it will be a thing for which they will gladly sacrifice everything, and a man will become its servant. To others still it will be a thing of joy and a source of happiness, the only possible way of life on earth, and a man, in the glory and wisdom of his talent, will become the faithful servant of his people.

Every actor must realise that for a creative artist there can be no question of sacrificing everything for his art, for all creative work is a series of life-affirming situations. The moment an element of negation or dictation enters into creative work, it results in an immediate suspension of creative life. It is impossible to reach the peaks of creative genius by saying to oneself, 'I renounce life, I give up its beauty, its joys and pleasures, because this act of renunciation of mine is the "sacrifice I make for all mankind".'

The opposite is true. There can be no question of sacrifices in art. In it everything is fascinating, everything is interesting, everything absorbs the mind. Everything in life exerts a tremendous attraction on the artist. In life the artist is always feverishly busy. His heart is wide open to life's troubles, struggles, and conflicts; and no artist can exist if he is expected to renounce life like a monk.

The heroic act of an artist consists in his disclosure of the secrets of creative life; the revelation to the ordinary man who possesses no special talents of that grandeur which the actor has discovered in the nature of things. The actor is the force that reflects all the mysteries of nature, revealing them to the men who are not endowed with the gift of seeing all those spiritual treasures themselves.

Now I hope I have made it clear to you that if an actor, too, has to perform some act of renunciation, it applies only to his inner life. The act of renunciation of an actor finds its expression in beauty and purity of heart and in the flame of his thoughts. But that does not by any means imply any dictation or any negation or renunciation of life and happiness.

It is the revelation to people of resplendent depths and great truths.

I am afraid I have talked to you rather at great length of the high mission of the creative artist, and I should like now to return again to the question of how you are to prepare yourselves for this high mission, that is to say, for creative work.

Imagine for a moment that each of you has suddenly grown older by twenty-five years and that life has, let us say, put you in the same position as that in which I am at the moment. You are, that is, engaged in working with some group of actors according to my 'system'. Now, how are you to awaken in the actor the sort of consciousness which should make him realise that the condition in which he is able to perform his creative work does not in the least resemble the condition of the man in the fairy-tale who possesses the magic hat which can at any moment render him invisible; a magic hat which one can always keep in readiness in one's pocket so that one can take it out the instant one has to walk on the stage and be ready for one's creative work. I have told you repeatedly that everything of a picturesque and vivid nature an actor picks up in life, that everything he learns and comes to realise in his ever expanding consciousness, is only an approach to a more flexible liberation of his creative 'I' from the clutches of his egoistic 'I' that exercises such influence over him in his private life. It is this little egoistic 'I', that is to say, the passionate, petty and spiteful impulses, vanity and its fellow-traveller, the craving for pre-eminence, that is never at peace. It, too, has a firm grip on man.

This constant struggle within oneself, like the struggle between what is useful and harmful in attention and imagination, lies at the very root of an actor's achievements.

If an actor's work on his part demands the conjuring up of a whole series of visual images, then an actor's work on himself—in the struggle between his high and low instincts—demands that he should find much more complex moving pictures. One aim—the achievement of a state of complete self-control, the state of calm which precedes the creative work of the actor—is not enough. He must at one and the same time set another aim before him, namely, the aim of awakening in himself a taste for life in the quest of the beautiful, a taste for hard work on his parts and characters, without any irritation, with a feeling of goodwill towards men, and an inner experience of all contemporary life as the expression of the highest example of beauty.

The ultimate value of the part and everything else an actor contributes to the stage always depends on the inner life of the actor himself, on his acquired habit of living either in chaos or in harmony. A state of constant chaotic rush, picking up one part after another, lack of orderliness in his daily occupations and an inability to introduce discipline into them—all this finds its way as a bad habit into the mind of the actor, and becomes the atmosphere that surrounds the actor in his creative work.

All this is primarily a matter for the actor's education, or rather self-education, and every talented actor must realise that his work on his part will be a direct reflection of his work on himself. Whether the work is carried on in the foyer or the theatre, or on the stage, or in the rehearsal room, the important thing is not the level the work itself has reached now, that is to say, the reading of the play, the analysis of the part, or the first stage rehearsals, but what is going on in the mind of the actor. What kind of thoughts had occupied his mind when he was on his way to the rehearsals and what was the nature of the mental images that accompanied him to the theatre.

If his talent whispered to him, 'You are mine!'—the actor would be able to rise to that perception of beauty and the beautiful which would in due course enthral the spectators. If, on the other hand, what he heard was only the voice of the instincts of his egoism saying to him, 'You are ours!'—then he would never be able to discover in himself the ways to creative work. Art takes hold of the whole man, of all his attention. It is futile to offer it only bits of life; one must offer it the whole of life.

It may be argued that by saying this I am making such demands on the actor which justify the accusation that I want to make an anchorite of him. But I believe I have already explained to you what I mean by a talented and creative artist. And I should like to add to that definition one more element of creative art which is no less important than the rest, namely, taste.

An actor's taste determines his whole life. It is quite enough to see a man, his way of walking, his way of dressing, speaking, eating or reading to form an idea in one's mind about his taste, about what he likes most.

There are actors who prefer tidiness to everything else in the world—irreproachable, pedantic, petty tidiness. All their life goes on in accordance with a carefully devised plan and heaven forbid that anything in their homes should be moved from its accustomed place. Such an actor may be a very kind-hearted man, and he may even be capable of performing rather important work both in the theatre and at home. But that paltry kink in his mind gets in his way everywhere. If a stool is placed on the stage one inch nearer or farther away, if the curtain over the window is not hung along the indicated line, the actor or producer of that particular order is capable of shutting himself out of the world of art and plunging into the petty irritabilities of ordinary life.

Taste determines not only the external life, but also the whole inner life of man, that is to say, those of his impulses in which either the petty and conventional or the organic need of high emotions predominates.

To enable the actor to attain to that state of perfection in which he appears to the spectator on the other side of the footlights like an artist in an ecstasy of creation—a state in which the actor reaches out through the conscious into unconscious creation—he must possess a taste for the beautiful, a taste that shapes his life not only out of the ordinary forces required on any ordinary day, but also out of the heroic efforts without which life loses its charm for him, and the stage, as an arena of creative art, becomes inaccessible.

Taste helps the actor to overcome all the obstacles of everyday life, all the philistine habits which loom so large in the life of the common or garden man. And it is only because taste transfers the actor with lightning speed into the world of beauty that he can attain that pitch of enthusiasm, those high transports of passion, in which he is able to feel that he and his part are inseparable and can boldly say to the spectator, 'I *am*'.

These are the profundities of the human mind on which the heritage of living art is based. There were unhappy periods in the history of the theatre during which living art ceased to exist, being replaced by dry-as-dust, dead form. But it revived once more as soon as artists appeared whose taste for life in art brought their love to a state of entirely selfless loyalty to it, to a point when they were ready to give up their greatest treasure of heart and soul to the service of art.

In my system, according to which I am conducting my work with you, I am always trying to rouse your enthusiasm for the examination of the nature of your own creative powers. I want to eradicate all your hackneyed stage conventions and replace them by new principles of creative art which prevent the actor from getting into a groove. An actor often believes that the palette of his paints is a brilliantly flashing cloak, while in reality it is just an old dressing-gown on which innumerable stains can be discerned with the colours made up of hackneyed theatrical conventions running into each other.

I hope you will get rid of every kind of overacting as soon as possible and always be natural in your parts. May you always be clad in cloaks made of scintillating, genuine feelings and thoughts. By this you will not only force the spectator to follow everything that is taking place on the stage, but there will also be in all your songs the true expression of thought-word-sound, and then I with the rest of the spectators will say, 'I believe in you'.

CHAPTER V

Every man who wants to become an actor must first of all answer these three questions:—

1. What does he understand by the word 'art?' If he sees in it only himself in a sort of privileged position as compared with his fellow artists; if in this idea of art he does not seek to express those things that trouble him like some faintly perceptible creative forces, groping blindly in his inmost soul and filling his mind with vague apprehension, but is merely out to make a great name for himself; if petty middle-class prejudices merely arouse in him the desire to overcome all the obstacles in his way by an exercise of his will so as to achieve success as a popular and important stage figure—such an approach to art spells disaster for the man himself and for art.

In enrolling new student-actors, the studio must clearly distinguish between those whom it can educate and those whom it cannot, those, that is, on whom all its efforts of spiritual education will be wasted by failing to arouse in them the consciousness that their creative work is merely a way of adding to the general good.

2. Why does a man who takes up any artistic profession, whether it be opera, drama, ballet, the concert hall platform, painting or drawing choose this particular branch of art, and what is the idea he wants to, and indeed has to, contribute to that particular branch of art?

If he does not realise sufficiently how much suffering and disappointment he is likely to experience and how hard his struggle for recognition is likely to be, and if the only thing he sees is the rainbow bridge which will, by the sheer force of his imagination, carry him beyond the earth and beyond life to the land of dreams, then it is the bounden duty of the studio to disabuse him. From the very outset the student-actor must understand that there is only one source of inspiration for him, that there is only one road he has to follow and one star that must guide him

114

on his way—hard work, work on and for, and not above, the earth.

It is the duty of the studio to discover those extraneous aids that are most likely to suit each student best; it is its duty to develop his awareness of those forces that reside in him alone. Its first task is to keep a watchful eye on the work of each student-actor. For the unsupervised work of a student which he himself is left to apply to his artistic problems is always a mistake, a maze of prejudices which he will find much easier to enter than to leave. Right from the very beginning the student-actor must realise that the profession he has chosen means hard work not only till his 'career' on the stage is assured, but to the very end of his life; work must become the source of that energy with which, in a series of interesting and absorbing problems, the studio must fill the mind and the heart of every student-actor.

3. Is the man who goes on the stage inspired by so unquenchable a love of art that it can help him to overcome all the obstacles he is bound to meet in the course of his theatrical career?

It is the duty of the studio to show by the example of its directors how the passionate love of art in a man's heart can be used as a constant stimulus for whatever the tasks of the day may be. This work is of the utmost importance; it must be carried out in a glow of enthusiastic devotion to the art of the stage. Only when a man's love of art is the oil that is poured on the flames of his enthusiastic devotion to it, can he hope to overcome all the obstacles he may encounter and reach the goal of pure art, free from all conventions and achieved by the creative forces every man has to develop in himself. Indeed, it is only when love of art has overcome personal ambition, vanity and pride that the actor can attain the fullest possible flexibility of his will and a free correlation of a deep understanding of the basic principles —the germ—of his part and its through-action. Only when the actor has fully grasped the meaning of the harmony of stage life, can he present—in action purged of 'self'—the truth of the passions in the given circumstances.

By means of the exercises according to my system, the studio must bring about this renunciation of 'self' and the switching over of the actor's entire attention to the conditions supplied by the author or composer so as to reflect in them the truth of the passions.

System and Methods of Creative Art

But may the great forces of life save and preserve the studio from the reign of boredom and pedantry! For if not, everything is lost; it would be much better to close down the studio altogether, dismiss the teachers and send the students home, and in fact give up the whole thing. Otherwise it may lead only to the poisoning of the minds of the young actors and their final undoing. For in art one can only inspire. It is—I cannot repeat it too often—a flame of unquenchable love. Teachers who complain of fatigue are not teachers; they are machines working for money. A man who gives ten lessons a day and does not know how to devote his love as well as his mind and body to each of them is a mere mechanic and not a craftsman: he will never become a real teacher of a young generation of actors. Love is sacred just because its fire is never quenched, however large the number of hearts it kindles. If the teacher gave freely of his creative genius —his love—he would never notice the hours he spent in work, nor would his students notice them. If, on the other hand, the teacher is merely doing a job of work, his students, like himself, cannot help getting tired and bored and generally taking little interest in their work. And neither does art in them—eternal art natural to all human beings and existing in them as love— penetrate through the dusty windows of the humdrum business of the day; it merely remains smouldering in the heart.

Every hour, every minute in which teacher and student achieve the closest possible union of minds must appear like a fleeting moment in their consciousness, an eternal movement in the rhythm of surrounding life.

Feeling-thought-word, the spiritual image of thought, must always bear the stamp of truth; it must be the law that enables every man to communicate facts as man sees them. Truth and love are the two things that introduce you into the rhythm of art's whole life.

The studio must arouse a feeling for truth in man as well as his love; it must nurture and cultivate them with great care. And to teach the student the art of self-observation, the studio must teach him the laws of correct breathing, the correct position of the body, concentration and watchful discrimination. My whole system is based on this. With this the studio must begin the training of its student-actors. And the first lessons in breathing must become the foundation of the development of that introspective attention, on which all the work in the art of the stage must be built.

*   *   *

An actor, I have been telling you over and over again, must be a man of education. Why do I dwell on it so often? Because I consider an actor's education, too, as one of the elements of his creative work. What does it consist of and what are we to understand by it? On what plane does it come into contact with the creative work of the actor, and in what way can it be said to be an element of it?

By an actor's 'education' I mean not only the sum-total of his exterior manners, his polished competence of deportment, and the beauty of his movements, which can be easily acquired by training and drill, but the twin forces of a man developing on parallel lines, and the result of internal and external culture, which makes him into an individual human being.

But why do I consider education of such tremendous importance to the creative work of an actor that I go so far as to call it one of the elements of his creative work? Because no actor can hope to express all the traits of a character in a play, if he has not first acquired a complete mastery of the art of self-possession. If self-possession and inner discipline have not brought the actor to a state of complete repose before he walks on the stage, to a harmony in which the actor must forget all about himself as an individual and yield his place to the character in the play, he will paint all the different characters he is representing in the colours of his own personality. He will never be able to be preoccupied with the life of his part as a genuine artist should. He will transfer his personal idiosyncrasies to every part: irritation, stubbornness, touchiness, fear, intractibility or irresolution, irascibility and so on.

Harmony of which the actor must think, that is to say, his creative 'I', can only be achieved as a result of the total work of his organism, the work of his feelings and his thoughts. The actor who is also a creative artist must be able to grasp all that is truly great in his time: he must be able to understand the great value of culture in the life of his people and feel himself to be an inseparable part of his people. He must be able to understand the highest cultural aspirations of his country as expressed by his greatest contemporaries. If an actor does not possess complete self-control, if his inner self-discipline is not strong enough to produce creative discipline or an ability to disregard everything of a personal nature, how can he be expected to find the necessary powers to reflect the highest achievements of the social life of his time?

When I was working on the part of Stockmann, it was Stockmann's love and his craving for truth that interested me most in the play and in my part. It was by intuition, instinctively, that I came to understand the inner nature of Ibsen's character, with all his peculiarities, his childishness, his short-sightedness, which told me of Stockmann's inner blindness to human vices, of his comradely attitude to his wife and children, of his cheerfulness and vivacity. I fell under the spell of Stockmann's personality, which made all who came in contact with him better and purer men and revealed the better sides of their natures in his presence.

It was my intuition that suggested to me Stockmann's outward appearance: it grew naturally out of the inner man. Stockmann's and Stanislavsky's body and soul fused organically with one another. The moment I thought of Dr. Stockmann's thoughts and worries, his shortsightedness appeared by itself; I saw the forward stoop of his body and his hurried gait. The first and second fingers were thrust forward by themselves as though with the intention of ramming my feelings, words and thoughts into the very soul of the man I was talking to.

The whole basis of an actor's life and work consists of the impossibility of separating his worldly 'I' from his actor's 'I'. If an actor does not always find it easy to discover the outward appearance of his characters and show it to the spectator, he will always find it easy to grasp the essence of the dramatic conflict of the character he is representing, provided he has been successful in achieving a stable and creative degree of self-possession. The greater an actor's self-possession, the more vividly will he be able to depict a man's passion for beauty or his inability to withstand the fascination of evil.

An actor's strength, his ability to rise to the heroic heights of thoughts and feeling, is a direct result of his education. From the point of view of the creative basis of an actor's life, education as well as self-possession are as important as the other element of creative work—love of art. However high an actor rises in his art, it will always be found that if he suffers from a lack of culture or from an inability to achieve the state of heroic tension, he will never reach the pinnacle of his profession. And only those achieve the state of heroic tension who have mastered the art of absolutely stable self-possession. Self-possession as a creative element on the other hand is only attained by the actor who is no longer under the influence of his personal passions, such as envy, jealousy, rivalry and a desire for pre-eminence, which have been replaced by his enthusiasm for art and an unselfish joy at being able to transmit from the stage the great raptures of the human soul, and show them and not himself to the spectators.

It is only then that the flame which brings about a complete fusion with the audience is kindled in the actor. It is then that the actor becomes the object of admiration of the whole people, and not only of a small number of people, every spectator recognising in him the better parts of himself, suffering and weeping, rejoicing and laughing, and taking part with all his heart in the life of the character in the play.

What therefore must the actor's work on himself be like to enable him to achieve this tremendous power of bringing about a complete fusion of the stage and the auditorium? In the actor himself the culture of his feeling and thought must be merged into one. For it is this singleness of purpose that leads to the initial steps of the creative art of the theatre.

How does one acquire this singleness of purpose which comes as a result of one's love of art and one's self-possession? Can it be achieved just because I say to the actor, Think in this way !

It is impossible to raise the actor's consciousness to a higher level by the exercise of someone else's will. Only the actor whose development proceeds along harmonious lines can, quite independently and through his own acquired experience, raise himself step by step to a wider consciousness.

What therefore must be the role of every teacher, including

119

my own, if the experience of one man in this field does not teach another man anything? In all branches of science, such as engineering or medicine, we observe how the experience of some becomes the treasured heritage of subsequent generations. Only in art, and perhaps in life too, people refuse to accept the results of the experience of those who warn them against their errors and illusions. I am trying to show you the way to a higher conception of creative art on the stage and in life. What must I do to achieve this? I must not only point out to you—actors—the nature of the creative feeling and its elements. I must bring all that ore which I have obtained throughout my life to the surface, and show you not how I obtain my results in each part, but how I look for the best way of achieving those results, or in other words how I dig for my ore.

By a whole series of tasks and exercises aimed at the attainment of concentration and attention, and the creation in them of the circle of public solitude, I have made you understand the two fundamental principles of the creative art of the stage, namely work on oneself and work on the part.

Before I begin to concentrate on a definite part, before I think of the creation of the circle of attention, before I attempt to include in it certain new 'given circumstances' of my part, I must myself get rid of the various coatings and layers of that private life of mine which have adhered to me during that very day and up to the very hour when I have to begin my work on the stage. Up to that moment I have lived simply as a member of a certain society, or a certain city, or a street, or a family and so on.

'If' I fail to break the bonds of all my own given circumstances of the day, 'if' I fail to free myself from my preconceived notions so that I become aware that 'in addition to being part of all those daily affairs of mine, I am also part of the whole universe', I shall never be entirely ready for the perception of my part, neither will I be able to reveal in it those organic feelings which are common to all humanity.

To transfuse the energy, concentrated in the part, into the audience, I must first of all get rid of the energy produced only as a result of the particular circumstances of my life. But what is the simplest and easiest way to rid myself of the circumstances of my private life? And how can I enter in the quickest possible way into the new conditions of my life on the stage?

In art 'to know' means to be able to. The kind of knowledge 'in general' which fills your mind with all sorts of observations and leaves your heart cold, is of no use whatever to an actor who is also a creative artist, an actor who experiences everything felt by the character of his part.

CHAPTER VI

The studio is no place for a casual going over of one's part. An actor should never go there for the purpose of studying a certain part at a certain time and for a certain urgent reason because life, which is never at a standstill, has driven him at that very moment into a blind alley, and he feels the need of the advice of a producer, and hence his desire to resort to the aid of the studio.

A student-actor regards art as the sole concern of his life, and for him the studio is his home. When a student-actor comes to the studio to learn his part, he must forget his personal life with its failures and worries. As he approaches the studio his thoughts must be concentrated only on his work, and on entering it he must shut himself up in the circle of beauty and of unselfish and pure thoughts of his work, and he must rejoice that there is a place where he can work with people who, like him, devote all their time to the pursuit of beauty.

A student-actor represents that highly developed consciousness of man in which the idea of love of art, having become the guiding principle of life, never places those who associate with him in an environment that is dull or arid because of too much cerebral work or too great a disposition for philosophic enquiries, but in one where the mere knowledge of the presence of beauty in oneself spreads the knowledge of it among everyone else and tends to create an atmosphere of mutual respect and goodwill. On arriving at the studio, an actor must never waste his time in inane talks with his colleagues, but must always bear in mind how precious those fleeting and irrevocable hours of one's youth are when energy seems inexhaustible and a source of perennial strength.

So pay heed to every passing minute! Make the best of every meeting! And remember to devote the greatest possible attention to the slightest sign of depression in yourself! For if you let despondency steal into your heart today, you can be sure that

122

your work will never thrive, either today, or tomorrow or the day after. By his whole behaviour during the working hours at the studio, the student-actor must seek to develop the better qualities of his character, and above all, let him be gay and cheerful and take things easy.

A tragic face, a heroic exterior, a wish to work out in yourself the external 'style' of your own particular character parts—all this is old-fashioned theatrical nonsense, which should long ago have been banished from an actor's ideas of his art.

No curb must be placed on the full and unimpeded development of an actor's thoughts and feelings; an actor's mind must be wide open to the new ideas which express the hopes and aspirations of his time. He must apply all his efforts to the attainment of greater depth and purity of thought, and concentrate all his attention on stimulating the creative powers of his heart at any fleeting moment. It is only then that 'the circle of public solitude', in which the actor must perform his creative work, will be achieved simply, effortlessly and joyfully.

The habit of devoting his attention to all the manifestations of life on and off the stage will endow the student-actor with the conscious power of observation of everything that is taking place outside and inside him. Guided correctly and step by step by his teachers in the studio, he will come to realise that for the beginning of his creative work he needs: (1) attention, internal and external; (2) goodwill; (3) absolute peace of mind and complete repose; and (4) fearlessness. If from the very beginning the studio does not check quarrelsomeness, touchiness, hysteria, envy and ill-will it will never produce competent, let alone great, actors who are able to attract the wandering attention of an audience.

The stronger the actor's circle of public solitude and the more intent his attention and thoughts on discovering the beautiful in himself and in those around him, the greater his charm, the stronger the vibrations of his creative work, and the more powerful his influence on the auditorium. The studio must reveal to the actor all the mysteries of the art of the theatre. The first of these mysteries is this—the more talented the actor himself is, the greater his creative powers, and the wider the range of his inner spiritual ideas, the more of what is beautiful will he find in

others. And if he discerns much that is beautiful all around him,
if he finds something worthy of admiration in every man, his
creative circle will grow richer, the flashes of his energy brighter,
and the chances of his ability to reflect all life on the stage bigger
and better.

The worst stumbling-block in an actor's work is that dreadful
habit of mind which always seizes on a man's bad points and his
most glaring faults, and completely overlooks the beautiful that
is hidden in him. This is generally true of all poorly endowed and
weakly developed artistic natures—to see the bad side of everything, to suspect persecution and intrigues everywhere, while
in reality suffering from an undeveloped sense of the beautiful
which is insufficient to discern it everywhere and to absorb it.
That is why their own stage images are so one-sided and false, for
there are no men who do not possess a grain of the beautiful in
them—the important thing is to perceive and understand it.

The switching over of your inward attention, though difficult
at first, gradually becomes normal. What is normal becomes, not
at once but again gradually, easy, and finally what is easy becomes
beautiful. It is only then that the beautiful in yourself begins to
evoke corresponding vibrations of the beautiful in every man,
and the way to the stage as a reflection of life is then open in the
actor.

Without such a thoroughgoing and voluntary self-preparation
it is impossible to become an actor—the reflector of the treasures
of the human mind. First you must yourself be able to open up
your heart to all the encounters of life. You must learn how to
devote to each of them all your creative attention. Only then will
the way be open also in the actor to the characters of his parts
and the powers of expressiveness in voice, gait and deportment
will be ready too, because the right feeling is ready in yourself,
because not only your mind but also your heart is ready to form
the right perception of the whole of the man whom you have to
represent on the stage. Thought-feeling-word—everything is
rolled round the familiar cylinder, round the attention you have
to devote to the man whom you are now concerned to depict. All
love is shifted on to the character of your part who becomes inseparable from yourself.

System and Methods of Creative Art

From the very first the studio must wage war against the feelings of fear and agitation among its students. Many hours should be devoted to this work not only in individual cases but also during the general studies. It has to be made clear that all these agitations, which are so characteristic of the actor, have their origin in pride, vanity and self-conceit, and are caused by the fear of appearing worse than the rest. The actor must be made to realise that he has to set free his inner powers so as to render them flexible and capable of coping with the problems inherent in his part at any given moment. The desire for pre-eminence, like the personal feelings already referred to, must be got rid of as a caste prejudice. In the studio all are equal. All alike are creative units. And the diapason of the actor's genius, permitting one actor to play leading parts and another secondary parts, is merely a matter of external contingency. Tomorrow someone's external data may suffer a change, he may fall ill, lose his voice or an eye, or go lame, and instead of playing the lover become an actor playing secondary roles. What has changed is only the character and diapason of his roles. What is of importance, however, is whether his talent and his spirit have also undergone a change. If he accepts his misfortune courageously, as an obstacle which his love of art must overcome, his talent will go on developing and growing in strength because his love of art has stood the test of a purely accidental circumstance—the stroke of bad luck that has befallen him; and at some future date he may obtain a part remarkable for its quite different type of characterisation, a completely new character in fact, and gain even greater popularity because he has risen in his misfortune to a state of heroic tension. The heroic era of our time demands a different kind of actor too. Every actor who is a servant of his state and a loyal son of his country must possess that power of self-renunciation that teaches people to rise to the heroic efforts of the spirit. He who knows how to survive a personal disaster without turning traitor to art, and to accept the new form of his creative work not as a curse imposed on him by fate, but merely as an obstacle that he must overcome with the help of his love of art, will be able to go deep down to the very source of his creative powers and discover the immutable and organic in each of his parts, what in

125

fact is characteristic of all of them. Such an actor will always give us the living image of his part, because his heart too has, through suffering, grasped the real difference between counterfeit and genuine love of art; he can be said to have understood art not just as a dry idea emanating from his mind, but as something that brings about the fusion of mind and heart into one harmonious whole.

Another mystery of the art of the stage the studio has to reveal is that an actor can begin to create only after achieving complete self-possession and repose. It must train the actor by a series of appropriate exercises to obtain such a degree of self-possession that he is able to enter the circle of public solitude naturally, flexibly, and with the greatest of ease. The studio must teach him to concentrate all his attention on one group of nerves and muscles; it must teach him so to concentrate on a certain thought that nothing around him should distract his attention from the direction it has once taken. But should the teachers fail to find an easy and enjoyable way of teaching my system, if they should convert it into something that is indistinguishable from the most tedious kind of despotism, and if happy laughter no longer resounds during the exercises, then the studio will never become a temple of art, but merely a place of refuge for those whose sole desire is to show off and be rewarded and paid according to the highest rates.

A teacher who introduces an atmosphere of fear and trembling into a studio instead of making his students feel at ease and happy, should not be allowed to teach in it. He does more harm than good. And the same is true of a conductor who does not know how to attract the attention—the love—of opera singers, and who issues his orders in a sharp and uncivil manner. He should not be allowed to teach in a studio either. For he is only a feeble kind of artist who is always looking for some external outlet for his prevailing feelings: irritation and personal preference of one man to another. The images created by the composer leave him cold. He does not even make any attempt to discover them, but is satisfied with finding the bare notes in the characters of the opera.

A superior attitude to the actors, a perfunctory nod or greeting coupled with a show of exaggerated respect to people who matter —all this is nothing but theatrical bad manners, and ought to be banished from the studio. It is, indeed, quite inadmissible among us.

The most important of the truths of the art of the stage— absolute self-possession and repose—must become firmly fixed in the mind of the actor. One must get under the skin of a character so thoroughly that, for instance, Anna Karenina should cease to exist merely as a part that has to be presented on the stage, but instead should become a certain woman-actress who shares the same thoughts and ideas as Anna Karenina.

In communicating these thoughts to you, I hope that each of you possesses the sort of love that will teach him to devote all his life to the service of art. Do not try to push your way through to the front ranks of your profession; do not run after distinctions and rewards; but do your utmost to find an entry into the world of beauty. If you find it in yourself only once, having achieved only for a few hours during your studies the fullest harmony of mind and heart, you will already be able to bring undeniably creative treasures into the life of the stage. And even if these do not reach the stage in your person today, they will not be entirely lost, for they will remain in your subconsciousness, and while mute today, you will project them into life tomorrow in some other part and strike a responsive chord of beauty in the people around you.

CHAPTER VII

Let us devote our talk today to the actor who begins consciously to develop his artistic powers in the studio. What ought he to begin his lessons with? What should be his approach to all those subjects he will receive and accept as the knowledge that will fashion him into a definite artistic unit?

To begin with, he must have complete trust in his teachers. He must, in addition, not only be full of the joyous consciousness of having begun his work as a creative artist, but also be fully aware of the fact that every minute of his life helps to fan the flame of creative art in him. If he is unable to grasp the usefulness of a certain exercise immediately from the very first steps, it does not mean that he does not possess sufficient talent to understand fully the meaning of that exercise. All it means is that for the time being he has not reached the required stage in his development; but energy, the energy emanating from the feeling of joy and love that art inspires in him, and not the feeling of despondency which leads at once to despair and tears, not the surly stubbornness of will, is sure to bring him within a short time to an understanding and a proper appreciation of the usefulness of this necessary exercise.

It is absolutely wrong to do any of the exercises laid down in my system mechanically and unthinkingly. It is absolutely wrong to speak your words to no purpose. You must acquire the habit of putting the greatest possible meaning into every word you utter. You must be fully aware of the value of every word. You must concentrate all your powers of observation on the organic and not just the generally accepted qualities which you wish to express in your speech by a combination of the various meanings of the words you utter. You cannot fling out words without first realising the differences between their shades of meaning. The value and the flexibility of each word lies in the intonation—incidental and temporary—you have given to the bare meaning conveyed by the word because that is what your part demands at that moment.

Your decision to take up a stage career implies first of all your willingness to open your heart to the fullest possible perception of life. An actor who devotes his talent merely to the reproduction of the facts he has observed in life, cannot, however talented he may be, cast so strong a spell on the imagination of the spectators as to force them to shed tears and remember long afterwards not only *what* they had seen, but also *how* they had seen and heard. This can only be done by the actor who has mastered his desire for self-admiration, achieved the highest possible degree of self-possession, and trained himself to show the utmost possible good-will to his fellow-men: it is only such an actor who can detect the organic as well as the accidental traits in human passions, and can split them up into those which are less important, that is to say, those that apply only to the character he is representing at the moment, and into those permanent ones that are inherent in the very nature of the feelings. But he can achieve this fusion of himself and the character he is representing only if he learns to love him and if he distinguishes what is only accidental and unimportant in him from what constitutes the very substance of the man on which the entire through-action of the part can be built. You will never obtain a proper understanding of the character of the person you are expected to represent on the stage if you are dissatisfied either with your part or with your position in the theatre, or if you are envious of the position of another actor, or, finally, if there are dissensions among the members of the cast.

Everything that distracts an actor's attention from his part or his work in the theatre or studio, everything that interferes with us while we are engaged in our business—everything of that nature is bound to have a most grievous effect on the actor's work. For under such conditions the actor is unable to do justice to his talent; intuition, the real source of an actor's creative temperament, is silent, and only his instincts are alive, those instincts which lead to overacting, to that hideous exaggeration in which the actor's self-admiration and not his part is what counts.

In such a state of mind it is quite impossible for an actor to grasp the ruling idea of his part or indeed of the play as a whole, its unity of action, or the need for subordinating all those who are taking part in the performance to the unity of the through-action of the play. All you can do is to be the bright spot in a good cast which is firmly knit together by its internal unity, and a brilliant personality, 'carrying the whole performance on your shoulders', as the philistines usually put it in the case of a really talented man—in a third-rate company.

The choice of men of exceptional talents does not represent the standard for the practical application of my system. Many people say that my system is only meant for people of talent, while others contend that it is only useful to actors of average ability who find it difficult to get jobs in the theatre. I, on the other hand, would like to make it perfectly clear that what people call my system is not my system at all. At least I did not invent it, but merely took it from life, from my own observations of the nature of the creative powers of the men of the theatre. It is intended for living people, for those who are able to understand that to live in art is not equivalent to trying to find a good job in it, but to give up their most precious possessions for it—love and the best qualities of their minds. Without love of man there is no way of being successsul in art. Nor is success in art to be had without joy and a feeling of fellowship. To withdraw into your shell, thinking, 'What a priceless pearl I am carrying within me!' is the fate of almost all failures. It is the fate of those who are quick to take offence at every remark of the producer, of those who are always under the impression that they have been misunderstood or under-estimated, or that they are being persecuted, while all their troubles are really due to the fact that, being full of themselves and thinking themselves great men, they are in reality small men eaten up by cheap vanity. And what they consider to be of such great worth in them is nothing but an idle dream, ending in disappointment and bitterness.

Much of what an actor is in the habit of regarding as a cardinal fault in his part is only something he has failed to observe in himself, and in himself only. A way out of the difficulty must be sought not in external efforts, in increasing the power of your voice or the sweep of your movements or the rapidity of your speech, but in listening in silence to the voice of your sub-consciousness. Think over the unsuccessful places of your part in solitude and silence—today, tomorrow and the day after—and the right nuance of the word, its value, its significance as an organic conception, its force in the circumstances accidentally provided by the play, as well as *your* intonation—all this will become gradually clear to you, all this will become easy, simple, and your very own. And the producer's hints you found so difficult to understand yesterday, will also become simple, clear and intelligible.

CHAPTER VIII

The commonly held opinion that the theatre is a cesspool of intrigue and oppression arises from the fact that there are so many people in it who are not only untalented, but also absolutely incompetent, people who have no real love of art, but who have plenty of love of anything that concerns them personally. How do they manage to get to a place where, so it would at least seem, only those who love art and are creative artists can work? The all too common conditions of life, such as the influence wielded by persons in authority, or by relations, acquaintances, and friends, helps many people who possess no acting ability of any kind to get jobs on the stage. And it is these people who are responsible for transforming the place where the company of the theatre has willy-nilly to live into a veritable morass. But what ought you student-actors to be who express the artistic aspirations of your generation? To begin with, you must be living people who possess all those new qualities which will help you, men of our time, to bring a new consciousness into being. What is this new consciousness you have to develop? It is a consciousness which does not regard life for the general good as an unrealisable dream, but which fills you with selfless devotion to your work in the theatre. It is a consciousness which, if you possess it, will bring with you to the studio peace and not intrigues, honour and not hypocrisy.

That period of sheer rapture when your enthusiasm produces a particularly strong affection for the theatre, the studio, and the creative work of the stage, will soon pass away, if there is not in it a strong feeling of joy that comes from the realisation that you have the chance of conveying the best qualities you have obtained by your conscious efforts to become a good actor. You may be dreaming of the fine conception of beauty you hope to convey to your fellow-actors today ; you may be well dressed; you may be young and handsome; you may have made up your mind in the morning, when going over your part in your mind,

132

to enrich the world with the wonderful gifts you possess; you may be smiling happily as you leave your house, thinking joyfully of how soon you will capture everybody's heart at the rehearsal by your fine looks and the excellence of your acting in the chief part in the play. But suddenly you learn that the chief part in the play is not being rehearsed by you today, but by X, and that you are expected to play a secondary part. All your noble 'ideas' evaporate in a twinkling; you look gloomy, you can just manage a sour smile, you can hardly bring yourself to utter the words of your new part which is not so bad at all, though it may not be the leading one in the play. Why has this sudden transformation come over you? Why have all your good intentions suddenly become the floor with which hell is said to be paved? Simply because only your brain, only your mind, was active when you were trying to find the solution to your problem: 'to give expression to beauty today'. Your heart was silent. There was no real love of the theatre or of art or of work in your mind or in it. You were only inspired by a feeling of admiration of your own precious self. That was why your conception of your secondary part was not that of a flame which should have kindled your word-thought-image, but of something that was unworthy of you. You despise those who are responsible for your caricaturing what you had intended to give today, and as you utter the words of your part mechanically, you can only think of them and the wounds inflicted upon your self-esteem.

Once again therefore we return to the primary educational task of the studio. Why is it that all the higher educational establishments of our country have so many students who are not corrupted by the desire to show off or create an effect? Because there every student is preparing himself for a career in which the only thing that counts is work, and not for one in which he may be singled out by the crowd just because he has caught its fancy; because in the case of a scientist who discovers a new and rare material, a better dye, etc., the results of his work can be tested by objective facts, while the student-actor works in an art that depends entirely on the passing of time and is inseparable from his own body and heart, for he is himself the result of his work. He only works when he is acting

133

subjectively. And his power to influence people—mostly due to a combination of many lucky external qualities as well as to intelligence—assures his victory over the crowd. His natural exhibitionism, however, makes acting too easy for him, so that he can do it without having recourse to his feelings. A real artist, on the other hand, is he who has grown into art with all his being, with his heart as well as with his mind. Not the actor whose only desire is to become an object of general admiration, but the actor whose only desire is to convey to the spectator through himself the idea-thought-word or sound is the real artist. Such an actor thinks little of leading parts, but is anxious to dissociate himself as an individual from that self which is to absorb the particular qualities of the part, grasped objectively, appraised and purified by his nobility of mind, so that they may grow into the personality created by the author.

The labour of education in a studio is equal to, if not indeed much greater than, the labour a family spends on educating one of its members. The student-actor must be trained to concentrate the powers of his attention on himself or rather on that creative element in himself—the immutable spiritual core of the man that is his shining glory—which will remain after the various personal characteristics, such as envy, pride, vanity, self-conceit, and the desire for pre-eminence, have been shed.

The work of drawing the creative circle in which the actor on the stage should live as though in public solitude must start with the control of his thoughts, his physical actions and impulses, which distract his attention from the real artistic problems inherent in the part. One should start with an analysis of that irrelevant feeling that destroys the sense of harmony and beauty in the student-actor whenever he succumbs to it as a protest against the producer's instructions and the proposal to rehearse a secondary part.

CHAPTER IX

A man's artistic development is a slow business. The whole range of a man's perceptions switches over from one field of creative work to another very slowly, and man as it were is born afresh in art. What is the part the studio must play in this new development and, so to speak, the second birth of man? Can the studio become that force which in a few years may transform him from the philistine he was when he came there into someone who is actively engaged in bringing beauty to everyday life?

What new vistas can the studio open up to a man for whom art is at present only a powerful magnet and who has no idea of the ways that lead to it, nor of the methods of attaining it? (The difference between enthusiasm and true love is, surely, that the first difficulty cools a man's ardour and forces him to choose an easier way of attaining his goal). The problem the teachers in a studio have to face is how not to lose those who are eager to embark on an artistic career on the stage and at the same time create from the very outset an atmosphere of hard work; and, moreover, how to make the student-actor realise that it is not talent, unorganised and prone to be swayed by all sorts of outside influences, but the work on it, that is to say, a constant process of strengthening the powers which have already been developed in the actor and the constant acquisition of new qualities and possibilities, which is the only way to art.

A man comes to the studio with his mind still clothed in the rags of prejudices he has acquired in his environment. Or he may possess the precious germ of creative art, but it is smothered by layers of personal incidental qualities from which he has to be set free. The studio is not only a house of culture to the man who joins it, but it is also the home of the wise teacher in which love stands guard over both teacher and pupil and presents both of them with a common foundation for creative work. If, according to my so-called system, a student-actor must be able to enter

135

easily, effortlessly, and flexibly into the circle of concentration, and can carry out his appointed tasks only when his attention is entirely focussed on his job, then the teacher too must not only be able to visualise the sum-total of all those qualities and powers of expression his pupil already possesses: he must also be able to recognise those of his qualities which are not characteristic of him as an individual possessing certain original and unique gifts of his own, but which have been acquired by the accidental influence of external conditions on certain sides of his character, and have, in the process, resulted in certain distortions of his true nature. It is this germ in every living man, this unique nature of his talents, distinguishing him from every other man, that the teacher must discern in his pupil.

When is he able to discern it? Only if his own attitude to his pupil is completely impartial and if in his relations with his pupil there is not a grain of personal predilection or personal considerations of a utilitarian character. It is impossible to be a teacher in a studio, that is to say, a man entrusted with the task of awakening new artistic perceptions in young actors, and remain an easy-going philistine, repeating the same exercises of my system over and over again as a lesson that has been learnt by heart long ago.

As there are no two ways that are absolutely alike in art so far as the student-actor is concerned, so there are no two approaches of the master to his pupils that are essentially the same. My system does not consist of written down 'rules' that can be applied indiscriminately; it teaches an art that is every moment different and that can be mastered only through concentration and through watchful discernment of the fundamental and unchangeable nature of things and persons so that they can be exposed to view in correct physical action with the aid of absolutely undivided attention. All the creative forces of a man, acting by means of these aids distinctly, clearly, and easily, are comprised within a circle in which he is always left as though in public solitude. Till he has entered this creative circle, the teacher himself cannot begin his lessons with his pupils. He is not a shopkeeper who, having made sure the scales are correct, is ready to serve his customer. It is his duty to remember that every fleeting moment irrevocably uses up not only his own, but also his pupil's powers. And if he himself is not armed from head to foot with the weapons of love and has not introduced himself as well as his pupils into his creative circle, he does harm to himself and to his pupils. This harm can be immense if the teacher begins in a purely extraneous way to 'show' his pupil how to act a certain part or a certain emotion, instead of first carefully relieving his pupil of his stereotyped notions, his prejudices, and his deep-seated theatrical pre-conceptions. The teacher must deepen his student's attention to the processes of thought in himself, and in this way help him to free his mind of conventional ideas.

From the very outset the student-actor must be taught how to concentrate all his attention upon himself, on certain contracted muscles in his body, and how to relax them at will and switch over his entire attention on another definite group of muscles. Such work cannot be boring. It is most interesting work, and in the course of it the student-actor makes the most surprising discoveries every day and finds ever new ways of overcoming his difficulties.

If only a teacher can avoid being a pedant, if he is quick to discern the organic qualities of a man's character, he will never be disappointed in the results of his teaching and will always be able to see the growth of the organic qualities in his pupil. Courage on both sides! Mutual respect and trust in each other's sense of honour will always prevent conflicts between master and pupil. Work in the studio is never an intolerable burden. Only uninspired and unobservant teachers find it difficult to rid themselves of the habit of exerting their authority on their students. During his lessons the teacher must always be conscious of the fact that every minute that has gone will never return; he must therefore value it above everything, concentrate all his powers on it, and not waste words on trifles, vulgar anecdotes, or flippant stories. The studio will become a real studio only if everyone in it brings his best to it, and if all are intent on preserving its high cultural level—each for all, and all for each. Only such a feeling of complete solidarity can make everyone in the studio equal as regards the rights and duties of creative art.

CHAPTER X

Whatever the student-actor may have been in his private life, he becomes a member of a new family on joining the studio. If he devotes himself with all his heart to the service of art, neither his family and friends nor his private affairs are of any importance to him any more. What is important is that he should not think that he can live outside the studio and merely come there to study. Only he is capable of overcoming all the hard trials of creative art and only he will be ready to take an active part in it one day who *lives* in the studio, who looks upon himself as its loyal son, and who does not forget its teachings outside it.

Having once made up his mind to take up a certain career and to devote his life to the pursuit of a certain branch of art, the student-actor must re-examine his decision again and again after the first three months of work in the studio. He has now learnt to appreciate all the difficulties and he has a pretty good idea of the enormous labour that work on the stage would entail all his life. If this labour fires his energy and forms, in fact, his only joy in life, then he should stay in the study and switch over once more on to new rails, for there can be no progress in his work if he sticks to the same inner problems. Indeed, whenever a certain stage in his training has been passed and certain results have been achieved in his inner development, results he has been successful in giving an outward shape and form, he has to apply himself to more difficult problems. It is here that the creative work of master and pupil run on parallel lines. A teacher should never take up an attitude of cold detachment to the progress made by his pupils. If the student-actor has devoted himself entirely to his work in the studio, his teacher must be more, and not less, devoted to his work. All his life is art, and the studio is the child of his heart that has grown up as a result of his complete re-nunciation of any personal relationships within the four walls of the studio where his main task is to provide a living example

138

of integrity for his students. The mutual love that emanates from the hearts of both teachers and students and their love of art can form an impenetrable wall that will protect their pure impulses towards beauty.

This passion for beauty determines the atmosphere of the studio; it raises everybody above philistine vulgarity; in it ripens the future unity of action of all the members of the cast for the purpose of achieving a harmonious performance.

The teacher in the studio, the producer, lays from the very start the foundation of a new conception of stage art not only in the minds of the student-actors, but also of all those who come to visit the studio. And it is from the studio and through the student-actors and their masters that a current of gladness, courage and youthful energy must constantly flow into life. Youthful not in the sense of young and immature, but in the sense that wisdom continually opens up new sources of power which had lain hidden under the enormous weight of all sorts of prejudices, and that the new consciousness of the actor finds its most fitting expression in hard work which only ceases with his last breath and which, even though his head be grey, always moves forward in the form of a series of forceful actions.

One of the chief and fundamental tasks of the studio consists in the creation of an atmosphere of general ease, simplicity, and peaceful collaboration, and not one in which a blind adherence to principle is the general rule and in which you feel at every step the dead hand of authority enumerating drily and stiffly the various shortcomings of a performance. In it initiative must be fostered, and not blind obedience to the teacher's instructions by way of imitation, or by way of demonstrating the external shades of 'acting', or cramming of references to erudite works, etc.

The only erudite work for an actor is his ability to observe the fundamental principles of the creative work of the stage, namely, the workings of his own heart and the nature of his own passions. An adequately developed attention, becoming the main stimulus of an actor's life, will lead him not only to the realisation of his ignorance of how to achieve the fullest possible control over his body and nerves; for if he observes life carefully, the student-actor will discover all the gaps in his education and will do his best to fill them, having grasped the important fact that at this time of his life there is nothing beneath his notice, since he actually knows nothing at all.

It is here that the teacher himself must form a clear idea in his mind as to the subjects he ought to teach his pupils. The worst possible error he can commit is to fill the heads of the student-actors with all sorts of fashionable nonsense. A course of general studies must be devised to stimulate thought and create the habit of using one's brains in one's work; but nothing should be done to overload the memory with senseless and compulsory work, such as the deliberate learning by heart which would merely produce a weakening of memory, a slackening of attention, and a feeling of general fatigue as a result of swotting up subjects which are of no importance whatever. The attempt to produce men of culture after a course of studies lasting only ten years cannot but be harmful. For if your aim is to produce men of the widest possible general education, you cannot possibly teach anyone anything in ten years. There are no subjects dealing with the art of the stage that can be stowed away in books and taught with the idea of turning out different categories of creative units A, B, C. Man himself, the whole of him, is the book of creative art. And the longer you give him the wrong kind of tuition at school, the less conscious does he become of the creative powers within him, and the more will he rely on textbooks and external circumstances to make a career for himself, forgetting what it was that first drew him to the studio and how great his love was of the career he had chosen for himself when he entered the studio.

CHAPTER XI

The methods of influencing the student-actor, and in turn his methods of influencing his surroundings, can never arise as the result of tension. What do we see when we examine man's activity in life? What is all his activity composed of? It is composed of his attention. A normal man's attention can be graphically represented by -.-.-.- and so on. That is to say, in a normal man there is always an interval of rest and reflection between each moment of attention. During these intervals the work of attention, no doubt, goes on, but it does not emerge from the layers of subconsciousness to the active brain centres which relay the action to the outside world. There must be some object to attract a man's attention to itself as well as time for the attention to assume the form of thought, which, communicated through the brain centres, finds expression in word and action.

In a mentally unbalanced man the rhythm of attention is broken. The intervals of rest, or the time during which attention relays its vibrations to the subconscious mind and gathers them together afresh, as the lungs inhale the air so that life can go on, do not exist so far as he is concerned. For him only the dashes exist, or in other words, attention, attention, and again attention, and his words pour out of his mouth without conveying any meaning to normal people. The speech of a madman is just a dance of thoughts without rhythm or control. He explodes in a series of disconnected thoughts—'I am the Emperor of Abyssinia—I am a great musician—here's the stove—the mouse is on the table—I'm wearing French slippers—it is raining—' and so on.

Every normal man tries to get as much out of life as he possibly can; he tries to merge with life and conquer it. The student-actor who has dedicated his life to art—and I am speaking of real actors and not of those to whom the theatre is merely a means to an end—must develop and increase his own value as an artist by developing all his inner creative powers.

141

System and Methods of Creative Art

But how is he to do it? What is it he ought to concentrate on in particular? The centre of man's creative work is his attention. It is on that, therefore, that he must concentrate. It is his attention an actor must do his best to develop and control. Indeed, the actor who has learned to control his attention and is able to focus it at will on certain groups of muscles, has also learned how to enter the circle of public solitude without any effort on his part. He can remain wherever and whenever he likes in public solitude with his creative problems. He has already set out on his journey not as an empty-handed seeker, no longer worrying about getting a job at one theatre or another, but as one who has formed a clear idea of the beauty of his artistic gift and is trying to use it as a means of communicating with the rest of the world.

We saw that in a normal man attention is subject to a definite rhythm. Is there anything else in man that is connected, according to the inevitable physical law of nature, with rhythm?— Why, yes—breathing.

Let us ask ourselves if there is not some analogy between attention and breathing. Not only does such an analogy exist, but every man, provided he is in good health, breathes rhythmically. The intervals between inhaling and exhaling the air are always constant, that is to say, when you inhale the interval before you exhale, if you are composed, will be, say 2; you exhale and once more the interval in your breathing before the next inhalation will be 2, and so on. Your breathing is strictly rhythmical. And it is only when it is rhythmical that it renews all the creative functions of your organism; your heart is beating regularly and responds clearly and harmoniously to the rhythm of your breathing.

But what happens to you when you are distressed, cross, irritated or when you fly into a rage? All the functions of your breathing are upset. You are not only unable to control your passions, but you cannot even control the rhythm of your breathing. It has become accelerated, the intervals between the inhalations and exhalations have vanished. One wave of breathing rushes on top of another. You do not breathe through your nose but through your mouth, and that still further upsets the whole functioning of your organism.

What do we see here? Is there any analogy between attention and respiration? Of course there is. The one as well as the other function of our 'I' is subject to rhythm. But a student-actor is not just an ordinary individual. He is a man who looks on art as the key to his life. This, surely, means that the development of his powers too—his attention and his respiration, the powers, that is, on which the whole of a man's creative work depends— must be placed by him under control, and that he must learn to manage them as centres of the utmost importance. The force that controls the movement of his lungs is beyond his powers of observation. No man can prolong his own life by one single day, if die he must, nor can he come back to life once he is dead. To develop one's mind and body at one stroke is as impossible as it is impossible for a rose to emerge full-blown out of its bud in an instant. But both the student-actor and the rosebud are *potential* flowers, provided they are carefully watched and tended. By the simplest possible examples, based on physical action, the student-actor's attention must be fixed on the unalterable analogy: calm breathing—healthy thought, a healthy body, healthy feelings, easily controllable attention; the rhythm of breathing upset— always an unsettled mind, always a sensation of pain, always complete distraction of attention. Suppose a student-actor comes to you, the teacher, and complains that he is the most unhappy, lonely, and persecuted creature in the world. You are his teacher; how will you react to his complaints? Will you examine the cause which he considers to be the reason of his unhappiness? Or will you try to discover in him the *whole* man, the *whole* of his life, the whole apparatus of human strength and the majesty of life? Will you do your best to clear away the rubbish-heap which he himself has introduced into his organism and which has driven him, day after day, into the pit in which he finds himself now? Well, of course being his teacher, you must also be his friend, his comforter, and the man who helps him to find a way out of his difficulties. You have no right to be influenced by his disordered vibrations, which are always highly infectious and harmful to the organisms of people who come into contact with them. You must be so courageous, calm and even-tempered that the atmosphere that emanates from you should first of all help the man who is talking to you gradually to find his own composed rhythm of breathing. And it is only when you see him breathing evenly and regularly that you should begin your talk with him about the matter that is troubling him.

But how can you, the teacher, so harden yourself that the smallest jolts from outside, the smallest shocks and interruptions in rhythm which constantly take place around you in the waves of human emanations, do not upset the rhythm and harmony of your own organism? You must always bear in mind that you can never give something you have not got yourself, nor teach anyone something you have not mastered yourself. You must yourself go through the whole course of studio or theatrical work and you must yourself know everything that is taught in the studio, for only then will you be able to be the principal or a teacher of it.

Rhythmic breathing is necessary to teacher and student alike as one of the methods of the ordinary regime of life, just as much as it is necessary to possess the fullest possible control of one's attention and be able to subject it to one's will easily when dealing with any creative problem. And if you could speak to your student about his own rhythm of breathing that he must learn to control, you the teacher, too, must clearly understand that you have to make yourself master of your rhythm of breathing and, furthermore, realise that the whole universe exists in accordance with a definite rhythm and that you, as a fraction of it, are also subject to the laws of rhythm. Having grasped the fact that not only yourself, but everything that lives, is an eternally moving rhythmic entity, you, the actor and teacher, will yourself, as you analyse a part, be able to detect the rhythm of every part and of every performance as a whole.

Only when you take as your starting point the law of rhythm, which remains unalterable for every living thing on earth, will you be able to begin your lessons on rhythmic breathing with your pupils simply, effortlessly, and cheerfully. And seeing in you a living example of love and truthfulness, they will follow you, not looking up to you as an authority, but sharing your enthusiasm, untroubled by difficulties, and only striving for new achievements.

CHAPTER XII

Let us now discuss the definition of the term 'creative circle', that is to say, let us try to find out what it means to create a circle in which an actor can, and indeed must, have the feeling that he is, as it were, in public solitude.

What is a 'circle?' It is that degree of concentration on one single thought in which all the nerves through which attention carries on its work are brought into focus. But is is not enough to bring them into focus; they must also be tied together by the exercise of the utmost alertness of mind, so that they should all be working in the same direction and the magnet of some thought should attract all the powers of your observation to itself.

Let us suppose you have a knife in your hand with which, according to the plot of the play, you have to kill your rival. Your thought, divided between the weapon (knife), and the action (murder), will not permit you to forge that unity of action out of your body and energy which should have for the audience the stamp of truth.

The only thought, the first one, with which you should enter your circle is your knife. Concentrate on the physical action: examining the knife. Look at it closely, test its edge with your finger, find out whether its handle is firm or not. Transfer it mentally into the heart or chest of your rival. If you play the villain try to estimate the force of the blow that would be needed to thrust the knife into your rival's back. Try to think whether you would be able to deal the blow, whether the blade should not have been a bit shorter or longer, whether it should not have been a little stronger, or whether it would stand the blow without bending? All your thoughts are concentrated on one object only: the knife, the weapon.

When you have gathered all the powers of your thought on the knife, you can begin to widen the circle of your concentrated thought. Do not attempt to change anything in your state of mind, but transfer your thought from the knife to its *object*, in this case to your rival. Here your thought will stumble by itself upon the memory of your first suspicion when he, who is now your enemy, was still your friend.

Do not change the circle. Widen it. Let your thought sink deep into your memories. Do not, however, look for sombre colours just because you are acting the murderer and you want to kill your enemy. Allow your memory, your thought, to paint you the picture of your former friendship with your rival. Transfer yourself in your imagination to the days of your childhood when your friendship with him began. Picture to yourself the loving faces of your mother and his mother; imagine that the two of them were good friends. Go on recalling the happy times you had with your present enemy, the games you played with him in the presence of your mothers, in the soft light of a lamp, in a cosy room, to the sound of music. And the moment when you are unable to make up your mind whether to kill your rival or not will not be spoilt by overacting, but will be marked by a true creative feeling just because your heart is full of forgiveness and love. You have widened your circle. You are no longer alone in it. You have peopled it with living, though invisible to anyone but yourself, assistants of your creative work. You remember the moment of your present enemy's self-sacrifice at the time when he was still your friend and saved your life. Invisible to the audience, these thought-images are alive to you, and through you they pass like a series of stages of your part, like the links of a chain that hold together all the separate scenes of your life-part and fuse them into one.

You have concentrated hard on your memories. You forgot all about the knife. But it is still in your hand. Suddenly you cut your hand with it, and all those beautiful thoughts of yours, fortified by the bright pictures of your past, are shattered. Your attention has once more reverted to the knife. And a whole gamut of new feelings, which are now aroused by the memories of your rival's betrayal, deceit and lies, start tormening you. Do not shift the circle, do not tear it apart, continue to concentrate your attention on the images already created by your thought, but widen the circle, invisible to the audience but intensely alive to you, and go on developing all the powers of your attention on the wrong you have suffered. Form your thoughts and the images of your imagination according to the text and the circumstances provided for you by the author and the producer; but as you have brought them forth out of the inmost places of your heart, the words of your part and your truth in it, your life in the circle of your imagination and the stage, will merge into one.

It is here that you will begin to enter into the initial phase of your creative work, that is to say, you will achieve the truth of the passions in given circumstances. Never forget that when acting the villain you must look for those moments of his life when he was good, when his love was unselfish, when a spark of innocence still glimmered in his heart.

The thought with the help of which you intend to form the creative circle must be active—all of it—entirely in one direction.

If you are a true student-actor, I have told you already how you should behave when entering the studio. If you have, as it were, immersed yourself into a purifying bath of love of your work, the studio, and your fellow-actors, then your life, as you retire into your creative circle, will introduce you easily into the work of attention; already on your way to the studio you have become aware of the best powers in yourself, and you have grasped the importance of the moments you will spend in your work; you cannot spare the time on idle talk, on silly gossip, and on the most vulgar preoccupation of all—stage-fright. A true student-actor knows no fear, for all his thoughts are entirely absorbed in the problem set him by his part, his teacher, or the producer. He just cannot afford the time to worry about whether he will be able to act his part, or what the people in the studio will say, or how awful it feels to walk on the stage where everyone could see and criticise him. Such thoughts can occur only to a man who, filled with ill-will and envy, himself finds fault with the actions of his colleagues. He feels constrained as he moves before a group of his colleagues because his heart and thoughts are not wholly pure; he does not become intent on the creation of the circle, being solely concerned with the impression he is making on the people who are watching him. The impression such an actor produces will always be a poor one. He is so pitiful just because he will never advance beyond overacting and the traditional conventions of acting. He is capable of developing the physical force of his movements and, externally, he may well achieve a high degree of technical proficiency as an actor; but his part, as an image, as a unit of the whole play, will not add another iota of happiness, warmth, or depth so far as the spectator is concerned. The chill of external proficiency and the celebrated 'inspiration' produce alike the same results. Only the closed creative circle, in which psychical and physical movements are harmoniously blended, is of any value as the expression of *total* attention, imparted to *every* circumstance of which the part is composed.

How does one draw up the plan of a part? Let us suppose you are Onyegin. What is the first thing you do when you start learning your part—if it is an opera? You have read Pushkin. You have been through the libretto. You know the text of the opera by heart. You have a very clear idea of what the composer wished to emphasise in the character of Onyegin, which, of course, does not mean that you have entirely lost sight of Pushkin's character.

While analysing Chaykovsky's characters you find in the first act, in the second, twice in the third, and in the fifth one and the same qualities, one and the same characteristic traits. You make a careful note of them. Furthermore, in the third and final scenes you again discover one and the same qualities. As you go on with your analysis, you again find general features in the second and the third acts. You note them all down.

At the end of your analysis you find that you have jotted down 37 different qualities. A further examination shows that 3, 5, 10, 18 are really only one and the same quality, and you mark them now with one number. After analysing once more all the 37 qualities, you reduce their number to 17. Then you again discover some general features shared by some of the 17 qualities, and reduce the total to 10. After reducing still further the remaining 10 qualities to more fundamental ones, you get out of the original 37 qualities only four, and finally you detect one, or two, or three out of which you compose the unbroken line of your part, from which you deduce the through-action of your part in the whole play. Now you have also obtained a clear conception of the ruling idea of the play, according to which you must shape all the actions of your part. Now it is no longer Pushkin's nor Chaykovsky's characters who are before you, but it is you— Ivanov, Petrov, or Sidorov—who are Onyegin. You are the life, a fragment of which was revealed to you through Pushkin and Chaykovsky, and it is through their synthesis in you that you have revealed yourself—Onyegin— to the spectator.

But to be able to dissect a character in your mind does not mean that you are a talented actor. There are many actors who can analyse their parts very well, but are unable to play them satisfactorily. You can learn nothing in the art of acting except the bare text or the notes. All you can do is to put the little word 'if' in the circle of your attention with the help of your thoughts and your imagination before the start of your creative work and in this way begin to live with the images of your inner life, as we have demonstrated in the scene with the knife.

If I am Onyegin, how do I arrive at the country house of the Larins on my first visit? Do I represent a pompous, starchy coxcomb who, in appearing before an audience, is afraid to forfeit his reputation and the dignity of a leading actor who is used to be met with applause on his entrance as 'darling' Onyegin? Such an actor will, while waiting for his cue in the wings, have thought a hundred times how his voice sounded that night, having already tried how he would 'take' the word 'dreams' in the third scene; he is constantly worried about his appearance, but he has forgotten the most important thing of all: he has forgotten that it was not in his dressing room that he put on his make-up, that he was really living in the country, that Lensky was the dearest person he had met since he had begun leading the life of a bored country squire, that his friendship with Lensky had started before his visit to the Larins, that he was now anxious to meet Lensky's friends, his fiancee's family, that it is *they* who are the living thoughts-images, invisible to anyone but himself, with whom his creative imagination will people the circle of his public solitude in the subsequent stages of his life on the stage that night. And it is them he has to scrutinise attentively, physically, at his first entrance.

System and Methods of Creative Art

What is the creative imagination of an actor? Does it bear any resemblance to the imagination of an ordinary man, and what is the difference between them?

The creative imagination of an actor must, if it is to be active, first of all possess the indispensable quality of every creative art—repose. That repose in which alone the harmony of thought and action can be achieved. It is quite impossible to form any creative circle, that is to say, a place where the imagination must be set in motion if, on the one hand, the actor's thought tells him, 'I am Onyegin, I must act as a young man who is in love with himself and who wants to escape the boredom of his life in the country', and if, on the other, the actor's mind is oppressed with the memory of some unpleasant family scene or with the fear that the theatrical management will not give him a leading part in the next play, or will not pay him as much as it pays X.

Both forces—heart and mind—acting in repose, can by the concentration of attention bring about so great a renunciation of the personal 'I' that a state of complete harmony can be created in the mental make-up of a man.

Let us once more recall what I said about the behaviour of an actor on the way to the studio, and about his thoughts when he is getting near it and when, finally, he enters it. He has been preparing the ground in his consciousness and nerves for embarking on his creative work. Now he has been called out by the producer or is sitting quietly and watching the work of his colleagues.

The first thing an actor must do on entering the rehearsal room is to shed all the ties that bind him to his private life. Ivanov's, Petrov's, or Sidorov's life has come to an end behind the door of the rehearsal room, and the man who is sitting there now is the man whose part the actor has come to rehearse. A feeling of great calm must fill his heart. Here he is beyond life's worries and troubles. Here, in this 'now', there exists no other life than his creative life; here is only the powerful life of his spirit which enables him, through concentration, attention, mental alertness and self-renunciation, to transform himself into the character of the play, and the given circumstances into real ones.

What constitutes the real value of every actor is not the number of parts he plays, but the quality of the characters he creates, that is to say, the breadth, power and integrity of the circle in which he lives in public solitude on the stage or at a rehearsal. There is only one difference between a good and a bad actor: the ability or inability to renounce his ego, to concentrate the whole of his attention on what is taking place in himself and in those who are admitted into his circle, and the degree of the *total* bestowal of all his powers on the transient 'now', without a thought of how he will act and sustain himself till the fifth or sixth act.

During the first rehearsals the experienced producer can already clearly perceive the differences between the psychological tendencies among the student-actors working with him. One is entirely in the power of the fleeting 'now'. He immediately grasps the significance of every remark made by the producer and tries promptly to switch over all the powers he possesses in the new direction the producer has indicated to him. All his powers, thoughts, and feelings are inextricably bound up with his creative work; he has long ago forgotten that he is a student-actor or that he is rehearsing; he has become the man whose soliloquy he speaks; his 'now' is filled with nothing but the thoughts of his part, and all his life is concentrated on them alone.

Another actor will, in answer to your remark, say, 'Yes, sir', 'I'll do it', 'I'll do it tomorrow', 'I've understood everything', but you can depend on it that neither tomorrow, nor in a week's time, nor during the performance will he do anything of the sort. This is a bad actor who has not only failed to prepare himself properly for the creative work that should be sacred to him, but to whom no work is sacred; he belongs, in fact, to that old-fashioned type of actor who looks on his art and his country merely as a means of enriching himself, and not as sacred altars on which he should lay his offerings.

Still, the teacher in the studio must be careful not to pay more attention to those who are true actors than to those who do not as yet realise the whole responsibility of the obligations they have undertaken towards art by their decision to take up a stage career. The teacher must not discriminate between his students.

but dedicate his work to all of them; nor must he devote all his energies to teaching the art of the stage, but must also devote them to the creation of an atmosphere of selfless work in which the actor should be free to develop all the different sides of his genius in accordance with the process of gradual evolution, resembling the gradual opening up of flower-buds. If the gardener fails to protect his flowers from the scorching sun in the initial stages of their development they will all wilt and perish; if he does not protect them against night frost they will freeze; if he does not shield them against hail, they will be broken, and so on. For it is not only the teacher's love and the magnetism of his personality that helps every student-actor to achieve a higher degree of development in his art; it is also the atmosphere of simplicity and truthfulness that should remove all the barriers between the teacher and his pupil, so that the student-actor should not hesitate to come to his master with his problems and questions, and that the whole of his life should find an echo in the teacher's heart. The teacher should always be ready to give his advice to the student-actor, as a friend, a more experienced friend, no doubt, but otherwise his equal in every respect.

Kindness and simplicity of address, and civility never prevent the teacher from introducing strict discipline in the studio. On the contrary, it is just these things that make people accept the discipline of the classroom without protest and help to develop in each student-actor his powers of self-observation.

It is here in the studio that the foundation of self-discipline must be laid in every student-actor. It is here that one must strive to develop and widen a man's consciousness by demonstrating to him that the higher the discipline of *his* thought, the stronger his circle will be. The wider the circle of his consciousness, the wider the circle of his imagination will be and the more vivid the images of his fleeting creative 'now'.

Everyone ought to realise that the multitude of failures occur just among those actors who do not know how to observe, create and build their creative 'now' without thinking of tomorrow. No other artist can possibly have so clear a conception of the unrepeatable fleeting moment as the actor, for the actor must in that fleeting instant of time grasp the full significance of a remark or of a sudden impulse of his intuition and promptly incorporate it in his part. Never again will he get exactly the same flash of inner illumination, for it is only in that 'now' that he has acquired all the powers that are active in him; his own personality is no longer a hindrance to him, and he has attained what is rightly called inspiration, that is to say, the harmoniously active powers of the mind and the heart, freed from all the influences of everyday life, except those given in his part.

The mind of an actor and a producer is a mighty force. But an actor who does not possess the magnetic power of goodness and—as an indispensable condition—the capacity of complete renunciation of all commonplace and conventional ideas, will never in his work with living people accomplish a complete union either with his colleagues or students, or with those hundreds of thousands of men and women whom his creative work must influence by the power of beauty.

CHAPTER XIII

Controversial questions of stagecraft will always remain controversial. No man has been able to find a final solution of the problem of the creative art of the theatre ever since the theatre existed. There have been geniuses whose art has drawn thousands of deeply moved spectators to the theatre, but they had no time to share the mysteries of their creative work with those who wished to dedicate themselves to the stage. It is impossible to imagine Shalyapin, Salvini or Yermolova in the role of teachers. They were full of their own problems, their creative art demanded all their attention, and to the very end of their lives on the stage their work could not be separated from their subjective role in art, if by this we understand only the series of actions in which their 'I' became fused harmoniously with the characters they were representing.

Your love for the stage must be so great that it should always fire you with the desire to get as many people as possible to take an active part in its life, and, besides, you, as a living example and a teacher who has sacrificed everything to his calling, should take so deep an interest in every student-actor as to make his life in the theatre as pleasant and easy as possible. What is it you have to impress on the minds of your students first of all when starting your lessons with them? It is what I myself, when starting my lessons, if they may be called that, with you am trying to impress on you. There is one quality about all the great actors I have had the privilege of seeing and observing that has always struck me most forcibly, namely, their extraordinary freedom of movements, their ability to control their bodies with such an astonishing simplicity and flexibility that it almost seemed as though they were not 'playing' before an audience, but were living in their own room, without noticing anything that had no relation to their immediate physical action or to the people with whom they were acting in the play. Movements on the stage that are absolutely free and unhampered—that is the first thing a student-

154

actor has to master. Having concentrated your thoughts on a definite problem and your attention on a definite group of muscles, you have to acquire the ability to move about in such a way that it should seem as though all your energy had been concentrated on those muscles.

Let us assume you have to cross over from your place by the window and hide a letter you have just received but not had time to read through properly, so that those who are listening to your every movement in the next room should not notice it. What are your problems? First of all you have to get up without making any noise. But your chair creaks. How will you carry out that particular stage 'business'? Will you 'act' fear—'Don't for heaven's sake let me make a noise with the chair?' No. You will try, in the circle of your creative consciousness, to set in motion the energy in your feet and knees by directing all your powers there and not looking round, as is usually done according to the conventions of the stage. You concentrate all your attention on that particular section of your problem. You are searching intently for help inside you, and the entire audience is with you, for it too is intent on the same task as you, drawn into your circle by your intense concentration. You get up. Oh, what a relief! You have succeeded in getting up without making a noise! Your smile of relief conveys to the spectators the immense effort you had to apply in order to set your muscles, your will, and your thought working in one direction, and it also reveals to them the new shade of joy you have discovered in the relatively unimportant scene: 'to get up without making a noise'.

Your second problem is to move across the room noiselessly. How many times does one see actors on the stage in just such a position! What do they do? Why, they raise their shoulders, draw in their heads, bend forward, and step heavily on each foot in turn, rolling their eyes about the room, all of which, according to the hackneyed conceptions of the stage, ought to express agitation.

But what have you, a student-actor to do? You have to transfer all your energy to the tips of your toes, you must concentrate all your attention on them, setting the rest of your body free— shoulders, arms, neck. Your head, neck and shoulders must always be held up straight, so that your head and back form one straight line, while your sacrum feels as though it were the end of a sharp stake on which your trunk had been stuck, leaving your extremities absolutely free to move about, so that you can set them in motion at any moment without the slightest effort on your part, but simply by the force of your will.

As soon as your entire attention is concentrated on the tips of your toes, you find it easy to manipulate them. You stand on tiptoe and move across part of the room. Make up your mind beforehand where your place of refuge is to be if the door should be suddenly opened, so as not to look like a man caught in the act. Your way across the room leads you to a small dressing-table, but your real aim is your cigarette box on your desk. You tiptoe gently and effortlessly to the dressing-table. You reach it without mishap. Your box is within your reach. Should you go on tiptoeing as before? No. Having reached the table, you start humming a tune, as though forgetting the door leading to the next room. You glance into the looking-glass, smooth your hair, as though you were dissatisfied with your appearance today, and then walk, not on tiptoe, calmly to your desk. You take a cigarette out of the box, light it, rummage in the box for a while, and then put your letter in. But suddenly the door opens and in comes your jealous wife. What do you do? Do you betray your fear so that your wife's jealous glance should at once see through your manoeuvres? Here the secret of your creative art can once more either ruin the whole scene by loading it with all too familiar stage tricks, or you may—in the given circumstances—attract the spectators into the circle of your agitated state of mind. According to the author, your problem now is to carry off successfully the scene of your wife's suspicion. Your attention is divided: (1) you must not show the letter and (2) your wife's suspicion must be allayed. But it is impossible to find room in your attention for two different problems. What, therefore, ought your first problem to be, and how are you to solve it? If, being too anxious to distract your wife's attention from the place of danger—the cigarette-box in which your letter is hidden—you move away from it quickly, her suspicions will be redoubled; if, on the other hand, you remain where you are, she may attempt to search the cigarette-box and your letter will be discovered. But your agitation is hidden inside you. You have admitted into your circle the image of the woman from whom you have received the letter. You do not think of the letter, but of 'her', the woman invisible to us, but alive to you in your circle.

Your annoyance with your wife arises from the comparison which you cannot help drawing between her and the invisible and enchanting image of 'her' in your mind. Try at this moment to love 'her' so ardently and to defend 'her' from your wife's attacks with such pure and chivalrous thoughts in your heart, that your own unfaithfulness should never strike you as in any way inconceivable.

What thoughts will be uppermost in your mind all the time as you play this scene? You have to present your attention with the task of preserving the fullest possible self-control and repose. Repose, repose, repose! And this repose as you play the scene must always coincide with the repose of your creative problem. The greatest possible precision in every—even the tiniest—fraction of your part can alone save you from overacting and arouse your powers of intuition. You know already how to analyse your part, how to find its most characteristic general qualities by gradually integrating those that possess common features, and how to discover the through-action and the ruling idea of the play. You divide up the whole of your part into small pieces exactly in the same way. In each piece you look for that theme which can be expressed by a predicate. In spite of the fact that all life is one continuous action, that 'I want to' is present in man every minute, it still remains true that the most difficult thing in the world is to express by a verb your wish in every piece of a part you are asked to analyse.

Let us take an example from Pushkin. It is possible to say—

I have a gilded* *monument* to myself erected;

I have a gilded monument to myself erected;

I have a gilded monument to *myself* erected;

I have a gilded monument to myself *erected*;

or finally,

I have a *gilded* monument to myself erected.

* The actual word used by Pushkin is 'unwrought by hand'.   (D.M.)

And in each case the meaning will be different, in accordance with the word we desire to emphasise. The emphatic word is the centre of attraction. In it the whole meaning of the sentence is hidden, and as a result of the combination of attention, strength of the voice, and the amount of feeling put into it, the feeling-thought-word the actor expresses is capable, like a spark, of kindling the enthusiasm of a crowd.

But has the external force any significance at all? The effect produced by the voice and the movements? The only thing that possesses any significance is the force of your attention and your sensitiveness, the 'how' of your different 'I want to's' in any particular piece of your part. You have been given your part. Never read it for the first time if you are in a bad mood, for if you do, you will never find those places in it in which your heart and mind can fuse harmoniously, that is to say, you have yourself destroyed all those salient points of your part in which you could have achieved true creative work. Having at last reached a state of complete repose and self-possession and being in an excellent mood, you read your part. Do not during the first reading of your part even attempt to mark those places in it which at that moment you think you would be able to make its culminating points. For very often the most important places of your part will escape your attention during the first reading. After you have read through your part, you should put it aside and do something else. Only after you have had a rest from it, should you read it a second time when you can start cutting it up into pieces, in each of which you must try to find your particular 'I want to'. Let us assume you are Czar Fyodor. You are thinking of your first entrance. What is it that you, an educated man, want? Are you going to look for photographs or try to remember how a certain actor used to play that part?

You must get some history books and look up the reign of Ivan the Terrible, so that you could enter together with the historian into the life of that age. All the various facts about that life, the powerful figure of Boris, the boyars, the whole mode of the life of that time long before the reign of Fyodor himself, will help to give you an inkling of the real life of that particular period. And it is there that you will find the roots of your part, and as you assimilate them in your heart, you will find not only the roots of your part, but its image in your imagination, that 'you-Fyodor' which will make plain to you the meaning of your various 'I want to's' which you are engaged in selecting.

CHAPTER XIV

HAVING cut up your part into its principal pieces, you start putting them together, seeking out those in which you find your 'I want to' expressed by the same verb. You then proceed to put them together, making a careful note of how many times you have expressed the inner movements of your hero in the play by one and the same definition.

From this you will deduce the main reasons and motives which caused the inner life of the person you are representing on the stage to assume certain outer forms and what the nature of those outer forms was. This will become apparent to you from those qualities of his character which you have already noted in the part and chosen earlier.

When you have put together in your mind and heart, harmoniously, effortlessly, and simply, all the movements of your hero's energy and given them their physical expression in accordance with all the signs and characteristics you had discovered during your first analysis of the qualities of your part, you will get what is called creative art, that is to say, you will disclose the truth of the passions in the circumstances given to you.

The moments of instantaneous illumination when you suddenly see what has so long been obscure to you, what you have tried so hard to find but could not get to the bottom of, what was so clear to you and yet did not seem to hang together, only come as a result of the concentration of your entire attention.

It is impossible, however great your talent, to enter the circle of creative work by means of extraneous aids only. All my system amounts to this: to understand the organic moments in your part and to be able to group them logically, reflecting them in a series of truthful physical actions. And to do that you must set free from the restraint of conventional qualities, by means of the exercises laid down in my system, those forces in which the whole mystery and secret of creative work is hidden, or to put it

160

differently, your love of art must be so selfless and pure and you must protect it by so impregnable, though invisible, a wall of constant craving for beauty that beauty should become the first circle of your public solitude in which you enter in order to form that temporary and conditional creative circle which your part offers you now. The physical liberation of the body alone will not produce anything of a creative nature. Only when your mind is free and not oppressed, when you are full of courage because you know what untold riches are comprised within you, will you be able to achieve a state of complete freedom both inwardly and outwardly from all the accumulations of accepted habits and customs and be able to begin your creative work on the stage.

But what is your idea of the best way of beginning your work? Will you again look for it outside? Will you again deceive yourself by the belief that one has to be somebody or be recognised somewhere or somehow? To become an authority and be lauded to the skies by someone? You must get it firmly into your head: the way to art is in yourself and only in yourself!

A man does not find himself in certain situations because of some extraneous circumstances, but because his energy always leads him where he can give expression to it, provided of course that he himself loves art and wants to live only in it, and if he is pure of heart. In the course of my life I have come across thousands of instances which confirm what I am saying to you now, and I daresay I shall find not a few such instances among you too.

In every branch of art there are at first hundreds of people who wish to study it. Many come in response to the bait of 'learning creatively", but having realised how much of their time they have to devote to it; how difficult it is to achieve the complete freedom of the body and all its parts; how long it takes to control and develop one's attention and to learn to transfer it entirely— at one blow—and instantly from one group of muscles to another before you even get to the psychological problems; how difficult it is to develop a sense of rhythm in oneself and change it in the most extraordinary way to the rhythm of the music before you even start on your exercises for collecting your energy and distributing it in different directions—having grasped all that, the majority of those who have come to study the art of acting will leave the studio. Many of those who stay behind will also very soon leave, for the temptation to earn money by slipshod work is very great. In these times of general want only a few of you have stayed behind, and we shall do our best to get more students. All those who have from time to time found their way here, seem to have long forgotten where our studio is. But that is something that happens over and over again and we need not be too discouraged. We shall always have a nucleus of students who have stood the test of every possible trial and whose love of art, like the germ of the part, provides the start for the theatre of the future.

Let us now return to the definition of the creative road of the actor. Are there any generally accepted and recognised rules which can teach you how 'to act'? If I have just told you that an actor can be said to have embarked on the road of creative art only when he finds in himself the never changing, unshakable, unquenchable love of art which thrives on difficulties and failures and which always burns with a steady flame, then will you please tell me this: do you think it is possible to lay down generally accepted rules, according to which every actor can learn 'to act', that is to say, to express *his* feelings, in the same way as any other actor? Every man discovers for himself *his own* germ and his own love of art and sets them free for his creative work by a special and unique method, which constitutes his individual uniqueness and his own secret. For this reason the secret of the creative work of one man is of no earthly good to another and cannot be handed to anyone as a model for imitation. For imitation is the most deadly sin of all. It is something that is completely devoid of any creative principle. And by imitation I mean teaching someone to imitate someone else's voice, or manner, or results, or to give an exact copy of the deportment of a well-known actor. That is not the road of individual creative work, that is to say, it is not the way to awaken in an actor an ever new perception of life and its problems, but the choking up of the purely organic thought by an accidental mode of expression which has become the established manner of one actor.

The actor's road in art is he himself. The 'himself' who

162

knows how to throw overboard such intolerable habits as self-conceit, pride and envy, in short, the accumulation of the all too common human failings which conceal his love and goodwill towards men and which he has first to overcome before he can release his own inner powers for creative work.

But if the creative art of the stage is so individual and inimitable, what is, or rather, should be of general application for all those who wish to set their frozen talents free for creative work? I am not talking of those who want to learn how to act a certain part in the studio. The studio is no place for learning parts; it is meant to supply a living need, it is the servant of those who want to free their nerves, thoughts, and all the centres of their bodies from all constraint so as to enable the living forces of life within them to unite with the same living forces of life in each spectator. The aim of the studio is to achieve through the stage a union in beauty and in the best and highest human forces among all who take part in a performance on both sides of the footlights. It forges its own weapons for the achievement of this union in beauty, namely its actors.

But how are we to find something of a general nature that is applicable to *all* as the road to the achievement of the final goal of creative art by everyone individually? Let us see if we cannot find in the nature of the human feelings themselves steps that are common to all and on which, as on the rungs of a ladder, everyone can climb up so as to attain the desired end of becoming a creative artist of the stage. Everyone must sooner or later put his foot on one or another of these organic steps. But how is he going to climb them, what kind of shoes will he be wearing (or whether he will be wearing any at all), where will he perceive the ladder to be standing, what will the steps themselves look like to him and which steps will be his, whether green, white, yellow or red—that is the secret of his whole art, of his organic creative ego.

Through my system we try to achieve a state of concentrated attention. We begin it with physical actions, for instance, with the minutest possible examination of some object, so that everything about it becomes familiar to us. It is here that the beginner realises how unused his thought is to discipline. While examining his right hand, he has found time to look round about ten times, he has heard the noise in the entrance hall, and he has caught his teacher's words addressed to someone by the window; his thought was jumping about all over the place, except on the hand he was holding in front of him.

A Hindoo sage once compared a man's mind to the mind of a monkey. You all know very well how restless monkeys are. Let us accept this hardly flattering comparison of a man's mind with the restlessness of a monkey. Now, the Hindoo sage went on, give the monkey some wine to drink. Its movements will then resemble the movements of a whirligig. Let us further assume that such a monkey has been stung by a scorpion, and the undisciplined mind of a man will be like these movements of the drunken monkey that has been stung by a scorpion.

Even if your mind is not as undisciplined as that, it is at any rate sufficiently so to justify such a comparison. If you gave a man a magic mirror in which he could see his own thoughts, he would realise that he was walking about on a heap of broken pieces of his begun, unfinished and abandoned thoughts. Just like a shipwrecked vessel. Pieces of torn velvet material, bits of broken masts, floating boxes with nails sticking out of them, boats crowded with people, and every sort of flotsam and jetsam.

This is what the thoughts of a beginner in the studio, who can neither concentrate his attention, nor keep it fixed on one object, are like.

And so we have now come to the first step of the creative art of the stage, a step that is unalterable and common to all— concentration of attention, or to put it more briefly, concentration.

CHAPTER XV

HAVING grasped fully the idea that everything in your art is contained only in yourself and that the way to your art lies through yourself, you will not find it difficult to understand the meaning and significance of the development within you of all the qualities of your inner powers and all the physical movements of your body that correspond to them.

Your endeavours to become an educated and cultured man are not due to your desire to shine, but to your desire to widen the possibilities of your consciousness, to grasp with your mind the new conceptions which enable you to reflect on the stage not only the narrow circle of the life of your family, your studio, the interests of your theatre, or your street, but lead you to an understanding of the life of the universe as a whole. For it is only then that you can feel that you too are part of the universe, and that your art can reflect not only the narrow, ordinary life of your street, but the whole range of human feelings and thoughts.

We have already discussed with you the steps of creative art which are common to all those who take up an artistic career, and we named the first of these concentration.

Let us see how we can here and now find the answer to the question: what is concentration? I told you already that the most difficult thing of all is to express each problem of each separate piece of your part by a verb, by a simple 'I want to'. It is not so easy to define an idea in a few words. It is hardly to be expected, therefore that you will be able to define concentration in a few clear and concise words which would be intelligible to everybody.

First of all what sort of condition is it? Is it an inner or an outer one? For, you see, it is quite possible to sit motionless staring at some object while your thoughts are roaming freely over any limitless spaces you like, jumping about from the moon to your cat which you forgot to feed, then to Jupiter, then back to earth, and then the thought of your appointment with "her" will flash through your mind, then again your thoughts will wander about aimlessly all over the part that you would have liked to play, and so on and so forth. Would that be concentration? For don't forget that outwardly you are qu'te motionless!

We have, therefore, come to the conclusion that concentration is a condition, or rather an inner action. So here we have all at once discovered two definitions—an action and an inner one. All right, let us carry on. Is it an active or passive action? You know from your own experience that your attention can be of two different kinds, a passive and an active one. And I am sorry to say that you are making much greater use of your passive attention than of your active one. So we have further found that concentration is an active action. To sum up—concentration is an inner active action. But what kind of action is it? What is it that acts? Thought. So let us once more sum up: concentration is an inner active action of thought.

Is such a definition of concentration sufficient? No. Why not? Because every thought is an inner active action. What peculiarity, therefore, must the inner active action of thought possess to become concentration?The thought must be fixed *entirely* and *absolutely* on one object or idea, and only on it, without breaking the circle of creative attention for anything else.

Now we have found the full definition of concentration: a thought enclosed in the creative circle of attention and fixed entirely on a definite point by will and choice will be concentration.

Thus we have defined the first step, common to all who wish to embark on the road of the creative art of the stage. The first germ over the development of which we have all to work is concentration.

Let us see what exercise will be the best and easiest with which to start our work on the discipline of thought so as to transform it after a period of hard work into concentration. You have five fingers on your hand. Now, sit down straight in your chair and let drop your shoulders, arms and legs. Make sure that your muscles are completely relaxed and that your head, neck and back form a straight line without any deliberate attempt on your part to straighten your trunk. As I have already told you, the sensation you get when you do that is as though your sacrum were the pointed tip of a stake on which your trunk had been stuck.

Now raise your hand and spread out your fingers. Having spread them out as far as they will go, start merging their movements with your breathing, that is to say, bring them together slowly, finger after finger, and at the same time slowly exhale your breath. Then again spread out each finger separately till all your fingers are outspread, and while doing it, inhale the air.

Never slacken either your attention or your respiration for a single moment while engaged on this exercise, but make sure that the rhythm of your breathing absolutely coincides with the rhythm of the movement of your fingers, and moreover that the rhythm in which your thought-attention is active in its attempt to reach the stage of concentration should not waver, and that your breathing and its purifying wave should all the time merge into the similar rhythm of the action of your fingers.

You have now achieved a concise rhythm of breathing as well as a full harmony in that part of your being on which you had decided to concentrate, in this case—your hand. Now you must make sure that the whole force of your attention should find its way to the circle you shall have created for your concentration: the parallel movement of your lungs for the inhalation of breath and the movement of spreading out your fingers; and the parallel movement of your lungs for the exhalation of breath and the joining of your fingers. Remember that only *this* particular circle interests you; the rest of the world, including your body, with the exception of your fingers, do not exist for you in this 'now'. Gradually, when your entire attention has been firmly fixed in this circle and when nothing any longer interferes with the full harmony of your work either in or around you because you are no longer aware of anything outside the circle of the business in which you are engaged, start widening the circle of your attention exactly as you did when widening your circle while working on the various sections of your part. Do not change anything. Do not break the circle, but widen it. Introduce a new task, but remain in the same rhythm of breathing and make sure that its absolute repose is not broken. Introduce the new task without the slightest effort or strain: bend over three fingers towards the palm of your hand, leaving two fingers outspread, and change the rhythm of your breathing. Press three fingers to the palm of your hand and inhale, join the two outspread fingers and exhale, and at the same time raise the three fingers which you had pressed to the palm of your hand. And once more you will achieve full harmony in this quickened breathing as compared with your first slower breathing. Then widen your circle still more by raising your second hand and working with two hands together, still in the same rhythm, either slower or quicker, but always equally steady and calm.

Note that no sooner is the rhythm of the kind of breathing you have chosen interrupted than there is a hitch in your concentration. What is the conclusion we can draw from this? The conclusion I have already mentioned to you: rhythm is the basis of creative art.

The studio ought gradually to introduce music into the exercises on the concentration of attention. The music, coinciding with the rhythm of your breathing, that is to say, with the basis of all your life on earth, should increase your concentration by bringing your entire being into harmony. The music should merge your thought and feeling into its own rhythm and gradually help you to achieve what we call true inspiration, that is to say, the awakening of your intuition or subconsciousness.

Till you realise that the whole basis of your life—respiration— is not only the basis of your physical existence, but that respiration plus rhythm forms the foundation of all your creative work, your work on rhythm and breathing will never be carried out in full consciousness, that is to say, as it should be carried out, in a state of such complete concentration as to turn your creative work into inspiration. For unless you do this, you will never become good actors. You can, no doubt, find a substitute for this work of awakening your intuition by developing your more or less noble instincts, but if you do that, you will never arouse the enthusiasm of the spectator and leave a lasting impression on his mind of yourself as the living image of the part that would compel him, remembering you, to look for better and nobler ways in his ordinary life.

Concentration, the first of the steps common to all creative artists, is the most difficult one. In mastering it and in learning to concentrate all the powers of your organism on some particular part of it, you learn at the same time the art of transforming your thought into, as it were, a fiery ball. Your thought, strengthened by your attention and put into words, in a definite rhythm will, provided it is spoken by you in a state of full concentration, break through all the conventional stage situations you may have to deal with, and find its way straight to the heart of the spectator. For if in rhythm and concentration, you have succeeded in harmoniously blending your consciousness, feeling and physical action, then you will be frightened by no obstacles that may arise before you, nor will you find any difficulties insurmountable.

That is why I am always telling you that opera is much easier than drama. For in opera the rhythm is there, and all there is left for you to do is to be clear in your minds why the composer wrote your aria in 3-4 time and not in 6-8 time, and why he has made these and not those words operative ones. Once you have realised that, your task is clear: to adapt your physical and psychological data to the ready-made rhythm of the composer. In drama, however, you must carry the composer within you. You must create your own rhythm, for if you do not or if you create the wrong rhythm, your part becomes a yawning gap in the play. The same is true of the producer who fails to create one rhythm for the whole play; if he does not succeed in creating out of all the parts of the actors, that is to say, out of the separate rhythmic particles of the play, a full and harmonious rhythmic chord, then his production cannot be regarded as entirely successful. In a straight play even the introductory music which, as a rule, helps to build up a rhythmic performance, can completely destroy it if the ideas of the producer and the composer do not follow the same rhythmic pattern. The creative art of the stage as an expression of the influence of beauty upon an audience is quite useless, if it is not founded on the law of life common to all mankind—on rhythm.

Opera, on the whole, is easier than drama. In opera everything must be subordinated to one rhythmic idea which is already implicit in the score. The main thing in opera is to subordinate all the separate and physically correct actions of all the characters to one ready-made tonality, expressing the nature of the feelings by sound. All that remains to be done is to embody it in truthful images.

We have just referred to the question of the opera producer. What does a producer of straight plays require most if he turns to the production of operas in accordance with my system? Is it at all possible to choose at random a group of people who can only sing and produce with them even some small musical piece without first making them understand the most elementary points about the nature of the creative work of the actor and the methods each of them has to apply if he is to find his own way of mastering the art of the stage, and without having been through the exercises with imaginary objects with them? 'Of course not', you reply. Very well. In that case you must, before starting the musical work with visible or living objects, devote some time to exercises on concentrated attention with imaginary objects, and during those exercises point out every incorrect physical action, the gaps in attention, and the omissions by the actor of a whole series of sensations because they had escaped his observation.

Sometimes a producer who leaves drama for opera is puzzled by a maze of different ideas: the musical image, the dramatic image, the vocal image, the poet's image, the librettist's image, and so on. All the trials of a producer who does not know how to blend all these 'images' into one are due to the fact that he does not realise that the first thing in opera is the music, and that it is with the music that the actor-singer and the producer himself have to start their work. The music, in fact, is the dramatic contents of an opera, provided in a ready-made musical form. It is in it, and in it alone, that one has to look for the nature of the action. The dramatic construction of an opera contains the meaning of all the creative motives for the framing of the logical line of the actor's actions.

Before starting on the dissection of the characters of an opera, you must grasp the essence of the music. You must understand its rhythm, the connection between all the composer's images, and you have to render a full account to yourself what it is you are dealing with. Is it a work of art in which the life of its characters forms the main element that lends it its sense of unity, or does its sense of unity depend solely on the music, or is it merely a series of scenes or acts illustrated by the music, and not subordinated to the general rhythm of a work of art but possessing only a general plot knocked together by the librettist?

Let us take as an illustration something we all know very well, say, Chaykovsky's *Queen of Spades*.

In the *Queen of Spades* the musical images are extraordinarily well defined and homogeneous. Not a single note, it seems, could be added or taken away from the main characters of Lisa, Hermann or the Countess. So far as homogeneity and finish are concerned, they seem to be perfection itself. They are so closely knit together by the music that if you eliminated only one of the characters or scenes there would be no tragedy.

The same is true of Eugene Onyegin. If you left out the letter scene or the scene with the nurse, there would be no drama. Tatyana's letter alone without the prelude—her conversation with the nurse—and without its ending, will not reveal the spiritual tragedy, the conflict, the agitation of the pure and innocent girl who once again becomes a child before the eyes of the spectators. Tatyana and the nurse form one inseparable logical line, and the acting of the letter scene without the nurse is fatal to the musical, dramatic and vocal image of Tatyana. For Tatyana's image we must have her singing and inflexions, the contrasts between her behaviour before and after the letter, the very sound of her voice in all the different variations of her mental and emotional alarms, her search for tender sympathy in the familiar and settled conditions of her life, and her dissatisfaction with these familiar conditions—all that forms the chain of her emotional states of mind, the moving pictures of her mind, that will bring the actress playing Tatyana to the letter and make her forget about stage conventions.

The impulse to share in a common human experience will be the most important thing in Tatyana's own impulse, its point of departure—her first tragedy: *she can find no support for the creative longings of her heart in the daily routine of her life.* And for the illustrated moving pictures of the actress herself as well as for the spectator and listener a glimpse into Tatyana's daily life is absolutely necessary. For it is only then that her yearning for the unknown and fascinating world created by her imagination will be fully understood.

Tatyana's musical image, like the musical images of Lisa, Hermann and the Countess, which are so closely knit together, is inseparable from the nurse, and indeed forms one indivisible whole with it. The scene in which Tatyana says, 'To another I've been given, and faithful to him I'll ever be', is born here, in the fusion of her life with the life of her nurse, in the intimacy of her ordinary and familiar relationships.

The belief that it is possible to grasp the full meaning of a 'musical' image by cutting it out of the other bars of the opera is as great a delusion as the belief that it is possible to grasp the image of Boris Godunov just by reading Alexey Tolstoy's play, and without taking into consideration the particular epoch in which the action takes place, or the character of the people and the customs and usages among which Boris lives and acts.

What matters is not dissection but synthesis. Music and vocal art merely form the basis for the third art—the art of the stage. And it is impossible to grasp the general synthesis of the data of a hero of an opera without first letting your consciousness and your feeling be permeated with the music. This, however, cannot be done by everyone. Not every man of the theatre can be expected to be so musical that the music should live in him. That does not mean that an opera producer must needs be a singer. But a man who produces an opera must be endowed with such a keen inner perception of musical values that he should be able to think and feel through music. Just in the same way as it is not necessary that your private life should be a model of external beauty before you can bring beauty on the stage. But you must carry it inside you exactly as you do your circles of attention— from the very first stages of your work till the last finishing touches have been put to your part—during all the rehearsals and performances.

Life in beauty within himself is absolutely necessary to the creative artist of the stage, and is similar in all respects to the duty of the opera producer to live, to visualise, and to compose the illustrated moving pictures of his actions in music, knowing the music from beginning to end always through them in all the scenes. Without it all talk about 'images' is useless to the actors or the producer.

It is important that the producer should constantly remind the young opera singer that he must never say his lines to no purpose and that he must always be able to discover the meaning between the lines of his text, the 'I want to' without which he will never get the thought-word-sound, but only the sound, taken correctly or incorrectly from the technical point of view, but always empty and quite devoid of meaning. It is active thought that will enable him to read between the lines of his text, and it is only then that the inner intonation will emerge, that is to say, the synthesis of feeling and thought and warmth of performance, and not merely notes as notes of vocal craftsmanship and brilliance.

The great majority of singers make everything depend on sound, to which in one way or another they add the words just as it suits them best, often changing them because they find it difficult to produce a good sound with certain letters.

The producer who takes the inner image for his starting point must concentrate the actor's attention on the most important thing the words he utters express. And provided the actor's entire attention is fixed on that he will forget about himself as a singer, and the correct feeling will produce the correct sound, and in this way he will direct his attention on the right road to the given circumstances of his part.

As soon as the producer has succeeded in catching the actor's attention with this bait, that is to say, as soon as he has succeeded in making the actor realise the importance of the value of each word, he has made a good start with the real studies. Further on the problems become more and more complicated. The actor's powers of observation are awakened, and his attention is transferred to his partner, to what he is saying or doing at the moment, what he is talking about or feeling. No doubt, opera singers are immeasurably luckier than we, dramatic actors, are. They are given both tone and rhythm. The composer tells them 'how' to reply to their partner's cue. But it would be a mistake to think that this 'how' is everything. The composer provides the form, that is to say, the music depicts 'how' in the same way as the word says 'what'. In other words, music will always be 'how' as the word will always be 'what'. *

But the main thing, which may or may not be expressed in the actor's response, is the synthesis of the 'how' and the 'what', that is to say, the living actor who has infused life into his response because for him the music and the word have already become merged; for him 'the part and I' no longer exist, but what exists is 'I—the part', since his own individual 'I' has disappeared, leaving only the 'I' of his creative intuition. You know very well the form of the duet between Gilda and Rigoletto, you know the rhythm in which Rigoletto will say all his words. But the fiery temperament of the hunchback, his passionate love of his daughter, and his anxiety about her, the impassioned ardour of Gilda's love and the agitation into which she is thrown when she realises that she has been deceived—all this is *your* way of interpreting the meaning that is hidden between the lines of your text, all this is *your* creative intuition transfused into the life of your part.

If your various 'I want to's' are properly fused with your correct physical actions, it is not only my heart that will say to you 'I believe', but all the hearts in the auditorium will identify their own feelings with certain feelings of the people you are representing on the stage and become one with them. Do not forget what I have told you over and over again. The significance of the word is not born when the time comes for you to say it on the stage, but when you have been evolving the image of the character of your part in your creative circle. You ask me whether there is any difference between the application of my system to drama and opera. Such a question does not exist so far as I am concerned. I am not writing out prescriptions for one or another method of teaching. It is exactly such an approach, such a purely formal approach, to my system, that gives rise to all

---

* The word is the subject for the composer's work, while the music is his work, i.e., the experience of the given subject and the composer's attitude towards it. (K.S.).

sorts of aberrations and dryness, which can result in nothing but harm and boredom for everybody.

What I am trying to do is to reveal to the actor those untold riches in himself by making him realise the importance of getting to understand the nature of the creative feeling. The producer must do all he possibly can to evoke in the actor the feeling for real life so that the actor should come to understand how wonderful it is to be alive during the rehearsals instead of memorising in a purely mechanical way the various instructions the producer has given him, the way in which he has to walk across the stage, how he has to bow, sit down and so on.

At first it is perhaps easier to arouse the attention of the students to the conflict of the passions in their parts. This the students will understand better than anything else. Having caught their attention on that hook, it should not be difficult to apply the comparative method. To show them how to remove the physiological coarseness from a certain experience, from a particular feeling of happiness, spite, frenzy, intoxication, etc., that is to say, how to get rid of the sort of overacting that has become sanctioned by stage usage, and try to get them to portray true and correct physical and psychological action.

While developing an actor's powers of observation, one must also teach him to observe his partner's face, his mood in the particular situation of his part, his inflexions which express the 'I want to' of his part. And at the same time one must watch the actor carefully to make sure that he finds the right kind of aids that will facilitate his communication with his partner and that will not disrupt the link of the single logical line for the sake of his own so-called 'individuality'. Opera singers must achieve such a fusion with the characters they are representing as has been indicated by the composer, that is to say, they must express his truth, which they have to make their own instead of giving their own particular interpretation of their parts.

During this stage of their studies, they must be taught to forget their own personal 'I' and put in its place that entirely new man of the part whom the actor ought to be able to understand from now on. It is at this point that one must strive to awaken in the opera singer not so much his will which takes the form of a stubborn desire to make himself proficient in something, as his enthusiasm for entering the circle of life of the heroes of the epoch with which the music deals and to search for life-like expressions in the sounds of his own voice.

The actor's desire to obtain a vivid picture in his mind of 'how a certain man lives', is capable of awakening, in a subconscious way we can hardly understand, the intuition which takes hold of the imagination of the actor who has already obtained the necessary training in the course of his studies with imaginary objects. An actor who follows these methods will no longer 'play' but act, that is to say, create.

But none of the exercises in my system should be done before the actor has first been made to understand what the particular exercise is for and what conclusions could afterwards be drawn from it.

A young actor must be trained to work under any conditions. It must be dinned into his ears that in our profession 'to know' means 'to be able to'. And one is able to do a thing only if the flexibility of one's will, imagination, and attention, as well as one's energy, is subordinated to one's love of art.

If the actor is fully aware of the reasons why all this physical and psychical drill is so important to him, he will find none of these exercises either uninteresting or boring. An actor ought to understand that anyone lacking in self-control will never be a creative artist because he will never get the better of his own character and personality, that is, of the sort of man he is in his private life. Such an actor will never be able to compel the ordinary man in him to occupy a secondary place, while leaving the first place to the man-artist who is endowed with intuition and possesses the kind of creative emotion that brings a sense of beauty into the life of the spectator, helping him to develop and to understand life in a new way by widening his consciousness by a display of works of art in a series of vivid and living images.

CHAPTER XVI

One undisputed step of the creative work of the stage, which applies equally to all men of whatever epoch or idiosyncrasies, we have already found, namely *concentration*.

Let us go further. Is concentration alone sufficient? If you are to direct your attention exclusively to one section of the internal and external problems of your part, then your attention, already in an active state, must also possess the quality of such alert observation as to prevent a single stray thought not belonging to the circle by your concentration from interfering with your particular problems.

You have concentrated your attention on your hand, on the movements of your fingers which blend harmoniously with the rhythm of your breathing. But that does not solve your problem. You still have to examine carefully the *nature* of your fingers, that is to say, in what way they differ from the fingers of any other man and what peculiarities they possess that the fingers of any other man do not possess. Are they short or long, thin or thick? What are their nails like? What is their shape or colour? Here it is not enough for you to concentrate, for your consciousness has now been given a new task, the task of comparing, making deductions, and drawing definite conclusions. You need all the power of your attention to enable your concentration to dwell on each separate aspect of your task, and your attention to fix the definite form of your thought by a precise idea or word. Let us call this power of your attention *mental alertness*. Steadily, step by step, you no longer absorb the organic qualities of your fingers as if they were the fingers of any man in general, but only those qualities which, so far as you are concerned, are characteristic of them alone.

How does one work on the development of this second general step of the creative art of the stage? To begin with, you concentrate all your attention on the first joint of your thumb. You examine most carefully its size as compared with the second upper joint, you examine its skin and the hairs that cover it, you notice the tiny cavity, you observe the hardly perceptible scar. The scar attracts your attention, and you begin to call to mind the circumstances which led to the appearance of the scar and the time when they took place. It takes you back to the terrible time of starvation and cold you endured. You were sawing wood for your small stove, and the saw slipped and cut right across your thumb; you remember the spurting blood, the awful pain, the consternation of your people, etc.

But, you will ask, what has this got to do with mental alertness? Well, let me ask you in turn whether you have gone on with your original task of examining your fingers till you know all there is to know about them. You have not. You have weakened your mental alertness by letting yourself be carried away by the memories of your past, and have thus interrupted your attention which has been diverted to something else. Now you can see why mental alertness is so important to you. For unless you exercise all the alertness of which your mind is capable in order to concentrate all the time on one and the same task, you cannot provide for your work those always precise conditions in which the process of the creative art of the stage takes place, that is, choose only those problems you need and endow them with your own individual qualities by merging them with those given you by your part. Here only uninterrupted attention can help you, i.e. the sort of mental alertness which protects you from any impulse of your imagination that might divert you from your direct task.

If an actor cannot focus his thought-feeling-word with the utmost alertness and if he does not know how to make all the powers of his organism act in *one* direction, he is like a flickering light that hurts your eyes. An actor who does not possess this simple power of alert attention and who is always in two minds about his tasks is a stage-hack and not an artist. An opera singer who during the intervals in the wings powders his face or smooths his hair when that is not, according to his part, the business of his creative circle, or who has a cup of tea, or puts drops into his nose, has not only broken his circle, dissociated himself from his part, and distracted his attention, but also gone back to the preoccupations of his private life, and will never be able to enter afresh into the life of his hero. He has shattered the whole chain of his inner powers, which it had taken him so much time and labour to put together. Even if he is under the impression that he has again entered into the life of the stage and that he has recaptured his inspiration, he is making a mistake: he is sure to substitute for the work of his subconsciousness, that is to say, his intuition, the more or less harmonious work of his instincts. For owing to the fact that his alertness of mind had disappeared, the original task he had set out to carry out when he first went on the stage has also disappeared; and those moments of his life on the stage which might have been transformed into priceless moments of illumination in art, have been brought down to the level of any ordinary experience of life, while he himself has come to resemble those actors who judge the value of their performances by their ability to take the 'top C', and by the length and brilliance with which they hold it.

You must prepare yourself for your first entrance on the stage while you are still at home. Do not clutter up the day on which you are due to perform with all sorts of unimportant things which have nothing whatever to do with your part. Think of your part always. You must try to be the person you are acting throughout the whole day of the performance, and by means of rhythmic breathing achieve a state of the utmost harmony and repose. On arrival at the theatre you must not waste your time in idle talk with your fellow-actors; you must forget about life as a whole except that slice of it which is resounding in your heart as the life of the stage. The circle of your artistic problems, your inspiration, and hence also your success, starts when you are putting on your make-up before the glass. As a consequence of your state of health, your mood and the power of release from 'yourself' which you have already achieved at home, your problems are no longer the same as they were the day before.

There is nothing fixed in creative art—once and for all. As all life is perpetual movement, so your creative problems too cannot remain stationary but must move together with your living spirit. Otherwise you will drift into artificiality, overacting and false exaggeration.

Suppose you are Tatyana. You are standing in the wings and getting ready for the first phrase of the duet 'Have you heard?' If you did not leave your dressing room as Tatyana, and exchanged greetings on the way to the stage as Tatyana; if as you put on your make-up you did not experience in your alert attention the dark wintry evenings you used to spend listening to your nurse's fairy-stories; if the rhythm of your heart does not beat in unison with hers; if the old woman's caresses have not evoked in your imagination a feeling of cosy comfort, or the consciousness that among the worldly-minded Olga and her mother, who are so alien to your—Tatyana's—spirit, you possess in your nurse a person who loves you dearly and whose love you reciprocate with the same tenderness—the stage will never become your home in which you have spent so many years, and you will never get those inflexions of voice which are full of charm, nor will you ever be able to reflect in them the newly awakened powers of love of a pure and innocent young girl. So far your nurse's love and friendship have served you as a substitute for that fatal moment when your love will blaze forth like a flame because the time has come when you, pure in heart as you are, have to love. So far your nurse has been to you all the comfort of your home. You must remember how on a moonlit night your nurse told you romantic fairy-stories, and *your* moon, the moon of your alert imagination will be a soft, pale disc in the invisible haze of your poetic dreams.

Your 'Have you heard?' was not born just now when you are twenty-six and a prima-donna of the Bolshoy Theatre, but when —in the alert concentration of the problems of your part—you were only sixteen. Your wish, expressed by the verb 'I want to' will be: '*If* I am Tatyana, I want to give my love, I want to disclose to you the inmost secrets of my heart, I want to explain to you that I am the singer about whom my song tells, that I am waiting for love, that my mind is in a turmoil, that I am overcome by anguish, and that I am full of forebodings'. This is what your mood is like; these are your intonations of the first act. Not to get your voice ready to take the first note, for, being trained, your voice will take the first note by itself as it should be taken, provided your feeling is right. Correct action depends entirely on correct feeling,

And what about Olga? Is her task of mental alertness the same as yours? It is the same inasmuch as it is an inner action meant to bring all the actor's thoughts and feelings to the necessary degree of tension, but the problems of her creative circle are diametrically opposed to yours.

She has no time to think. All her instincts are in a state of violent agitation. All her life consists of this happy, ephemeral 'now'. She is all a whirl of happiness, and her moon is a huge red ball; her meeting with the man she loves is nothing but the egoistic expression of a mind that lives for the moment, a young girl's escapade, a desire to tease everybody and everything, and to find delight in everything. Her 'Have you heard?' means 'I want him to be here soon! What a shame to be without him even for a few minutes! I want everybody round me to share in my happiness'. And her intonations of the first act express energy, cheerfulness, kindliness, and simplicity. Not singing in a low voice and throwing the listener into a panic when taking the contralto notes in 'Everyone calls me a child', but devoting the whole artlessness of your alert attention to the problem of 'diverting Tatyana and making her join me in my happiness'.

We have now, therefore, found the two steps that are common to all who wish to become proficient in the art of the stage, namely, concentration and mental alertness. Let us now discuss the applications of these two steps to the sustaining of a pause on the stage.

If you are in opera you have your rhythm given to you, and all that is left for you to do is to break up your music into sections and, having traced its statics and dynamics, bring your individual problems of physical movement or repose into harmony with it. In the pauses you require not smaller but greater precision and keeness of attention. All your powers must not only become part of your creative circle, but be intensified to such an extent that in it you should feel as though you were behind a stone wall. It is not from outside, through physical action, that you must hope for an intensification of your methods of acting. What you must do is so to develop your attention that not a single extraneous thought, as for instance, what you look like now, or how the lights fall on you, or whether the spotlights make you look older or younger, should interfere with the only life that exists for you at the moment, namely the life of the stage. All your life now is merely the movement of your spirit among the different circumstances given to you by your part, and the rhythm holds you within those limits in which you can easily establish harmony within yourself, that is to say, true creative work.

If you are in a straight play, you will find it much more difficult. You cannot act without rhythm, which you have to create yourself. How is it to be done? You, together with all the other actors in the performance, must sound in *one* rhythm. This one rhythm, as you know, will result in a harmonious performance only if the whole play is acted either in a minor or a major key, that is to say, when the tonality of the whole play is found, or to put it differently, if its ruling idea, through-action and unity of truthful presentation have been found.

However well versed you may be in my system, even if you know it a lot better than I, you will never be able to get any rhythm out of it. You can only find it in yourself. How? By the love which helps to evolve the sensitivity of your subconsciousness. The love of your profession, the love of art, is the very basis of your life, and it will supply you with the rhythm of all your vital energy on the stage. If your love of the stage is genuine, you are always full of energy and strength. This love is the very centre and foundation of your 'I', that higher 'I' which creates and is always aflame, and not the one which eats, drinks and is immersed in mundane affairs. No doubt, we cannot do without all this, for we live on the earth and we can only live in accordance with the laws of the earth. But the thing we regard as the foundation and the most valuable part of our life can be divided into our immutable love of art and the constantly changing, though inescapable conditions which surround us. If your loyalty to art is unshaken, your higher creative 'I' will always introduce you into the right rhythm. And if the same kind of rhythm— arising out of love of art—is alive in all the actors of your play, because they, like you, are genuine actors, then you will merge with them in one single rhythm. The right feeling of all the actors will produce the right rhythm in everybody, uniting in it all those who are taking part in the performance.

CHAPTER XVII

We have now established the nature of the two general, inevitable and necessary steps which lead to perfection in the art of acting. Let us see if we cannot find something else of a general nature which is characteristic of certain moments in the work of an actor. If your mind is troubled and oppressed with fear, you can hardly be expected to negotiate even the two initial steps we have just been discussing. Now you have developed your introspective ability of self-concentration and you realise how all-comprehensive your inward sense of freedom must be to correspond to the parallel sense of freedom of your body so as to enclose the whole of your being within the creative circle, that is to say, and I cannot repeat it too often, to achieve the fullest possible harmony of all your physical and mental abilities.

Fear, depression, a negative attitude towards life, lack of confidence—all these qualities of the human mind are not your personal qualities only, but are parts of your creative work as a whole as well as of all your actions. But your mind, too, if it is unable to free itself from the petty preoccupations and worries of everyday life, and your heart when there is no feeling of goodwill towards your fellow-artists in it, will, like fear and depression, impede, if not altogether interrupt, your creative work.

If you come to rehearsals full of love and devotion to art and to people, but with a heart burdened with anxiety because of some private difficulties of yours, you will never be able to complete the creative circle within which only the facts inherent in your part exist.

What conclusion can be drawn from this? Why, that another step of the ladder leading to perfection in the art of the actor, whether in drama or opera, is *fearlessness*.

This step is of enormous importance for creative work. You must be absolutely clear in your mind that fearlessness has nothing to do with self-conceit, or with that intolerable boastfulness and impudence which are mostly a cloak for inner cowardice. Fearlessness in creative work is the ability to set your mind free from everything that has any relation to your private affairs; it is that atmosphere of gladness and freedom which is your own contribution to creative art; it is the expression of the energy with which you set yourself to overcome all the difficulties of your part and to solve all its problems. It is certainly not that state of mind in which your heart is constantly in your mouth and in which all your strength is dissipated in agitation. By saying to yourself, 'Don't be afraid! Don't be agitated!' you not only waste your strength, but also intensify your fear. Instead of diverting your attention from your fear and in this way weakening it, you merely present it with a new and utterly wrong problem, the problem of 'overcoming fear'.

You know already what the first two steps of creative work are—concentration and mental alertness. Once you realise that fear impedes your movements on the stage and prevents you from setting yourself free from the influence of any extraneous matter that bears no relation whatever to your work on your part, you must redouble your watchfulness and intensify your mental alertness so as to be able to deal with the different qualities of the character you are required to represent. You must divert your attention from yourself and engage in a more minute and con-scientious examination of the organic qualities of your hero, and wherever possible, you must seek to infuse greater daring and courage in your part. If you do that, your attention, weakened and diverted from your part because you have set yourself the wrong problem of 'overcoming fear', will again be concentrated on your part in an effort to discover a living problem in it, and in this way the creative circle you are trying to achieve will be strengthened.

The direct result of all that is *courage* in creative work.

Every part, even the one in which you are required to present on the stage the highest type of human love, namely maternal love, must always be built on the foundation of courage. The most reprehensible feature of the creative work of an actor is exaggeration and overstatement. Whatever the nature of the part and whatever external forms it takes, your conception of it and your representation of it on the stage must always be characterised by the quality of courage.

Let us illustrate our meaning by an example. Let us see whether our rule applies equally to all parts and to all actors. Let us assume you have to act the part of a villain and a traitor. Your representation of such a part will never be convincing, neither will it produce a lasting impression on an audience, if you fail to discover for yourself where your villain has shown courage, or where—if only for one brief moment—he has been good. In short, you will never succeed in the part of a villain if you fail to find one positive quality in him. A mass of black and grey colours will produce nothing but boredom. A display of a large number of negative qualities will never hold the attention of an audience. It will merely weaken it. For what happens to your own attention when you present it with a wrong problem, happens to an audience too. You intensify the external attributes of your part, you raise your voice, you hurl the operative words at the audience as though wishing to stun it with them, but your words fail to hold its attention and, instead of listening to you, it starts examining the shape of your nose, your hands and feet, your eyes. People begin to move about uneasily in their seats. They begin to cough. Do not blame the audience or your partner on the stage. Rather try to re-examine your own approach to your part, your own conception and execution of it, and you will find that the colours which predominate in it are of unrelieved darkness. The more forcibly you want to convey to an audience the depth of a villain's depravity in his pursuit of evil, the more courageously you must strive to emphasise the positive sides of his character and to bring out those fleeting moments of innocence in his nature. And the more strongly you stress his courage, the more will the audience reward you—the embodiment of the part you are playing—with its undivided attention. For you are not acting a certain part in a play just because your talent and your training make it possible for you to do so; what you do is to submerge your consciousness in the currents of those agonies and torments that pass through you into the audience, and you show up the bottomless pit of moral iniquity into which your hero had been cast by the passions over which he has no control: envy, hatred, bad temper, discontent.

Only a courageous presentation of your part, and courage as a quality, however infinitesimal, in the part itself, will enable you to concentrate the undivided attention of the audience upon yourself.

Let us take another example. Let us suppose you have to play the part of a mother. Now, according to your conception a mother's love is identical with self-sacrifice. You yourself have lavished all your care on your child to make his life as happy as possible. Your child has claimed all your affection, all your tenderness. Your love has made you his slave. When he fell ill, you were beside yourself with anxiety. You used to find fault with his nanny; you kept ringing up the doctor; you sent for another one; you drove your cook to distraction; you could not control your fits of weeping.

What will your representation of a mother on the stage be like if this is your attitude towards your own child? You will presumably introduce into the circle of your creative problems all the mental chaos in which you were accustomed to live at the bedside of your own boy. However much you have tried to free yourself from the shackles of your own personal experience by enclosing yourself within your creative circle, fear and general confusion will be sure to colour every single aspect of your part if you will not concentrate all your imaginative powers on a mother's courage as the foremost problem of your love. Only if you are courageous will the other problems of your part and, above all, the tenderness of your love for your child, touch a sympathetic chord in the hearts of the spectators. They will be moved only if you do not overdo every caress of yours, and if you do not over-indulge in baby-talk while playing with your child, thinking in this way to express the whole depth of your love for him.

Moreover, it would be a serious mistake if you were to take only that moment in your son's life which is given by the part in the play. You must re-live in your imagination the whole of your son's life and not concentrate only on the tragedy that has occurred in his and your life when your son is, say, thirty years of age. Here he is lying in his cot as a baby. Here your courage has helped you to snatch him out of the jaws of death when he fell dangerously ill. Here is his first attempt at talking, the first pair of trousers he wore, his first lessons at school—and at every phase of his life it was *your* courage that helped him along: your strength in him. In this way you will gradually arrive at that phase of his life which is given in your part. But in this case you will no longer have to deal with the accidental circumstances contained in your part, or with stock situations of 'how to play a mother', but with the most essential part of the whole matter, namely with those passions which you have yourself discovered in your heart and which, as the palpable image of your thought, you put into the words given you by the playwright.

Now, if you take the idea of a mother as you yourself perceive it to be and, in addition, purify and ennoble it by courage, you will find the whole of *your* truth in the action of the play. And the audience too will find it with you. Only bad actors have to force themselves to play certain parts. A good actor, on the other hand, takes as his starting point the universal human passions that lie hidden in his own heart and brings them into play. In other words, he first concentrates on the nature of the passions and only then tries to adapt them to the given circumstances of his part. And it is for that purpose and for that purpose only that my system exists. It is based solely on that, its aim being to teach the actor to fuse physical and psychical action so as to achieve the fullest possible harmony between them.

Let us take yet another example. You are a lover. The force of your passion has made you completely its slave. You cannot think of anything else; *she* is the centre of all your being; *she* is the only meaning of your existence; *she* is the sole aim of your life. You are obsessed with one single thought—to give up everything and to be only with *her*.

How are you to present this sort of passion on the stage? Werther, whose love proved his undoing, could not wait another minute for his happiness. All Charlotte's sufferings and torments made her only one minute too late when she rushed in after the shot to find Werther already dying.

If the whole gamut of Werther's emotions were to bear only the character of a man obsessed with love, if Charlotte's reproaches were expressed only in tears, if all the suspense of

187

separation found expression only in tears, could you hope to hold the attention of an audience to the very end of the opera? What does hold the attention of a spectator and helps him to experience with you every incident in the lives of the protagonists in the drama invented by Goethe and Massenet? What will induce him to break through the circle of your public solitude and forget all about you as an opera singer, seeing in you only the character you are playing and with whom you are living through that particular moment of your life? Only your courage. Only your inner perception of what sort of courage you would need in order to live a life without her. All the scenes in which you appear without *her* will contribute to the final tragedy which brings about the fatal conclusion of the opera. The boredom, the sheer waste of the days spent without *her* will emphasise your love for her. Indeed, the tragic denouement was only caused by the fact that your courage—your resolve to live without *her*—had suffered a crushing defeat. Your—Werther's—conflict with life, his conflict with God, his fight against the various obstacles, all this has been built on the foundation of the first problem you have to solve: a man's courage. And only after that come the problems of Werther's passion, jealousy, despair, etc.

These are the three general steps of the creative work of the stage. In the next chapter we shall discuss the most important of all the principles of good acting—creative repose.

CHAPTER XVIII

The conventional notions about creative work and inspiration make actors who have not the faintest idea about the nature of the creative powers that are active within them, look for and cultivate in themselves a state of 'creative agitation'.

Already from the first three steps of creative work of the stage common to, and one might almost say shared by, all men, you can see that there is no question of any 'agitation', even if it were a hundred times creative. The actor who is immersed in the creative problems of his part, has no time to think of himself as a personality or of his agitation. His attention is completely occupied with the selection of the qualities he needs so as to adapt them through a whole series of physical actions to the particular circumstances of his part and the truthful embodiment of himself in those circumstances. Truthfulness is not dealt with in my system as an independent quality because it is the very foundation of the creative art of the stage, and because it has its own qualities in every actor. Truthfulness is the blending of all your powers and thoughts with your part through the little magic word 'if'. For it is only when you have achieved the fullest possible harmony within yourself that you are able to merge truthfully through that word with the character you are representing.

The rhythm of your heart has assumed the rhythm of your hero. Your thought tells you, 'If I am Raskolnikov, what will arouse fear in me?' And by a process of the deepest possible self-analysis, you try to establish those of your organic qualities which you could project into the conditional circumstances of your part so that the force of your attention should isolate only a certain scene from Raskolnikov's life.

How can you possibly be successful in this kind of work if you have quite a different set of circumstances in your mind or memory? For instance, if you cannot get the fact of your being in the studio out of your head, or if you cannot forget that you are surrounded by people, or that you are on the stage and people are looking at you, and so on? As soon as these extraneous thoughts occur to you, your creative circle is broken and you are no longer in full possession of your creative repose. Your world—the world of those images which are invisible to us but which are so vividly real and alive to you—with which you have peopled your circle has disappeared, and you find yourself in a circle of trivial excitements and irritations, and so far as you are concerned none of the first three steps of the creative work of the stage exists any longer. Everything has to be started all over again. The circle of public solitude has to be built up afresh, and you are again faced with the task of getting yourself, the producer and your partners into it.

Even if we disregard the time you and your teacher have wasted, think of the great harm you do to yourself and your will as an actor and a man. Your will grows and begets attention every time you achieve results, however small they may be. Every time you strain your will and fail to achieve the necessary results so that the plan of the part you are trying to work out is destroyed by your fruitless efforts to give an external form to your thought-image, you are dropping behind both as actor and a creative artist.

What has prevented you from obtaining the required result? The absence of creative repose, of course. You have to walk on the stage and sing Hermann's aria, 'Her name I know not', and instead of your problem of despair, 'express the torment of being "without her",' instead of giving a vivid representation of the inmost thoughts of your heart filled with the passion which harmonises with the enchanting sounds of Chaykovsky's music, which is depicting to us the rhythm of your heart, you are all the time thinking of the conductor, worrying about keeping time with him, or about how to take the high note so as to earn the applause of the audience. Your thoughts and your eyes wander anxiously to the box of the board of directors. You are wondering whether the director on whom your fate depends is there, or whether those you are interested in are listening to you tonight, and so on and so forth. This is the hopeless situation into which you have allowed yourself to be ensnared, a situation composed of the trivialities of your lower 'I', which has prevented you from reaching that state of concentration in which your higher 'I', your creative intuition, is waiting for you.

Standing in the wings, you were actually there, you were actually yourself, X, and it was you who have just been taking a sip of wine which your dresser has offered you. You were not even thinking of 'her', let alone of your despair at finding yourself without her. Most likely all you were aware of was your feeling of dissatisfaction at not being in good voice tonight.

You are now, I think, able to realise clearly how your creative agitation has led you astray and how important it is that you should keep your repose so as to be able to achieve those heights of moral purity and peace of mind where alone you can find complete renunciation of yourself, the actor, X, and merge into one single image: I—Hermann.

The conventional conception of 'creative agitation' must be abandoned. No such organic action exists. What does exist is *creative repose*, that is to say, a state of mind in which all personal perceptions of the passing moment have disappeared and in which life—the whole of life—is concentrated, clearly, forcefully and definitely, on the circumstances given in your play and only on the given piece of the scene.

Let us see what creative repose means. What are its component parts? It is merely the result of the first three steps. If you have worked conscientiously to achieve the first three, you will automatically mount this fourth step.

It is time you realised that there are no secrets in your art which exist outside you and which you have to conquer as an army conquers a country in a war, by making them submit to your will. The more you exert your will, only your bare will, the more surely will you be creating new obstacles to your mastering the secrets of creative art, which appear to you like alluring heights existing in some way outside you. All the secrets—the entire road to creative art—are, as I have told you so often, in you alone. Only in yourself, by means of concentration, mental alertness, and observation of your powers, can you solve successfully, simply and joyfully those problems with which the conditions of the stage and your part present you. The repose of the creative artist is the absolute setting free of his consciousness from the pressure of personal passions. And it is only in this state of complete freedon that those images and passions, to which you have given all your attention, can and will live.

The fourth step—repose—forms the borderline and the transition to the further steps of the creative art of the stage.

The step of repose produces that break in the mental make-up of the actor after which any fragment of the conditional tasks given him in any sort of combination forms the entire world of his creative art. And he always achieves a truthful representation of his stage characters because he has introduced his own life, out of himself, into those moments of the life of the stranger the author has given him, and they have become *his* life without the assistance of any artificial stage effects introduced by the producer.

All stage effects are merely a manifestation of the poverty of inner life. If an actor's inner life had been very rich, he would need neither make-up, nor costumes, nor sets. All that would be needed would be the presence of the creative artist himself whose great powers of thought and attention would have begotten that irresistible wave of charm which would have kept the audience under its spell. All the devices of the theatre as a spectacle are only meant as aids to us, actors, so as to enable us to adjust our creative powers more easily to the requirements of our art.

CHAPTER XIX

We have now, as it were, crossed the Rubicon, and can proceed further in our discussion of the principles of the creative art of the stage, where what interests us is no longer the actor's work on his part or on himself, but the fact that in his work on his part he is now able to introduce all the qualities of his attention without dividing his creative problems into 'I' and 'if I'.

Now you know already how to gather together into one 'if I', for you have reached the stage where you can achieve a complete merging of yourself and the character of your part. Starting from this point, whatever part you may be acting—a father, a mother, a son, a lover, a villain or hero—what can you find *here* of a general nature that is applicable equally to all stage characters represented by people and to all people representing stage characters by impersonating them? If the thought-image of the actor is conceived as one inseparable entity and is not broken up by anything of an extraneous nature in his creative circle, and yet is not sufficiently intensively realised according to the inner exertion of his artistic powers, if, that is, the qualities represented by the actor are not sufficiently clear-cut and his inner movements do not rise above the beaten track of everyday life, the audience cannot be expected to give its full undivided attention to his acting. Everything in his inner life is correct, everything seems to be truthful, everything is gathered together into unity of action, everything is cleverly contrived, and yet something seems to be missing, some little trifle which will, however, make people flock to see X and not Y. What is missing? Has he found the right solution of all his problems? He has. Is his body completely relaxed? It is. Is the actor's life firmly entrenched in his creative circle? It is. What is wrong then?

What is wrong is what is commonly known as talent. But the difference between the talent of X and the talent of Y, according to the true meaning of the word, is not particularly great. In fact, there is not much to choose between them. And yet X seems to have something which attracts crowds and Y has not. In his embodiment of the part X brings all the powers of his thoughts and feelings, expressed in physical action, to the highest point of intensity permitted by the truthfulness of physical action. If he happens just to be sitting without uttering a word, his pose on the stage is brought to the utmost point of relaxation, clarity and plastic significance. He has grasped the fact that a bent or outstretched arm or leg must be bent or outstretched to the utmost limit. If, as he is watching someone from behind a bush, he cranes his neck, then his neck must be craned to the very limit, and must not just represent a craned neck.

Everything on the stage—posture, movement, word—must be distinct and explicit and never forced; it must be expressed in full tones and not in semitones. If your suspicion has aroused jealousy in you, you will not of course betray it at once by proclaiming it aloud with all the intensity of your being; you will unfold the whole range of your emotion gradually, beginning with pianissimo and ending with the most ferocious storm of your heart—fortissimo.

But what is it you must possess in *every* piece of your creative work from pianissimo to fortissimo? Every time, however brief the particular feature of your part may be, it must in every section of your part be brought to the highest degree of *heroic tension*.

Only that which you have experienced in such a form will make an impression on the spectator and will, in fact, appear to him to be a new and highly interesting interpretation of a play he has himself already read a few times and which he has not found particularly interesting; for you have not only presented it to him in a way that is quite different from the way in which he had understood it when he read it, but have also swept him off his feet completely. Just as the outward form of the body conveys a certain meaning to an audience only if the full extent of its plastic significance is realised, so does the inward meaning of a character get across to an audience, the frontiers of space and time that separate the stage from the auditorium are abolished, and the spectator is forced to believe in you, and weep and suffer as well as rejoice and laugh with you, only if your life on the stage bears no resemblance, however true or subtle, to ordinary life, but if your thought and feeling have become merged and have risen to an act of heroic tension.

Let us suppose you are representing a mother mourning the death of her son. You have already shed a flood of tears; there were tears of despair, tears of recollection of childhood, tears of happiness from the consciousness of the nobility of your son's character, his goodness, his filial devotion to you, his talents and so on. In short, the whole range of human relationships has been shown. The audience sympathised with you, and to a certain extent even lived with you, but . . . it remained just where it was, perfectly well aware of the fact that there was a stage in front of it, that it was in the auditorium of a theatre, that it was watching the third act, and that after the fourth act it would have to rush to the cloakroom and so on.

What is the trouble? All your tasks had been carried out in a most irreproachable manner, and you were not B, but the T, who lived in you as you did in her, in accordance with your part. And yet there was this gulf between you and the audience. The trouble is that you have failed to discover in yourself that part of your being where heroic tension lives. That side of your talent has not developed so far, and that is why you cannot express it in your part.

But how are you to develop that side of your talent? The whole talent of an actor is unfolded only through his own ordinary life. A man cannot be torn out of his life and at the same time be expected to become a real actor. An actor is the force that reflects life. What do we usually see on the stage? Who are the men who become great creative artists? Who are they who become our teachers and our models of the art of the stage? In the great majority of cases they are people who belonged to the middle classes and who have had to fight very hard and overcome a multitude of obstacles in their lives. Too great security as well as too great poverty almost invariably kill talent, with the only exception of men of genius; but we need not talk of geniuses, since they do not want my system. They are a system in themselves. They are themselves a heroic life. The stage is their whole life, and because of that it is the same to every spectator. Here everyone forgets all about time and space; their tears and smiles evoke tears and smiles from the spectators, and even such things as buses, galoshes and cloakrooms are forgotten!

But actors who possess talent and who are loyal sons of their country, you who love man, who desire to devote your lives to the service of a great art, and who strive to bring beauty everywhere, you must live your ordinary lives, learning and observing. Your road is the road of developing ever new qualities of sensibility, which come to you as a result of your struggles and victories. If you stop in fear and hesitation before every obstacle in your life, you are almost certain to be always defeated. You must always overcome every obstacle as it arises if you want to rid your creative powers of all worthless rubbish and every sort of impurity and reveal the organic and the true underneath it; for what is organic and true in you will emerge into the world of action only when you have discovered heroic tension in your heart and learned how to bring it to light on every ordinary day of your life. You have grasped the true nature of this action from your own experience of life; you have learned how to find your way to what is best in you, and you have realised that your ordinary existence has come to an end because you yourself have chosen the life of heroic adventure in art. So that now, when working on your part, you understand what the step of heroic tension means.

Note how false and unsound is the conception of this step of creative art of the large number of actors of the so-called 'inspiration school'. Realising how unavoidable this step is in the creative art of the stage, but not knowing how to find it, the actor begins to lapse into pathos and false exaggeration. He, so to speak, makes the welkin ring, while the spectator remains sitting very calmly in his seat and watches him: 'Getting himself all worked up, isn't he'?

Suppose you have to play a dramatic scene with your sister who has just taken away your husband to whom you have been married for twenty years. If you will build up the whole scene on your egoistic sufferings, if everything you do will be filled only with reproaches, spite, hatred and the injured feelings of a scorned and humiliated woman, your scene as a piece of creative work is a sheer waste. When can it come to life and rise to the heights of real art? Only when you have crossed your Rubicon, when you are no longer thinking of yourself and give the better side of your nature a chance of asserting itself, when you find the extenuating circumstances which lessen your sister's guilt, when you start wondering when and where you yourself had been unjust to your husband, when a current of love and forgiveness, the energy of the heroic endeavour of a woman's heart, and not of curses, pass through you into your part. It is then that you can be sure to gain the interest and hold the attention of your audience. You have risen to an act of heroic tension, you have discovered in yourself and revealed to the spectator a slice of life permeated with a new conception of beauty, and the audience has responded by giving you its entire attention, by its own awakened sense of beauty.

There is nothing in the world more eager for beauty than the human soul. In art it is only possible to inspire. Only the teacher whose love of it has excited your enthusiasm and in whom you saw an example of the influence of his living soul on yours will be able to introduce you into the circle. To reach this step of heroic tension in the creative work of the stage and to avoid lapsing into false pathos, you must first learn how to develop within you all the different sides of your talent through your daily experience of life, always remembering that it is impossible to stop short in your development as an artist, and that in art he who does not advance always retreats.

If in the course of the day you have shown the same measure of goodwill in your encounters with your fellow-artists as in your ordinary life, you have laid down the track along which you will find it easier to achieve a profoundly heroic attitude towards men and affairs in the decisive moments of your life.

Men and women who have come in search of creative work on the stage ought to ask themselves what is the whole meaning of their life? If it is not uninterrupted creative work that goes on hour after hour, then what is the sense of living?

I have told you over and over again when we were discussing what your behaviour in the studio should be like that the development of a feeling of goodwill towards men is of the utmost importance to you. Now I again draw your attention to this quality of your heart. Think it over again now that you have reached the stage of maturity. What can a man see in the world that surrounds him and how can he see it? He can see it, of course, only as his consciousness permits him to see it. The greater your goodwill towards men and the purer your thoughts, the greater the number of beautiful qualities that you will discern in your neighbour. The lower the level of your feelings and thoughts, the more evil will you see around you, for you have to make an effort to see what is good, while you need no effort at all to see evil.

Develop, then, your goodwill, and do not emulate the example of the theatres where the actors hate each other. Unite with people. When you meet them try to show them the beautiful in yourself, and awaken an interest in the beautiful in the heart of the man you are talking to.

CHAPTER XX

We now already know five steps of creative work common to all those who devote their lives to the art of the stage. It would seem that every aspect of truthful representation of human passions in given circumstances has already been sufficiently elucidated. But there is one more feature common to all representational art and without which the represented passions cannot exert their fullest effect on the spectators simply because they lack the quality necessary for influencing human consciousness, namely, charm.

Where does this charm come from? What is its nature and where must we look for its origin? For if you see a great actor, and indeed if you analyse a whole gallery of stage artists of high standing, you will be sure to find in every one of them, in addition to his ability to set free and relax the muscles of the body, also this quality of charm as an immutable feature of his art. And in every one of them his truthfulness and his charm will be conveyed differently and will also be perceived by you differently.

What does it all amount to? What it amounts to is that their art possesses no special secret, but that they themselves are endowed with a *nobility of mind* which purifies the passions they depict on the stage. By their wider sensibility they have discovered the most subtle organic qualities of their parts, by their concentration and mental alertness they have selected them, by their powers of observation they have cut their parts into separate pieces, by their courage and repose they have achieved the total merging of their own "I" with the character of their part, and finally by their heroic tension they have transformed every piece of their life on the stage into a clear-cut and truthful embodiment of life as a whole.

But how does your everyday life, which you have to depict on the stage, differ from the life of the stage? What is it that has to be introduced into the passions on the stage to make them glow, hold the attention of the auditorium, and strike a chord in the hearts of the spectators?

If in depicting suffering on the stage, you fail to purge the ignoble instincts and thoughts in which it is so often immersed by your nobility of mind, or vice versa, if in representing a hero you endow his heroism only with positive qualities, then neither his love of his country that you are supposed to show nor his heroic deeds will reveal in your action on the stage that which will also show that in his ordinary life, too, his behaviour was characterised by a high sense of duty. You will not, in short, succeed in showing him as a man of high principle in private life as well. All your attempts to deepen your attention and introduce a larger and ever larger number of new people into your creative circle will be of no avail to bring about a complete fusion with the audience. You will remain acting in the circle of your solitude, but you will remain as solitary in the life you are living in as when you presented your attention with the wrong problem. To make sure that the heart and mind of the spectator should pay the closest possible attention to your life on the stage and that you should not remain solitary in it, your whole work on your part must be imbued with nobility. Every quality of the character you are representing must be purged of everything conditional and fortuitous. You must discover the true nature of each quality, the organic nature of each passion, and not by any means only the accidental shade given to one or another feeling and the action arising from it, as you find it in the play.

Imagine a huge cupboard standing along the whole width of the wall of this large room. It is full of small drawers, each with a large number of compartments, and every compartment filled with innumerable beads of every possible shade of colour. All these drawers are the organic, and always immutable, qualities of human passions. Their numerous compartments are the different conditional aspects of your part, while the beads of different colours are your ways of adapting yourself to the part, the secret of your creative genius, *your* nobility of mind, with which you colour all the emotions of the hero of the play so as to endow him with the vividness and tension of real life. Now, let us say, you are standing before such a cupboard—your spiritual storehouse. You already know your hero as your highest creative 'I'. The producer tells you, 'Here you go down on your knees'. But you in your own reconstruction of the part have made up your mind to stand beside a column drawn up to your full height. Now, if you have grasped the point that really matters in the feeling which you have to depict, what difference does it make to you from which drawer you take out the pink bead? Whatever the attitude of your body in accordance with the external mise-en-scene, you have to give us your action—the pink bead.

All disputes with your producer about the mise-en-scenes are almost always a waste of time, except of course when your producer is a formalist pure and simple, while you are inspired in your creative art by the truth of life. The creative force in you suffers no diminution whether you sit, stand or lie down. The only point that may be considered pertinent in this connection is the extent to which your creative powers can be said to have been set free, and whether in a certain mise-en-scene your body does or does not obey your will because, somewhere inside you, you have not achieved the proper degree of freedom and have, consequently, failed to achieve the necessary harmony. But if that is the case, it is useless to be angry with your producer or threaten to throw up your part; what you should do rather is to check up once more your creative problems to discover where you have substituted one problem for another and instead of giving the organic quality, given its artificial counterpart.

Your nobility of mind, and only that, can be of assistance to you here too. If you observe the true passions of men, you will always find in them great moments of sorrow, during which man undergoes great suffering. In every passion to which man has become addicted you will always discover the presence of agony, and this is particularly true in the case of a passion that can no longer be controlled. A man who is entirely in the power of some passion becomes its slave. What, therefore, must you select in all those cases where you have to show a man possessed by a passion? The first task of your attention must not, of course, be the representation of that passion but of those fateful moments

201

during which man's spirit is striving to free itself from that passion. Your nobility of mind must purify all the critical moments of a man's struggle to free himself from the pressure of the passion. In observing the irresistible progress of the passion of a drunkard, you must make use of all those moments in his life when he is sober, you must emphasise his love of his wife and children when he is not under the influence of drink, and show his fight against a passion that is destroying his better self.

Now you can see that for you, as actors, it is not enough to dedicate your life to art; you must also know how to plan your whole day as one continuous creative current, so that every day should develop in you a new consciousness, always adding new treasures of experience and observations of life and yourself to your heart. And if you still decide that there can be no life for you except in art, and that your role is to merge your own life with the life of the stage, then pay particular attention to your own manner of living each ordinary day, for it is in it that you will find the last step without which life in art is impossible. This is *gladness*.

Low spirits, as I have already told you, leave an imprint of sickliness on all creative work both in life and on the stage; they exert a constant influence of your lower 'I' on all your actions and thoughts. It is self-love and not love of humanity that leads a man to depression and makes him a prey to fear. It brings into the circle of your creative work these harassing thoughts: 'It's damned hard; I'm feeling shy; everybody is looking at me; the others do it much better than I'. The treasures an actor carries within himself, as a result, flounder in the bog of these trivial preoccupations. Here the actor himself gets into difficulties because he is unable to set free the best powers in himself so as to enter the first creative circle with the help of his love and enthusiasm.

If, on the other hand, you just happen to lack the feeling of goodwill towards men, you must do your best to acquire it. Get rid of envy, doubt, uncertainty, and fear, and fling open the gates of gladness. You have many reasons to be happy: you are young, you are learning your art in the studio, you are employed in an excellent theatre, you have a fine voice. Concentrate all your attention on this day of your life. Promise yourself that not a single encounter today, now, will pass except under the flag of gladness. And you will see that, as though by the wave of a magic wand, you will succeed in everything you do. And what you never dreamt of being able to find and master in your part yesterday, you will find and express in it today.

And so, day by day, discovering more and more gladness in yourself, you will soon come to regard it as an unconquerable force. Examine the faces of the great actors. They always look inspired, calm and full of joyous energy. As a feature common to them all, you will always discern in them the energy of joyful endeavour, and not the energy of low-spirited will, concentrated dully upon itself. The gladness of the great actors is not derived from the secrets and mysteries of their genius. It comes from their knowledge of the presence of love and goodness in them, and their constant welcome of these qualities in the hearts of their fellow-men. Actors are never unhappy because of some inexorable decision of fate. They are unhappy because they put themselves, instead of love of life and mankind, in the centre of their life on the stage, and because they are full of a dismal stubbornness of will. All they are out to get is a leading part; all they want to do is to eclipse everybody else. They never think of expressing life through themselves in the given circumstances of the play.

Keep an eye on yourself, and you will see your talents grow steadily, as you start your day with a feeling of gladness that you are able to live in the work you love.

Now we have examined together all the seven steps which form the germ of your creative work.

CHAPTER XXI

YOU know already what constitutes the inner way of creative work which man carries within himself. All the steps of spiritual and creative development that are common to actors as a whole compose that germ of creative art which is the starting point for every actor who is a student of my system.

By concentrating all his attention on the powers which have been developed in him, the student-actor begins his work of creating his circle of public solitude which we have discussed every day. The germ of your inner creative work and the germ of your part as a whole must always merge and not move along parallel lines. An actor cannot do his work and at the same time keep himself under constant observation. That is why one of the worst methods of learning a part is to do it in front of a looking-glass. For having acquired the habit, while learning your part, of constantly dividing your attention, you will not open the door to real temperament, i.e. intuition, on the stage either, but will merely produce out of the drawers of your memory a representation of the life of your hero which has been previously fixed by you along conventional lines.

To see in creative art a stimulus for union in beauty, to introduce new problems into every performance, and uncover greater and deeper creative powers in yourself, you must live in the germ of your part as though the germ of your soul could not at that moment live otherwise than in accordance with the circumstances given in the play. It is only then, while keeping all the organic feelings of the germ of your part intact, that you will tonight find a new inflexion with which to enhance the nobility of a difficult passage in a soliloquy in which you were not successful the night before.

If last night your entrance as Othello into Desdemona's bedchamber seemed unnecessarily gloomy to you because your creative problems of that piece of your part were tinged with the intention of killing her, then you can rush into her room tonight full of passionate hope to save yourself from the horror of your position, and your face will perhaps be full of entreaty and not threats.

When can you say that your work on your part is finished? Let us suppose you have been successful in it. You have played it a hundred times. You have become famous in it. But is your work on it really done? I have told you many times that art gets hold of the entire man and of all his powers, and that it is only then that it can grant him recognition.

But however great his recognition may be, there are always more torments than raptures in the life of an actor. The raptures of an artist's soul are no doubt very great, but a man can rise to those moments of exaltation only when the germ of his life in his part on the stage is indissolubly bound up with the germ of the creative powers in himself; when his life on the stage fills his thoughts completely to the exclusion of everything else; and when the purity of his impulses has created the habit of doing everything in the theatre from the highest motives, leaving all trivial personal feelings behind.

The actor can only hope to progress and grow more proficient in his art when wisdom begins to develop in his creative germ, that is to say, when he himself begins to introduce his pure and self-denying love into every moment of his creative work, forgetting all about himself and thinking always of his business in the theatre. When you are in love all your powers are heightened. You not only want to keep an eye on yourself inwardly, but also to be smartly dressed outwardly so as to 'charm' her by your appearance. Your voice sounds better. You feel much stronger. Everybody seems better, kindlier, and happier to you, because you yourself are so full of gladness. You must be just as much in love with your theatre and your studio. Your first joyful greeting on awakening in the morning must be addressed to your theatre, your studio and your fellow-actors. To the last day of your life your love of the studio must preserve its purity and its fascination. For only then will all the parts you create be the fruits of your real love of art. And the creative art of the stage will be embodied in you, and you in it.

Love of art lives and grows stronger with advancing years when life frees you from the shackles of egoistic love and your heart grows gradually colder and your bodily passions weaker; it does so because you put more and more the wisdom of life you have acquired into it.

And not only must your love of art, a love that is without fear or reproach, be the foundation of your life's career, but you must also be in love with something or somebody every day: with a picture, a flower, a song, a woman, a profile you saw by chance which reminded you of Aphrodite and helped you to people your creative circle today with new glittering images, a landscape, or football match which produced in you a feeling of energy; with anything you like so long as your spirit is always in a state of exhilaration, so that the ordinary everyday life that surrounds you has always the power to light a spark in you.

Never forget that you live on the earth and for the earth, and not above it. You have yourself chosen the stage for your career, and your are therefore the servant of those who want to see you. Never think yourself higher than the common herd, but always consider yourself merely the instrument for influencing them on behalf of beauty, which reaches them through you.

In possessing the creative germ, you may count yourself a very lucky man, for you have found a way of applying your creative impulses, and you have discovered an outlet for them, without which life would be meaningless to you. And it is here that there always exists this cardinal difference between actors who cannot help being what they are because otherwise their hearts would burst from the great multitude of imaginary people and actions they carry inside them (their reason for going on the stage is that they could not live otherwise, and they are happy and grateful to life for their work because their work is both love and necessity for them), and the other category of actors who are only anxious to exhibit themselves before a crowd. Here, too, there may be men of talent. But here the actors see the meaning of life not in the application of their powers to the general harmony of life. They do not want to be the servants of the people, but merely famous and honoured individuals.

No truly great artists like Duse, Yermolova and Salvini ever ripen in such an atmosphere, but only a Sarah Bernhardt, a Rejane, etc.

If you have entered into action—into the life of your part—and have passed all its passions through the filter of your nobility of mind, you must never forget *the sense of proportion.* One can easily impair the whole emotional range of a part by too generous an application of sombre colours or too liberal a use of bright ones.

The great masters of stagecraft were never satisfied with a monotony of colours. The whole fascination of their genius lay in the fact that their intuition was so fine and their physical actions so true that they could easily and without the slightest effort shift your—the spectator's—attention from one colour to another. Their harmony enticed your attention entirely into their circle, and there was no break between your perception of the most profound and cruel hatred and of a sudden childish artlessness. No great gulf existed between these feelings so far as you were concerned simply because it had been bridged by the actor's genius.

You know already that the secret of the actor's genius is not to be found in the force of outward expressiveness, but in the force of life of the creative germ within him, in the force of his fullest possible attention to the passing moment. Shun monotony in the selection of your problems. When observing the state of your attention, when putting your problems together, and choosing your various 'I want to', pay particular attention also to your voice. If you have noticed that your voice generally possesses a tragic character and timbre, choose for your exercises the gayest possible comic problems, develop in your creative germ every possible shade of gladness, always remembering my words that gladness is an unconquerable force.

When you are preparing your part yourself, you must be careful never to overtax your memory or your attention. If you are tired, go out for a walk, or go to a picture gallery, or go and have a look at your favourite statue. Always remember the Indian story of the pupil who asked his teacher how to find the right solution of his creative problem. The teacher advised him to put his trust in his subconscious mind. 'Glance into the pocket of your subconsciousness and ask it, "Is it ready?" and if it replies,

207

"No", go for a walk. When you come back, ask it again, "Is it ready"? and if its reply should once more be, "No", go for another walk. And so you keep on asking it till you hear the reply, "It's ready." Then act'!

You too do likewise. Do not impose any unnecessary strain on your attention. Do not try to find a solution of some difficulty in your part by sheer stubbornness of will. Leave it alone for a time, achieve a state of complete repose, and change the problems of your attention. For then the creative germ in you will reveal to you where your mistake was and what changes you have to introduce into the problems of your attention.

CHAPTER XXII

When you come to a stage rehearsal, you must first of all, before you utter the first word of your part, redouble your attention towards yourself and check up whether your body obeys you freely. If all your muscles are relaxed and you feel at the top of your form physically, proceed to check up your inner world.

See with your mind's eye whether your consciousness is as free as your body, whether all your attention has been transferred to your higher 'I', whether enough places inside you have been set free for your creative work, and whether any personal misunderstandings or perceptions are interfering with your desire to give yourself up entirely to the life of your part.

When you have transferred all your attention to the particular piece of your part on which you had stopped at the rehearsal on the previous day, do not take *it* as your starting point for your inner work during your rehearsal today, but run over the whole part from the very beginning in your mind in a flash of complete concentration, and then from this starting point, build your creative circle of public solitude today.

Never treat a rehearsal lightly, rushing in when it is about to start, flinging off your overcoat and handing it quickly to the porter, and jumping on the stage just in time for your cue. Many actors think it bad form to be at the rehearsal before the appointed time; they consider their position in the theatre to be of such importance that everybody ought to be glad to wait for them. The more indispensable they are to the theatre, the more are they under the impression that they can disregard the elementary laws of human courtesy.

A student-actor who is not trained in an atmosphere of theatrical bad manners but in an atmosphere of love of art, must always be in good time at the theatre, and prepare himself, inwardly and outwardly, for the rehearsal so as to be able to say with all his being, 'I'm always ready'.

Salvini—whom the whole world so greatly admired and who was never in need of advertisements or *claques* to make people fight for seats at his performances—used to arrive at the theatre at five o'clock, though the performance only began at eight.

The scene-shifters had only just arrived to get the sets ready. On his way to the dressing-room, Salvini always stopped to exchange greetings with them. After chatting and cracking a few jokes with them, he went to his room to put on his make-up. In about an hour, with his make-up still not completed, he again went out on the stage, chatted to the workmen again, paced up and down the stage, and then once more went back to his dressing room. In another hour he appeared on the stage for the third time, this time fully made up, though not fully dressed for his part. He again stopped beside the scene-shifters, gave them some hints about the scenery, checked over everything he needed for his part in the first act, sat down in a chair for a few minutes, and after a short silence again went back to his room. Fifteen minutes before the beginning of the performance, Salvini was quite ready, and he went out on the stage for the last time, fully dressed for his part, and, indeed, as the character he was acting that night. It was no longer Salvini, but the character of the part who had completely ousted the personality of the great actor.

What do you think Salvini was doing during these hours before the performance? Why should he, who had played Othello a thousand times, think it necessary to arrive at the theatre at five o'clock? Did he have to go over a part he knew inside out? No, what Salvini did during these hours was to live through his part. The few hours of his *theatrical* life were his real life; he, Tommaso Salvini, entered into the feelings of his part every time he performed it, and as he familiarised himself with the sets and scenery and the figures of the scene-shifters that darted in and out of them, he drew them into the circle of his attention, adding them, the visible and living, to those images of his creative imagination, invisible to us but real to him, with whom he peopled his creative circle.

No doubt Salvini's genius lived in a way in which the talent of an ordinary actor cannot live. One must possess an enormous range of inner powers, such as Salvini possessed, not to tire one's attention by concentrating on the huge creative ladder he made for himself during those three hours so as to be able to enter his creative circle with all his faculties of attention fully alive. 'To each according to his ability', as the saying is.

But we can see from this example that all those who went and built their life in art in accordance with the life of their hearts and minds, and the harmony of all their beings, arrived just at this point—the point of the formation of the creative circle. They transformed the theatre, according to their plans, into whatever it had to be for them that night. All the scenery and sets and the living people among them—everything, in fact, became the *indispensable* parts of their circle, into which they included everything they came across on the stage.

Every student-actor must behave in exactly the same way on the day of his performance. Having his own range of creative faculties, he must not, of course, try to imitate Salvini, but create in himself his own rhythm of the life of his part.

You are Tatyana and you are singing tonight. All day, however, you have been busy with your private affairs. You paid a visit to your dressmaker. You rang up your shoemaker. You discussed your forthcoming concert appearances with two of their organisers, and all the attention you paid to your part was to run over the notes on the piano. You were at the theatre at half past six, while the performance was due to begin at half past seven. You rushed out on the stage at the last moment, not even after the third call, but after the repeated calls of the assistant producer. While in your dressing-room you kept chatting to your dresser who was helping you on with your clothes and at the same time shouting remarks to the other performers without thinking that you might be interfering with them. What, then, was your performance like today?

At best the conventional methods of your acting, which had fixed your nerves and passive attention, preserved the semblance of 'acting' today. But the charm of a sweet country-girl's life, the charm of a pure heart filled with the ordinary human desire for love, the enchanting range of the emotional life of a young girl in which everything is so new to her—'Where is he? Everything in me is calling for him!'—the inflexion of your

211

voice in your first phrase, 'Have you heard?' when the moon, the companion of your dreams, cast its mysterious light over you and—through you—over us, the spectators too—that you did not give us, for you had no time during the whole day to prepare yourself for it. Your attention had a hundred problems to solve today, and among them there darted occasionally the problem of 'singing Tatyana'. But that life, that creative life, which begins in you with the harmony of your heart and mind and comes to an end only when this harmony too comes to an end, you did not possess. You had not lived through Tatyana's life in your imagination, and that is why we, the spectators, could not see it in you either. There was a disharmony between you and the other characters in the performance. You had not time to fuse with them and live with them as people who are near and dear to you. You did not come out on the stage in good time to look round it properly, to live on it, to sit down on the sofa, to spend some time with your nurse—the only human being you really care about—to have a good look at your mother and sister and draw them into your creative circle as you find them on the stage today. You had no time in which to transform the stage into the organic home of your soul; you had no time to warm it and people it with the—to us invisible—collaborators of your individual creative work in that 'now'.

You are already experienced student-actors and you can once more make sure of the correctness of the important methods which you will apply in training your creative will and your creative attention.

We have already discussed the importance of habit in creative work. If you get into the habit of being untidy—everything in your room thrown about on the floor, your bed unmade unless some solicitous hand covers it up, all your notes heaped up on the piano, and to find the thing you have to perform today, you throw everything on the floor and fly into a temper if you don't find what you want at once, leaving half of the notes lying on the floor—then the whole of your creative work will most certainly bear the same character, for there are no barriers of any kind between your outer and your inner life: the *beginning* of all your habits is yourself. If you are used to being untidy outwardly, you will be exactly the same inwardly, in your parts, in your songs, in the sketches and plans of your part.

The force of habit must exert an equal influence on the purity of your thoughts and the purity of your appearance. Nothing in the outer appearance of the character of your part should grate on me when you are telling me of the beauty of your hero's inner impulse. You may be poorly dressed, very poorly indeed. Your shoes may have lost their original shape, but they are clean, and they have no broken shoe-laces tied up in knots anyhow. Your whole inner man, pure and joyous, is made plain to me in the case you are carrying which, cheap though it may be, is nevertheless as clean as your own thought. And my thought finds no difficulty in merging with yours; I have no need to overcome the dissonance between your inner and outer appearance, and find a special problem for my attention, namely, 'To overcome my disgust at the untidiness of this man'.

From this example you can gather that the aethestics of outward form are an indispensable quality of the actor, as it is, indeed, of any other man. But a mere outward prettiness that does not harmonise with the sense of the beautiful in the actor is liable to create no less a dissonance than outward untidiness. The wisdom with which you must invest your everyday habits consists of your doing whatever you are doing *thoroughly*, with your attention keyed up to the utmost. If you have to put together your notes, don't be lazy, tired though you may be, and put them together with all your attention fully concentrated on this work. If you have to go to the studio, get up earlier, tidy up your room, and take out your coat which you have hung up carefully the night before, and the whole range of your inner attention, deprived of its correct rhythm if you are doing things in a hurry, will become the firm and strong basis for your work. It will assist you all through the day to enter the circle of the problems of the studio without a break between your home, your journey to the studio, and your work in it, provided you have started your day with your attention fully alive to everything around you.

A series of habits makes up the entire scheme of your creative education. If you were born a Samoyed and were used to eating seal meat, living in an igloo, and wearing the skin of a polar bear, you would of course find it very difficult to be a Lensky and run the risk of being killed in a duel because you suspected your fiancee of unfaithfulness. You would most probably have preferred to throw her into the sea for the fishes to feed on.

I have taken an example of two diametrically opposed civilisations. But that does not mean that it is impossible to *change* your habits and assume a different form for the outward expression of your talent.

No breaks ever occur in the creative consciousness of a normal man. I have told you already that the attention of a normal man can be expressed in a succession of dots and dashes thus: -.-.-.-., that is to say, attention—mental assimilation—attention—mental assimilation, and so on. Talent is nothing but a prolonged period of attention and a shortened period of mental assimilation. In a genius the periods of mental assimilation have been reduced to a minimum, while the period of active attention have been prolonged to a maximum. Napoleon used to exhaust his secretaries and marshals because his periods of active attention went on almost without interruption. We here are not Napoleons. Our periods of digesting the facts that are attracted by our concentrated attentions are, as a rule, normal. And between our attention and our will to creative work there are only the walls of our conventional assumptions and prejudices which we are quite capable of overcoming ourselves by the acquisition of a number of new habits, called into existence by our new developing consciousness.

If we are lazy, if something in our work seems difficult to us, we must remember that everything in the labour of art is reduced for everybody, whoever he may be, to one thing only: to make what is difficult natural, what is natural easy, and what is easy beautiful. Everyone of us can achieve this beautiful, the time as well as the height he will reach in his selfless creative endeavour depending only on the extent of his talent and attention.

Now we have reached the signposts in accordance with which every man plans his creative life.

CHAPTER XXIII

The first signpost which helps to set free the whole man for his creative stage problems is, of course, the function of the body—movement.

The first impression created by an actor is an external impression, but external appearance by itself is of no importance whatever. The appearance of an actor in a state of repose may be charming, but the moment he moves, his gait which does not harmonise either with himself as a human being or with his part, may destroy the whole of the created impression. His gait, which was in conflict with the harmony of the actor's inner actions just because it was not an entirely free physical action, had attracted the attention of the audience and distracted it from the through-action of the play and its unity as a work of art and from that spiritual task which the actor had been carrying out just before it.

Why did this happen? Surely, there are many actors who have never mastered the art of walking on the stage, and yet they do not attract the attention of the audience to themselves, and they can go on acting without interrupting the attention of the audience. Gait is in general one of the weakest points of actors. For instance, of all the actresses I have seen, there was only one whose manner of walking on the stage I personally liked, and even then many people disagreed with me. But no actor's part, as the centre of the audience's attention, ever suffered from it.

Why then did the actor's gait spoil everything in this particular instance? Because it constrained and hampered the actor himself. His attention was not fixed on the problem on his part—'I want to show you the desperate and hopeless position in which this letter has placed me'. Hampered by his feet, he changed his problem and formulated it to his attention like this: 'How am I to get without mishap to the other end of the stage where the letter is lying'. The rhythm of the music was no longer in his heart, though the violins seemed ready to burst with sorrow and despair: both his spiritual and physical problem lacked rhythm.

What conclusions can we draw from this? First, each problem dealing with the actor's own attention must be formulated concisely and carefully safeguarded by his concentration; secondly, each problem which includes movement must be wholly included in the creative circle from the very beginning of its formation as an indivisible psychical and physical action.

The circle of public solitude which you draw will never become a slice of your life for yourself or for us, the spectators, if you construct it only as a series of subjective problems. Every life, whatever its shape or form, is always movement. It may be the movement of thought or of body, but it is always movement.

What then restricts movement? It is restricted both by space and time. Your creative circle will attract our attention, that is the attention of the spectators, only if, when you formed it, you were in full possession of *all* your mental faculties, that is to say, if, when you entered it, you were fully conscious of the place and the time in which the days of your part are passing; if all the movements of your mind have revealed to you the conditions of the epoch in which the action is taking place and its historical importance; if all the characters of the play who are with you on the stage at the same time have been clothed in your imagination in the period costumes created by the conditions of the time, and so on and so forth.

When you have made yourself familiar with all those conditions and fully assimilated them, you may be faced with two alternatives: (1) either you have at once identified your freed body with all the problems of your part, in which case all your movements, and specificially your gait, have achieved the fullest possible harmony and you have no need to waste your time on your physical tasks in that particular piece of your part, because your correct inner feeling has automatically transformed your physical movements into correct movements; (2) or everything in your inner world has disposed itself most beautifully and satisfactorily and flows smoothly, while your movements on the stage still interfere with you, interrupting the flow of your part and putting your gait or gesture somewhere in the centre of your attention instead of finding a place for them among the many other extraneous aids for your part. If you are in opera, you ought to listen carefully to the rhythm of the music. Go on from it with redoubled attention. Find out how you can transfuse your energy physically into a series of certain beats of music. What does this particular beat say to your heart? Is it dynamic or static? And after a thorough study of the music and yourself in its rhythm, you will invariably discover which group of muscles it was that pressed on your nerves and prevented your creative force from finding physical truth in your gait. A number of physical exercises to the accompaniment of this music will help you to find the correct physical action in your part and to fuse your physical and psychical actions harmoniously.

The ability to adapt *your* qualities to every part is no less important than the ability to select in each part your own 'I want to's' and unite them in a small number of organic qualities of your part.

Very many actors are capable of analysing a part, and very subtly, too; but creative work—the acting of a part in a play—is synthesis. And very few are capable of it. That is why many actors who are able to discuss their parts excellently, act them very badly.

The adaptation of your data to a part so that, so far from interfering with it, they should actually assist it, depends on the gift of synthesis, the gift of intuition, the gift of unique individuality in every man. I know of a case of a young actor of the Moscow Art Theatre who plays the parts of old men inimitably. Everyone got the impression that his data could express themselves only in the parts of old men, in which his weak voice, his frail constitution, and a certain stoop seemed to go perfectly with old age. But quite unexpectedly this actor expressed the wish to play Khlestakov. The theatre laughed. But I and a few others did not laugh, and let him play that part. In it he not only won the applause of the whole theatre, but also of the whole of Moscow. And later he created a whole gallery of stage characters, and won over a large number of actors to his side.

What happened in this case? The actor knew how to adapt his individual data in such a way that his attention and the attention of his audience became fused into one indivisible whole. There are no definite rules according to which a lover must always be tall and handsome. He may be neither tall nor handsome, but the heroic tension of his life in his part will redouble the attention of the audience to his words and his inner actions, and distract it from his appearance.

Your feet may not be beautiful, but if they move in rhythm with the whole of your being, that is to say, in rhythm with your inward and outward problem because you set them free from the attention of the audience as 'feet', they will never interfere with your life and action on the stage, and they will obey the general plan you have designed for your part while you are carrying out a piece of it. But as soon as the thought occurs to you that your feet are not beautiful, there is immediately a hitch in the rhythm of the life of your creative circle and you change the whole problem of your attention and attract the attention of the audience to your feet.

CHAPTER XXIV.

The attention of the public, whether in a positive or a negative sense, is always attracted by gesture. The actor must have the right feeling in every piece of his part, that is to say, he must set himself a number of correct problems, for only then will he find that his correct action will arise automatically from his correct feeling. In the same way will his correct way of walking and his correct gesture come to him only when his entire creative being is subordinated, naturally and effortlessly, to the rhythm of the whole performance. In other words, his union with all the other members of the cast will not be a union with people he knows and may or may not like, but each of them will be for him only what he or she represents in his or her part.

An actor must develop such an ability to adapt himself to the conditions of the stage as would enable him to see in the person who is performing with him not those human characteristics which he or she possesses as an ordinary man or woman, but only and *wholly* those which the conditions of the stage permit him to see in him or her. It is this feeling alone that will be correct and it is in it that he will always find that note or that rhythm in which he has to seek to unite with all those who are taking part in the performance. Because all of them—the performance as a whole and he himself in it—have already admitted to their creative circle that slice of life which is called 'tonight's performance.'

Now you can draw your own conclusions whether you ought to talk in the wings or in your dressing-room about things which have nothing whatever to do with the performance, or whether the theatre or the studio can ever be anything for you but a temple in which you contribute all that your soul possesses.

Gesture and gait demand a great deal of work, but let me remind you again that everything in the world of art depends on work and the ability to make the difficult natural, the natural easy, and the easy beautiful.

The habit of viewing the whole of your day through the prism of joy in life must be laid at the foundation of all your creative problems. Only if an actor is fully conscious of life in all its aspects, can he set himself those simple problems in his part which will be easily comprehensible to all and will find expression in a definite and correct physical gesture. A part must never be conceived in accordance with some external design, nor must an actor ever proceed from gesture to the inner life of the man-part, if I may so express myself. Everything external flows out of the heart of two factors: the actor and the part, and it is only when the two merge into man-part that the true life of the stage begins. Now, for instance, you are sitting here in definite poses, that is to say, in a certain gesture. One of you is even twirling a stick, another is smelling a flower, and a third is taking notes. None of you thinks either of his pose or his gesture, and yet all of them, whether beautiful or not, are lifelike.

It is this *naturalness* of pose and gesture that must be caught by your attention and transferred by your observation into all those cases where you will be projecting your inner world into the circumstances given to you.

A famous actor once told the story of a young man who one day entered his room looking terribly embarrassed and hardly able to utter a word because of his shyness. He began by apologising to the actor for the trouble he was giving him and then, rubbing his hands nervously, demanded to know whether he would ever make a good actor and whether the famous actor would give him an audition.

'Go out, ring the doorbell again and repeat the whole scene of your agitation and questions from the beginning', said the famous actor to him.

At first the young man was completely taken aback, then he looked terribly hurt.

'How do you mean, sir?' he said. 'I feel so awful. I'm practically out of my mind. I feel that I am at the crossroads. I've come to you for advice, and is this the kind of reception I get?'

'You'll never make an actor', said the famous actor to the young man, and in all probability he was right.

An actor must possess so keen a sense of observation and such a well-developed memory in his muscles as to be able to reproduce not only pose and gesture, but also harmoniously moving thoughts and body. The work of the student-actor must keep moving along parallel lines of inner and outer creative effort. You can see for yourselves how much we have to talk here about the importance of work. But if your thoughts of your work are entirely preoccupied with honour and glory, you will never fathom one of the most profound mysteries of the creative art of the stage, namely to see and to understand the heart of the man whom you have to represent in your part. You will never be able to transform your part into a man-part if your heart and mind are occupied not only with the problems of your art, but also with your personal ambitions, your desire to become the leading actor in your theatre, to get rewards, and so on.

If you know how to devote yourself entirely to art, renouncing all personal ambitions, everything, the greatest success in life, will come to you. You must understand that it is not intrigues, good connections, or lucky chance that create the actor's position in the theatre. There are no lucky chances in art; there are the fruits of arduous labour, if you know how to labour selflessly, regarding as your only aim in life the art of the stage.

When we examine closely the small signposts in an actor's career, such as his gait, gesture, and gaze, we can see that they too are merely the general signposts of the actor's work on his part. In their outer form no two parts can be indentical as regards gait, since the whole rhythm of the spiritual structure of every part cannot be repeated and cannot be taken as a whole as a model for another part. If Lisa and Tatyana might possibly have the same gait, Marie Antoinette and Anissya from Tolstoy's *Powers of Darkness* could not by any stretch of the imagination be said to have the same gait. And yet, according to the inner structure of these two parts, both these characters must achieve the maximum degree of heroic tension. Each of them must develop her body, be the mistress of it, and having set the body free, force it to carry out any task, whether it is the heroic or the ordinary side of life that has to be shown.

Are those actors right who do not consider our dancing class for every type of actor as important? You laugh because you know

221

that there are people among you who dislike troubling themselves with any unnecessary exercises in the rhythm of movement, the excuse they usually give being that they are 'character' actors. But there is no difference between one part and another for an actor who understands that the representational art of the stage is always the result of the fullest possible development of the powers in himself. The man who does not realise that the creative work of the stage, whatever form it may take, is a blazing torch and not a quiet backwater is not an actor; and to be able to carry it from the stage as a torch an actor's body must acquire the habit of carrying out easily and smoothly every command of his thought. For only then can you give the right answer to the spectator; only then can you give him a heart which is wide open to love of art; for then your body is no longer an obstacle to the expression of your inner powers. And it is only then that the union can be achieved between the stage and the auditorium which have become one in the communication of hearts and minds united in beauty.

*   *   *

Today we have finished the rehearsal, and you saw how many times we had to stop because this or that physical movement was not correct.

Well, let us once more discuss the nature of the actor's physical action on the stage. Why is it so difficult to achieve an action that is absolutely right?

The physical action of the man the actor represents on the stage is not only the result of thoughtful and deeply felt representations of separate pieces of his part, nor is it a talented representation of the inner life of the character of the play; it is rather the most thorough blending of the actor's inward visual images with that chain of external objects he sees round him on the stage.

When that is achieved, the figure of the actor himself as well as his personality are no longer of any consequence. It is as though they had been forgotten. Quite other movements emerge, movements in which the new 'I' find expression. The new, and to the actor very dear, man, to whom his 'I' has yielded pride of place in his existence, taking second place himself and serving him, the man of his part, with all the strength and joy he possesses, or in other words, living for him.

I live the life of this different human being, the man of my part, not because it gives me an opportunity to display some phase of my own art which I carry within me. I am grateful to him for the new life I, the actor, live in his image, because my life—the line of the incessant creative work of my heart—has not come to an end with my transformation into him, the man of my part. On the contrary, my own life has become enriched by my new creative experiences as the man of my part and those will unite my own past experience as an actor with those that await me in future in other parts.

It was not the world of imagination that interested me so greatly when I lived as the man-part. It was not the fascination of another existence that put such vivid colours on the palette of my day. I was happy and I was swept off my feet by the heights of beauty even while I looked for and found in him those primary noble passions which I knew I possessed myself. It was that that made me feel akin to the character in the play and indeed made me one with him.

The search for the highest qualities of human nature in the character an actor is representing on the stage, even though he were a villain, makes him come to life and infuses life into the conflict of passions too. It vitalises the torment that comes from the realisation of weaknesses and the joy of heroic impulses.

In the stage life of the mature actor every instant of creative work is of importance. That is why I am telling you so often that an actor must never follow the road of mere display and imitation. An actor's creative impulse dies in imitation. His attention is not directed inwardly, but is concentrated on the external form. The result is the substitution of the creative state of mind by the ordinary actor's 'feeling' which usually makes him show outwardly what he does not feel inwardly. I have played one and the same part in a Chekhov play hundreds of times and yet I cannot remember a single performance in which completely new sensations did not arise in my soul and during which I did not discover in the play itself new depths of which I was never aware before.

If the new creative impulse is absent in your ephemeral 'now' on the stage, then you cannot expect the inflexions of your voice to be enriched by the colours of some new experience, either. Singing will merely be a matter of pianissimo and fortissimo, the production of sound merely as a matter of vocal technique, corresponding to the imitative physical action. It is here that every kind of forced singing arises. A singer who has nothing but emptiness inside him forgets that the voice is a most subtle instrument which does not tolerate the slightest strain. Every opera singer must sing in full tone, but without forcing his voice.

However hard an opera singer tries, his voice, if he merely imitates and has not made for himself an inner illustrated band of visual images of his hero, will never be able to convey something that will come with a shock of surprise to the spectator, that is to say, he will never make the spectator see the depths of a man's sorrow or the heights of his happiness.

Why then is it so difficult to achieve that fullest possible expression of feelings which is so vivid that the spectators are enticed into it? Why, in short, is it so difficult to give them true art? Because art of the stage is the synthesis of all the achievements that man has gathered together in his spiritual 'I', that is to say, in the work of his heart. Let us call them *the culture of the heart*, and let us call all the experiences arising from observations and the habits of the physical body and of thoughts *the culture of the mind*.

To capture any kind of consciousness in the orbit of your creative emotions you must present your visual images to another man in such a way that he will not only understand them but also be swept away and fired by them. I must hold so bright a torch in my hand that it should melt the ice of all the accepted conventions, habits and repressions which close up the heart of the spectator whom I want to take an active part in my art.

Turning to our work in accordance with my system, one can express it like this: when the actor has made himself the band of visual images, when he himself is swept away by all his different 'I want to's' so much that they have become his real life, when he says with all his outer and inner actions—'I am'—then the first task of your creative work is to transmit your love of the man of your part to all those with whom you either sing or act in the performance, sweep them away by, or rather sweep them into, your own enthusiasm for the character you are representing.

It is only when this interest in your part has been aroused among the other members of the cast that the process of creative co-operation begins—the real life of the stage which as an already existing entity will draw the whole audience into this process of creative co-operation.

I have told you many times that I am deeply convinced that the theatre as an institution that has lost contact with the common people cannot and must not exist.

If a theatre that is really inspired by the great ideals of dramatic art is successful, then it can only mean that it was able to attract all those thousands of people who come to it.

I wonder if you realise how important an actor's influence on a crowd is. Have you ever thought of the atmosphere a creative artist of the theatre creates for a whole mass of people? Have you any idea what tremendous power an actor wields and how great his sense of responsibility must be? Have you grasped the great meaning of the theatre as such?

The Greek word —ἄγω—I act—already tells you of the great force of the word-thought flung into the crowd from the stage. The power of an actor's thought bursts like a high-explosive shell among the people.

We see that even simple cultural propaganda finds an echo among the people who pick up everything that is of general usefulness and of common human interest without the slightest effort just because it corresponds to the tastes and responds to the needs of the moment.

What then must be the influence of a theatre which gives its spectators immortal works of art! Works in which the whole aim and attitude of the actors is directed towards the desire to penetrate into the very heart of the organic passions and evoke feelings that are common to all mankind.

My system is merely the starting point for the career of every real actor and every real theatre. Neither I nor my system, nor a man's love of art can impose 'the burden' of a taste for art. Every man who is possessed by art has not the power to throw it off because it means happiness and indeed life itself to him. The actor's heart cannot obey any laws except the laws of creative work. It is only this rhythm that the actor detects for himself in the whole of the universe.

Harmonious artistic natures are what humanity needs very much. But they are only in demand when they respond with all the fibres of their being to all contemporary movements, tastes and needs. It is then that they find it much easier to represent vividly those characters in which the audience recognises its own negative qualities and is delighted to discover its own positive qualities. An audience eagerly looks forward to getting something new and beautiful, something that exercises a great power of attraction over them, something that is both accessible to all and possible for all.

It is through you, actors, that the forces which are understood by millions and that tell of everything that is beautiful on earth, find expression. The forces which reveal to people the happiness of living in a widened consciousness and in the joy of creative work for the whole world. You, the actors of a theatre, which is one of the centres of human culture, will never be understood by the people if you are unable to reflect the spiritual needs of your time, the 'now' in which you are living.

How is the theatre to find the means of reflecting these needs? How find the right kind of aids to transmit to the common people those forces, those new technical and spiritual principles, which the theatre has already discovered and which it can introduce into action as atmosphere?

Here only one method is possible, namely, to create a company of actors who have the same standard of education. The whole emphasis must be put on one fundamental action: to create actors who have been trained in the spirit of true art. One must realise once and for all that in our business more than in any other success depends entirely on people who have been trained as creative artists.

As for the aim of an actor's education, it should not only be to produce a man who knows how to be inspired easily and naturally by 'the given circumstances'. An actor must be steadfast in his ethical problems. He must be steadfast in his undivided and alert attention. He must be efficient in his work, and he must clearly understand that his work does not come to an end with the fall of the final curtain. He must bring high ideals and beauty into life.

All these are questions that affect an actor's whole life. In man's inspirations and dreams of a better life the actor must introduce the will 'to be' and 'to become' the thing his contemporaries regard as an ideal.

CHAPTER XXV

Every art in which the time element plays an important part must possess the power of attracting the unflagging attention of the spectators. An actor finds it particularly difficult not to give in to the temptations of his creative work in a long soliloquy or aria. Never by anything external or by any diversity of external methods will you accomplish such a fusion with the audience as to be able to hold its attention during a whole scene lasting half an hour.

What then can be done to make sure of holding the attention of the auditorium? The only method is so to strenghten your creative circle of actions as to make it impossible for any thoughts that have no relation to the conditions inherent in the scene to penetrate through its protective wall. I have already told you that your circle can be said to be truly creative only if it is alive in every sense of the word, and not if all you are trying to do when already in it is to find a solution to the problem of drawing a creative circle round you. What you have to do, having concentrated your attention on a definite task, is to start introducing into your memory those people who are sharing your life on the stage, though we may not see them. Let us suppose the problem of your part is to give us a stage embodiment of Faust. Now, if you concentrate all your thoughts on the horror and despair of old age and if Goethe's thought about the power and the majesty of man's spirit which, having changed its ageing shell, can preserve its desires undimmed, does not form the foundation stone of your part, you will only succeed in creating a hackneyed operatic Faust who is dreaming of a successful top C and who will all the time be going through the steps of the vocal and not of the creative art of the stage. And yet it is only the latter which would enable him to achieve a reflection of life in human passions which he has to express only in the circumstances set out in the opera.

Why does Mephistopheles show Faust the image of Margarita? Because by the magic of his art he has read Faust's passions in his heart, the passions which old age had been unable to quench. It is only from that blazing flame, from that starting point, that Faust's words will assume their value and significance. The significance of the word is not born when it has to be uttered on the stage, but when the actor created the image of his character in his creative circle. To find the correct operative words and to invest each of them with its inner meaning, one must proceed, in one's sentences and words, from the image and the passion as well as from the moment when the inter-relationships between the different characters on the stage have been established.

When the feeling of resentment at the passing of his youth has arisen for the thousandth time in your Faust's heart, you, having chosen your operative words, will make them your starting points; you must look on them not as a means for making yourself understood, but as bits of your own heart. You will not only show your affection for the word as a whole, but you will put a special meaning into each of its consonants—not one consonant will be lost, and that not because you have achieved a good diction according to all the rules of elocution, but because every consonant has become a bridge between the different parts of the word which is not a *word* to you, but your creative heart.

If you do not happen to know all the rules of elocution (this is no doubt very reprehensible and, as you know, I am present at all your elocution lessons and am learning together with you), but have understood what my system is for, you will have begun and finished your work on your part with love, the love which you carry into life out of yourself. And in this way you will also overcome your ignorance of elocution; love will help you to bridge the gulf in your knowledge by discovering in your heart an intuitive understanding of the value of the vowels and the consonants in a word. But do not for heaven's sake think that you can achieve growth in your parts without studying elocution, singing and dancing. To remain on one and the same level of inner development all the time is quite impossible. You often hear people say that in art you either go foward or go back. That does not at all mean that the actor who appears in many plays goes forward as compared with the actor who does not act as often. Even while you are not acting, it is quite possible to work hard on your

part, people your circle all the time with new details of its different problems, find the right expression for your operative words,
change them, and look for new problems because for the life of
your heart you want neither stage nor partners. Everything in
you is alive, and you go forward because you are full of courage
and energy. And that is why when your turn comes to act, everything on the stage comes to life *because of you*, because of what
has lived, grown and taken shape in you.

But if you act the same character so often that you have no
time to get under the skin of your part in a new way and merely
acquire the usual conventional stage tricks, you not only do not
improve in your art, as you may be inclined to think you do, but
you stop dead and very soon you will be going back. Once you
can afford no time to change your problems and find still newer
organic qualities of your part, then all you are anxious to do
is to repeat the old. Each ephemeral 'now' of a man in a part,
however, can gain the interest of the audience only when both
the man and his part are no longer preoccupied with the same
problems as on the previous day, but when the mood and the
meaning, comprehended today, have thrown a new light on the
part by new intonations.

The secret of the charm of an actor's new intonations, mistaken
by the audience for talent, is in reality only the sounding of new
notes in him as compared with his problems of the previous day.
And there is no end to the work on a part or to the actor's ability
to bring it to perfection, as there is no standing still in it, if the
man's own life is spent in obtaining an understanding of himself
as one who reflects the whole of life in his parts.

CHAPTER XXVI

The dissatisfaction of an actor with his theatre is mostly due to the fact that he is conscious of the presence in him of the powers he would have expressed in his creative work on the stage if he had not always been too much preoccupied and busy with all sorts of things and duties and so on.

Let us see whether the actor is right who is always complaining that life takes up too much of his time by the demands it makes on him. Is he justified in claiming that these demands prevent from moving forward in the life of art?

When anyone complains to me about his life or about someone, a wife about her husband, a husband about his wife, or a father about his son, I always try to make him re-examine himself. Has he been always absolutely fair to whoever or whatever he is complaining about? Has he always been just, and in having an argument or quarrel with someone, has he always visualised the living heart of him with whom he has had a misunderstanding?

So you, too, student-actors, should ask yourselves what it is you put first: your private life or art? If your life is your work in art, can you possibly divide your life up? Cut out a piece of it and call it 'studio' or 'theatre' and separate yourself from the rest of the life that goes on round you?

All your life will be true life only when your creative 'I' has been merged with it.

The day when, in the morning, a rehearsal and a meeting with a whole company of ardent hearts is awaiting me is never a miserable day to me. Remember that all of them are full to the brim, like leyden jars, with creative powers. And no sooner do you discover a word of love in your heart than each of those hearts responds by a powerful spark of its battery, a spark that is invariably creative.

The force that keeps you in a creative atmosphere is merely your own ability to reflect through yourself the life of the human

231

heart on the stage. But if you separate yourself from life, if you retire within your own shell and try to erect as many barriers as possible between you and the rest of the living world, under the pretext of devoting yourself entirely to the stage, what kind of life will you be able to reflect on it? Even the richest imagination must replenish its store-houses by a living communion with people. But it is impossible to observe people, their sufferings, their struggles and their loves and at the same time fence yourself off from them and, choosing a small number of intimate friends, move quietly inside the ring of the parts you have made for yourself, and worry about your part only when it is in danger of eluding you. The stage will never become a true reflection of life to you, if you regard the *day* of your life as merely a series of external actions and external comfort in it. Your day must mean living men to you, and your creative heart with them and for them.

How do we conduct our studies with you? By rhythmic exercises we seek to achieve a complete blending of the movements of your bodies with your different musical pieces. But where did we get those musical pieces from? We took as our starting point rhythm, word and sound. From the life which the composer has clothed in sounds and blended by the power of his genius and by the force of the fire in his heart with the rhythm in which each of his characters lived in his mind. We have tried to find out the secret of the composer's heart and discover why in one place the time is 3-4 and in another 6-8. What is the difference between Werther's and Charlotte's heartbeats? And why did their lives end in tragedy?

The sacred law of life they had violated—the right of every man to love and to live in his love—has divided the creative powers of their hearts and brought them to a climax of horror, to their 'doom'.

If we take Charlotte's letters, can we really imagine that our Charlotte lived as she is usually represented on the opera stage? We see a woman sitting quietly in an armchair, reaching out for Werther's letters from a box at the moment indicated in the libretto, and then proceeding to display her vocal art, at best showing an excellent knowledge of her part and enunciating her words correctly. Her whole attention will be directed to the task of singing her lines well, making no mistakes, looking pretty, moving about gracefully, and doing her best not to spoil the impression created by her womanly charm, and of course getting her voice ready for the difficult passage of her prayer. The life of a woman, whose thoughts are in agony about another tormented heart, the gradually dawning realisation that the marriage, which had been arranged for her by her parents and which she had accepted because of the conventions of her bourgeois education, was not at all her duty to life and that a woman's real duty is to follow the dictates of her heart and to fulfil the great purpose of life, i.e. to give the man she loves as well as herself a chance of a happy and contented life—all this is absent from an uninspired opera performance, from the conductor's time-beat as such, from the vocal excellence of the human voice, as such, and from the conventional mise-en-scenes, as such. The whole point is that they all do not matter, as such, but merely as *conditional* aids to the expression of the *organic* life of human hearts.

And indeed how could the whole scene possibly become the material of life, a piece uniting the spectator with the actor, if he had not introduced the spectator—I daresay long before Charlotte's letter scene—into the circle of his creative life on the stage?

We in the studio raise the curtain with the first chords of the third act. It is Christmas Eve. Charlotte is waiting for Werther. She had been watching the street for hours through the window. Every sound of footsteps makes her rush to the window again; in her mind she can see Werther as he was at their last meeting, when she had sensed his terrible despair. She lives in that memory with all her being. This is the cause of Charlotte's anguish and inner conflict. The heavy duty of her conventional, joyless marriage to which her heart cannot reconcile itself—and the walls of prejudices. At last, at the culminating point of the musical introduction, her despair, blending with the cry of sorrow in the music, makes her rush to the bureau and seize the box which contains her only precious possessions in the world—Werther's letters.

It is now that I, the spectator, also remember with you, Charlotte, that Werther promised to be here on Christmas Eve, that Christmas Eve has come but he has not. And the whole gamut of feelings—from the tense moments of your waiting for him to come to your reading of his letters, thrills me not as an opera scene but as young Charlotte's agony from which I cannot tear myself away.

It is not the action itself that is important, but the gradualness of the development of your—the actor's, the man-part's—steadily growing powers.

If you have to intensify the action by some tremendous gesture, will you produce it simultaneously with the word? No. The gesture has lived in you already, in your circle, from the very beginning of your soliloquy, like the closing chord of a song, if all the problems have been chosen by you correctly. Your attention is growing gradually not in obedience to your will, but in response to the word of your part at that very moment, to some fragment of your heart, to some fragment of your flesh and blood. If your feeling was correct, then the correct gesture will come by itself as the graphic conclusion of your soliloquy.

CHAPTER XXVII

The most logical and orderly system, however well-founded the cause and effect of its premises may be, can give nothing to the actor if he looks on it merely as one of the aids for helping him to embark on the road of his creative work. All my system, like no doubt many other systems in the world, can do is to assist the actor to discover the powers that he already possesses, and teach him to observe how they work, to find his way through the chaos created in the passions and thoughts of the actor himself, and, as I have said so often, to cleanse his creative life of all refuse and waste. But if you regard my system as the be-all and end-all of creative work then it means that you look outside for the main currents of your creative work. But you must remember that you yourself are the source of all the currents of the creative forces, and that to look for help from outside in order to awaken them means to ruin yourself as a creative force and never to find an entry into the rhythm by which everything around you lives.

When you have thoroughly mastered all the inner steps of the creative ladder, common to all mankind, you become aware that most of your life already belongs to the studio.

What only the day before you regarded as the most important thing in your life, is of secondary importance to you now. A little more time—and the centre of your attention has grown more concentrated on the studio and your work there. The things which you valued so greatly before have now given place to the heroes of your parts by whom you begin, as it were, to be obsessed.

What does it mean? What is happening in your mind? You have imperceptibly transferred the centre of your attention from your own personality to all those in whom the creative force of your heart has disclosed a new comprehension of the valuable things in life.

So we have now reached that stage of your creative development when you begin to understand from your own experience that the only thing that makes your life worth while is your creative work. Your childhood period of art has passed; you now enter the grown-up period of creative work, and the stage has become your life. In art is is impossible to give orders; it is impossible to force anyone to become an artist by the exercise of will; in art you can only inspire and be a living example of the influence of one living soul upon another.

The period of your creative courage in the theatre is full of all sorts of diverse occupations, if the teacher knows how to guide you, keeping your interest in your work alive all the time, and all the time making your studio exercises more difficult so as to make you realise the inadequacy of your knowledge and the immaturity of your development, for it is then that you yourself will learn everything easily and joyfully. Every day is a dead loss to you if you have not improved your education by the acquisition of some, however small and unimportant, piece of knowledge, and if you have not discovered some new and beautiful qualities in your parts or in your fellow-actors. Lazy stagnation today will not provide you with the creative link for your tomorrow. A normal man has no gaps in his consciousness that separates his today from his yesterday and from his tomorrow. As a matter of fact, yesterday does not exist as a creative emotion. It only exists in your memory and imagination, and is needed in creative work only as experience, as a necessary function in the chain of the logical conclusions of your consciousness. But as a creative principle yesterday is worthless. The most terrible thing that can happen to the creative powers of a man is for him to live in the past. Having made up your mind to become a creative artist, slam the door leading to your past, and remember that the past exists only in you, and that outside you it can no longer be found. Life has run on, and if you have been left behind there is a break, a gap, and perhaps even a gulf, between you and the life around you. If you will not raise yourself *above* your personal yesterday and enter—a purer, simpler and happier man because of your suffering—into the new day that is opening up before you, then you have yourself closed the door to creative work.

In the life of every man, of course, there only exists his ephemeral 'now', his 'today', and not his yesterday.

System and Methods of Creative Art

I spoke to you about the difference that could always be discerned in the work of actors. One actor, during his studio exercises or at a rehearsal, will at once and without the slightest hesitation accept the remarks made to him, being fired by the desire to grasp and correct the mistakes pointed out to him so as to achieve the required result without loss of time. His love of his work arouses all his powers to a state of heroic tension. He is seeking not himself, he is thinking not of his own hurt vanity, but the image which in his effort to solve the problem of his part has already become indistinguishable from himself. What is valuable to him is not his own personality, but the joy of finding one more organic quality so that it should pass, like a spear, through his own heart, and also pierce the hearts of those for whom his creative work is meant. Such an actor automatically looks for the best aids that will make it possible for him to express in the most efficacious and delicate way what he wants to say, and he is glad that his teacher has drawn his attention to the incorrect problem he has presented to his attention; he always overcomes his difficulties and achieves a more perfectly realised image; he knows the value of the fleeting 'now', of the unrepeatable instant of the concentration of all his creative faculties, and he will not miss it. And this means that on the stage, too, and in the auditorium, he will always find in himself that harmonious combination of all his powers and that creative repose where his *personal* qualities will not interfere with him, but will be transmuted and merge into the image of his part, and it will no longer be he but the man-part, that is to say, he who carries in himself all that is living in his part.

Another actor, eaten up by ambition, reacts to every remark made to him as though it were a personal insult, and is always quick to find some excuse for himself, pointing out the circumstances that interfered with him, or overwhelming you with promises to do everything next day, or the day after, or at the performance, but you can rest assured that he will not do it either the next day, or the day after, or at the performance.

Why have I come back to this question today in spite of the fact that I have already discussed it with you several times? Because the time of courage in your creative work has arrived.

And every one of you has to re-examine the steps and the sign-posts of his creative work. Everything is in a state of flux. And if you have stopped even for one instant, you are already lagging behind, and you have already increased the distance between you and your part. As a creative artistic force you are not a bit different from the pianists and vocalists who have to do their exercises every day. Your inner world cannot live on old problems. If you do not move forward in them, you will grow mouldy in them and most assuredly finish up by adopting the conventional and artificial stage tricks.

There can be no break between the stage and your current day. The stage is all of you. Not the you who walk leisurely to the hairdresser's; not the you who having dressed up and smartened yourself up go like a lion to your meeting with 'her'; but the you who are glad to be alive today because you see clearly where and how to communicate the agitation of your heart; the you who know the immense value of the creative urge in yourself, and knowing it understand the heart of the man to whom you will bring beauty from the stage today.

CHAPTER XXVIII

Do you need to give so much alert attention to your problems and to everything that surrounds you on the stage in the period of your maturity and your courage in art? It is only now that you have adapted all your powers in yourself so as to obtain a combination of the correct inner feeling with the correct physical action; now that you no longer rely in your part on the instincts that are active in you and that arouse the reaction of your brain and lead to physical action; now that your every physical action on the stage becomes the echo of your intuition and your higher creative 'I'—it is only now that your life in your creative tasks begins.

Suppose I give you, Miss X, the following problem: come into this room and pick a quarrel with every one of us who are sitting here. But, remember, the quarrel you are to pick with me must in no way be like the quarrel you will pick with A, B, C and so on.

What is it you ought to do first of all before you enter your circle of public solitude? Before you start developing in it all or some of the steps of your creative germ?

Well, of course, first of all you must find your bearings, you must ascertain for your inner creative germ how and where to open your campaign. At this moment you must feel both like a soldier who is doing the fighting and like a general who is planning the campaign. For you are not only a soldier, that is to say, you are not only your body that will do the actual fighting, or if I may put it differently, act physically; you are also the general who has his plan of campaign all mapped out, that is to say, you are also your inner creative powers. And your task will be to win the battle, or in other words, you must quickly and effortlessly force your mind to come to a decision, choose the right spot for your attack and order your body to act.

Theoretically, therefore, you the general, i.e. your intuition, must have a precise plan of action already before your soldier— your body and its instinctive reactions—begins to act.

System and Methods of Creative Art

If you had been a genius and possessed the gift of picking a quarrel with each of us that would be guaranteed to be most disagreeable to each of us, you would require only an instant in which to make up your mind. For you would have grasped in a flash of inner illumination, say, the most vulnerable spot in me and made up your mind to go for it. Being a genius, you would have needed the tiniest possible period of attention (dash) and the tiniest possible period to grasp its significance so as to convert it into action (dot). Again, being a genius, you do not need much time for making your plans to explore my inner world and find its weakest spot. All that would have been the easiest thing in the world for you. Your genius would have indicated my weakest spot to you and you would have got the better of me in no time. But unfortunately neither you nor I is a Julius Caesar. And to come, to see and to conquer you want not only time to gauge our characters, but also to bring all your acts and thoughts into the closest possible correlation with each other in a state of the greatest repose, i.e. to be both soldier and general at once.

We have already said many times before that creative work begins when your inner and outer powers act in harmony and comes to an end when that harmony is broken. What makes the achievement of this repose easy for you so as to enable you to start your creative work? The circle of public solitude, of course, in which you have already learned to begin to live long before addressing yourself to the solution of each of your creative problems.

Let us then start on our problem. So you have decided to make a scene with me because you think that I have been unfaithful to you? Well, as a matter of fact, I have witnessed many such scenes, but they have not got on my nerves to such an extent that they should be my weakest spot. You laugh because you think it funny that I should have allowed myself to be inveigled into so conventional a situation as the one Miss X has just proposed to me. Well, I too think it rather amusing, but I readily agree to imagine myself a handsome young man, and I promise you a good fight if I notice that, in playing this scene, you make full use of the organic features of a jealous woman. But I warn you that as soon as I notice any sign of overacting or artificiality

240

in you instead of the true organic expression of your jealousy, I shall resume my position of an old teacher.

'Oh, so that's what you make me out to be, madam? I am a despot, am I? I am a heartless deceiver! I'm too lazy to do anything except run after women! Is it my fault that you suffer from chronic indigestion? Oh, naturally, it is the result of your nervous upset caused by my habitual unfaithfulness! I'm sick of your reproaches and tears! Do you hear? Sick of it! Your suspicions are merely the inventions of your disordered imagination! She's the most innocent of creatures! She's beautiful . . .' Sorry, I give up! I've been caught out. You are again amused, are you? Well, learn how to plan your problems of attention and how to solve your difficulties in the given circumstances. Miss X had been attacking me. To stop the flood of her accusations, which I knew perfectly well I thoroughly deserved, I tried to find her weak spot namely 'She loves me and so she is sure to forgive me', and launched a counter-attack. But I'm afraid I could not keep my attention concentrated on my problem: 'I want to break through as quickly as possible to her feeling of affection for me'. I was carried away by my memory of what 'she' looked like and said something in her praise. By doing this, I barred my entrance to Miss X's heart and handed her a new weapon against me—her envy of her rival who not only does not suffer from chronic indigestion, but is also always well dressed. Instead of distracting Miss X's attention and, in a state of the greatest creative repose, presenting her with a new problem that would have taken her thoughts off her rival, I drew her attention to her rival and intensified her jealousy by a feeling of envy. Instead of discovering in her, Miss X's, already grief-stricken heart the narrow path leading to her kindness and love for me, I presented her attention with another passion—envy.

I lost my way and became insensible to the organic features of jealousy. What is jealousy? An ardent desire for affection and the fear of losing it. Instead of convincing Miss X of my love and drawing her attention to me, I have diverted it from myself to her rival, while all the time she was yearning for affection with every fibre of her being. I have made a mistake in mustering my problems. My soldier—my body and its instincts were fighting and obeying my commands in a campaign which had been wrongly planned by my general, my intuition, my creative 'I'. That is why I was defeated. And now I must be further punished for my own mistake and dry the tears and stop the flood of incoherent words with which Miss X will no doubt overwhelm me. So, I suppose, the best thing I can do now is to capitulate. Sorry. But it was all the fault of my unsuccessful approach to my problem. I made this mistake because my plan had been wrongly conceived.

Now let us see whether you have made any mistake in your problems. Where and how have you gone wrong? Everybody is laughing, which I am afraid is a bad sign so far as your dramatic scene is concerned. I can't help thinking that you have not acquitted yourself so brilliantly either. Very well. Let us analyse your scene.

Your entrance was excellent. You made me believe at once that you had not entered our studio, but my private study in your own home. I could read in your face that you were determined to have it out with me. You flew at me at once. You started *forte* at once. Well, you were of course successful: I gave up the fight. But surely you could have woven a much more subtle web of gradually developing feelings than your storm in a teacup. Now, confess, there was in your attention also this line of thought: 'How do you like that? They are five and I am one, and I, if you please, must have a different quarrel with each of them!' You laugh. Well, perhaps you did not put it exactly that way. But you did feel a little rushed because of the great amount of work your attention would have to cope with. Well, that was the first spoke you put in the revolving wheel of your creative life. And yet you knew very well that your creative life was your 'now'. It was with the help of this 'now' that you had chosen the scene with me. Why then were you thinking of what might happen *afterwards*, how hard it would be for you to go through five different scenes one after another, and how to find a subject for each scene that suited each of us in turn, and so on. All that would happen later on, while now, in our scene there are only you and I, and no one else in the whole world except you and I. You have not only destroyed the inner unity of your attention, but also the inner unity of your creative circle. If you wanted to live with the problems that bound you to me, you failed to plan your work in a way that would have driven everything else from the field of your attention. You were not trying to find a spiritual basis for your attack, but gave yourself up blindly to the action of your instincts: to fall on your prey.

I believe I told you before that when you are acting on the stage under the influence of your instincts, you resemble a cat chasing a mouse, or a dog in full cry after a rabbit, and so on. And it is this mistake of allowing yourself to be carried away by your passions and instincts without previously purging them by your consciousness, your nobility of mind, and the strength of your love, that you have committed now. But I am not a mouse and you are not a cat, and we have to act in accordance with the highest possible sense of beauty that we can discover in the nature of each passion. We have broken this law, and that is why our whole scene followed such a vulgar course, that is why we at once raised our voices, and I have been forced to make you the exceedingly ungentlemanly reproach concerning your weakest spot—your chronic indigestion. Your sensitiveness and mine missed our real problem, and the whole line of our original problem became distorted. You did not observe the rule of gradualness either in accordance with life or your part.

Your entrance was excellent. There could be no doubt that you were at home. Your behaviour, by its intimacy, was entirely in keeping with the assumption that everything in the room had long been familiar to you. You put right the cushions, the curtains, the flowers. But you fixed me with a glance of such an intense hatred that the least I should have done was to push away in horror the cup of tea you gave me, and assuming that you had put poison in it, pretend to be as terrified as I possibly could, if I were to do justice to that concentrated look of hatred on your face and the flash of enmity in your eyes.

Only a murderer who had made up his mind not to let his victim escape from the room alive, would have made such an entrance, which of course means that you had started the scene with what you should perhaps have ended it, having gradually made the circle of your problems more and more complicated.

You have broken all the laws of gradualness, of the sense of proportion, and of the feeling of precision in your problems, namely, the instant of time which was passing just now. You had not planned your action in accordance with the idea you had to deal with, that is a simple jealousy scene, but in accordance with a jealousy scene ending in murder. You were not in the circle of the life of your imagination which would have very accurately shown you the time and place and purpose of your scene. All these conditions you broke in your attention, and that was why you had diverted it from real life to a conventional perception of it: jealousy, that means excitement, irritation, and absence of logic in one's actions.

Yes, to be sure, excitement, irritation and absence of logic— all this is to be found in jealousy. But if guided by your sense of tact and adaptation, you had not approached me, your teacher with whom you had to play a scene, but me—your unfaithful husband —created by your imagination, you would have begun your scene with a tender smile and a kiss, with which you would have concealed your wish to find out where I had been the day before. You would have explored the ground very carefully so as to be able to ask me in the most natural manner why I had come back so late last night, and so on. And it would have been here that you would have led me and the spectators across the most complicated course of your feminine feelings. You would have just hinted at your suspicions, you would have suppressed your tears which would have prevented you, as an actress, from finding a thousand more devices for a display of your enchanting womanhood, its cunning tricks and its charms, and as a result, you would have enticed me into the mesh of passions according to my own system.

CHAPTER XXIX

When addressing yourself to physical action in your part, try to get as clear an idea as possible what the whole of your part really is like. If your internal canvas is made up of an uninterrupted series of 'I want to's', then your external plan will be an exact reflection of your different 'I want to's'.

It is indeed on the exact correlation of your desires and your external physical action that the success or failure of your part depends. The little magic word 'if' (if I am such and such a man or woman today) brings me to the conclusion that I *can* live only thus.

Let us take an example that anyone will understand—women's tears. Tears again! We certainly seem to be unlucky in our examples! I should have thought it was high time we had a little fun for a change. Ah, you find that it is easier to be happy, do you? Well, I am glad you have made this discovery.

And so, tears. Charlotte's tears or the tears of a leader of fashion who is ageing and beginning to realise that the time of her innumerable conquests is over and that she is no longer the cynosure of everybody's eyes, different as they may be, are still tears and nothing but tears.

If you are Charlotte today and a society lady tomorrow, what must you do? Could you perhaps try to find the common denominator of both their general organic qualities simply because in both parts you have one and the same action, namely weeping, and tears are the moisture that has to be removed by the same physical action, that is by wiping them.

No doubt the physical action is the same both here and there. But we have just been saying that the success of a part depends on the exact correlation of every physical and every inner action. Are the inner organic qualities of Charlotte's life and the life of the lady of fahion the same? No, they are not. Then how can the external action and its organic movement—the wiping of tears—be the same in both cases?

If you are Charlotte, your whole life, which brought you to the tears, is full of inner conflicts between your wrongly conceived duty and your love, and the whole canvas of your creative higher 'I' prompts you to conceal your depths. The secret which is tormenting your soul, filling your eyes with grief, fills you with apprehension and makes your hand tremble, and you are anxious to brush away the tears that suddenly come to your eyes so that no one should guess what is concealed in your heart. Your 'I want to' is to hide away the dearest thing you possess—your love—from any glance that may accidentally discover it. You are pure and innocent in your love and your suffering, and your whole behaviour is characterised by extreme timidity. You touch Werther's letters as though they were his living heart. And your tears, both when you are alone or with your sister, find expression in a physical gesture only in the form of a tormenting desire to suppress your fits of weakness and carry on as a faithful wife as long as your strength holds out. You think least of all of yourself; all your thoughts revolve ardently round Werther; your passionate wish is to avert the insane act of his death. You yourself are utterly incapable of putting an end to your conventional marriage, though the thought does now and then flash through your mind, 'I have made a mistake. This cannot be my duty to life'.

What kind of physical actions then can these problems that agitate your heart produce? Would you be thinking about your looks at that moment? Do you need a looking-glass now? Do you know what your future course of action will be? Your imagination has peopled your circle of public solitude with the, to us invisible, phantoms of your dread and fear for Werther. You imagine the likelihood of a duel between him and Albert. At the same time your mind is filled with memories of your walks with Werther in the stillness of the night when your soul knew no conflicts, when the nightingale and your duets with Werther at the harpsichord brought peace to you and him, and when you did not suspect that you were in love with him, but loved the purity of his heart in him, giving yourself up entirely to this feeling of love, to which he responded with fiery ardour. Your timidity and your passionate desire to conceal your tears and avert your 'doom', the thought of which is haunting you incessantly—these will be the organic qualities of your tears as Charlotte, and these will produce two different kinds of physical action: sometimes a timid movement, sometimes a tragic impulse, sometimes a quick glance in the direction of the door through which people may come in any moment, and sometimes a passionate desire to kneel down and pray. But it will never occur to you to lock the door of the room and so on.

Now let us see what your tears will be like if you are a famous society beauty who is ageing and losing her admirers. What has brought you to the point of tears. Rage! You are furious with old age that has come upon you unawares. What has brought on your fit of crying in spite of the fact that, being an experienced flirt, you know perfectly well that your tears will have a disastrous effect on your looks and are therefore a mistake? Spite! You were expecting a letter from the man you had taken so much trouble and wasted so much time to enthral. Only the day before you had used the deadliest weapons of your charms, which no man had ever been able to resist, and now you expected a letter in which he would declare his love for you, but the letter did not come, and you realise that it will never come.

What inner organic action have we here? 'I want to catch, to possess, one more moment of life. I want conquests and passion'. It is only egoism we are dealing with here. The man you were expecting a letter from is only a means to an end, namely to fill your own life which is getting emptier and emptier. You have no thought for him. Just a chance to bring your love affair to a successful conclusion. You, too, of course will want to conceal your tears. You will not hesitate to go to the door and turn the key and send every unwelcome visitor to hell. You too are facing your 'doom': old age is approaching and you can do nothing about it. But you are fighting it, and you will go on fighting it. You rush to the looking-glass, your constant companion, the only witness of the secret sorrows of your old age, and you look in it eagerly, as eagerly as you are trying inwardly to snatch once again at the sensual enjoyment of life; like a miser who sits trembling over his gold, you are trembling over your face; you forget the whole world while contemplating it. Having no idea of inner beauty, you only prize the smoothness of your skin—while wrinkles are appearing on it everywhere! You are in despair. You fling down your faithful friend, your glass, and burst into sobs. What sort of physical action is this? How do you sob? You might possibly throw yourself on the cushions of your sofa and start kicking it with your feet. Or you might stamp on your glass. Or you might be tearing your handkerchief or tearing up into little bits the photograph of the man who had deceived you and refused to fall a victim to your charms. (It's a good thing, though, he can't see you just now). You can choose any variation you like, so long as it does not go counter to the conditional circumstances of your problems or your part which has been given to you, and so long as you achieve a complete fusion of your inner and outer problem, selecting any physical action you like best, for all of them can change in accordance with the particular conditions of your play. But the organic qualities—your egoism, your callousness, your selfishness, your hypocrisy, your dissimulation and your greed—all of this will be shown by you in accordance with the manner in which your artistic sensibility and your sense of beauty, your nobility of mind and your sense of proportion allow you to create the plan of the scene of tears that one would expect from such a creature.

Now let us compare the two scenes, the two women, and see whether you would have chosen your different organic 'I want to's' for the two scenes simultaneously. Well, you say, 'No', yourself, so it is hardly necessary for me to dwell on the obvious.

Let me, though, draw your attention to two points: both Charlotte and the society woman rush across the room, one to her letters and the other to her glass. Both snatch up their most precious possessions, something that is more precious to them at that fleeting moment than anything in the world. But in pressing her box of letters to her heart, Charlotte also presses to it the living heart of the man she loves, a man on whom at that moment all her life is concentrated; she is filled with utter self-renunciation, and her thought of him is her temple of purest love. Her gestures do not express any desire to satisfy her passion, but loyalty and reverence; and the powers of her womanly charms grow as a result of the timidity and the misery of all her movements.

But in the scene where you are playing the faded society beauty, you snatch at the glass greedily, rapaciously, expecting to find in it the solution of your problem—victory or defeat. All your thoughts revolve only round yourself. As you peer into the glass, you realise how useless all the artifices of your numerous masseuses have been, and the eagerness with which you scrutinise your face gradually gives way to hatred and despair. And your physical action is a glass clasped in tightly twisted fingers, a head thrust forward and an intent, greedy look—and everything suddenly explodes in the one violent movement with which you hurl your glass on the floor, everything crashes on the floor, so as to give your hatred a chance of escaping from your heart.

Once more I must repeat to you that your part demands the concentration of all your attention on yourself. Having once found the inner and outer problem running parallel to each other, you cannot apply them to your other parts or to other living people in them. Your organic problems chosen by you in each part must be based on your own unique individuality. You must approach the creation of your circle through all the steps that are common to all actors, and you must enter it by mounting their ladder. But having entered the circle of your today's problem, you will be a creative artist only when your entire attention is concentrated anew on each piece of your part and when you do not repeat in your performance today the outworn theatrical trick that was so successful yesterday.

CHAPTER XXX

The throbbing life of the human heart, represented in every play and offered from the stage, cannot be included or described in any book or system.

It is absurd to assert that in a certain book the whole of life is described and all the laws laid down how to act a certain piece of life or a certain feeling.

It is quite impossible to act any feeling, for every feeling is by its very nature so sensitive that it hides away at the touch of your thought. All you can do is to learn thoroughly the nature of the feeling, analyse the substance of each thought, find out what shape a physical action takes under the influence of certain reactions, and how the conflict between thought and feeling grows, creating a disharmony in the human mind, and ultimately tragedy. But to set out certain conditional external rituals according to their different points and once and for all, like the divination rites of witchdoctors, is quite impossible in an art in which the element of time plays so important a part.

You can learn from books how to prime the canvas on which an artist will paint a portrait. You can also learn how to mix your paints so as to produce a vivid portrait, and how to put them on so that they should not run and interfere with the truthful delineation of the features. But the features which have been truthfully delineated physically because the canvas had not interfered with the painting, need not necessarily correspond with the inner truthfulness of the painted portrait. Why not? Because everything depends on the painter himself, of the range of his inner illumination, on his intuition which he never permitted his trivial personal feelings to interfere with.

The canvas, which reflects the slices of life, is the stage. You are its painters, and you can either be mere technicians—'high-priests'—who have thoroughly studied the whole external cycle of the rules of stage representation, or you can try to master the nature of the feeling itself and become the current which con-

250

ducts to the hearts of the spectators those forces which open up new vistas of beauty for them.

By getting up from your chair you can at once force me by your physical action to enter the circle of your inner life, and I shall understand who and what you are as well as what makes you happy or unhappy.

Let us see how it can be done. Please, Mr. Y, here is your chair, sit down, relax all your muscles, make sure there is no strain on your nerves, and see whether you are thinking that you are in the studio and that we are all looking at you. Forget that you are a student-actor; imagine that you are in a beautiful wood; the pines are rustling above your head, the sky is blue, you can hear the roar of the sea from the distance, and you can catch a glimpse of the shimmering waves. You are no longer young and not in the best of health.

You feel comfortable in your chair. Now try to imagine the days when you were young and how strong you were then. Now your hand is trembling, you are lonely, and saddened by your loneliness, you even feel like crying a little.

Why did you give such a wrong external representation of the inner life I have just described to you? What is loneliness? What is the nature of this feeling? 'There is no impulse for energy, and no desire to come into contact with certain aspects of life, for all the time the thought keep hammering in your brain, "I am alone; no one cares for me".'

It therefore means that your pose does not as yet express the despair whose nature we shall perceive in the form of the following thought: 'I am doomed to end my life in utter loneliness. I have been forsaken by everybody. I have no more strength to adapt myself to the demands of life. Everything is at an end because everything in me is dead, because I am helpless'. Your pose seems to convey that. Your hands are clenched convulsively, the corners of your mouth are drooping, and beneath your lowered eyelids there is just a faint glimmer of life. Ah, now you have corrected your pose. Your hands are no longer clenched, your eyes are wide-open, your glance is wandering aimlessly without expressing any keen thought or energy. The folds of your clothes which fall so carelessly on your figure make us

251

realise that it does not matter to you what kind of an impression you make on the people around you. But still there is nothing in your pose to make me believe that your energy has been organically destroyed by time and hard work; on the contrary, I can't help feeling that all sorts of desires may still awaken in you. In fact, you make me think of the saying, 'There is life in the old dog yet'.

Now change your problem. You are still full of life. You possess the energy and love of three men. But you have had a very hard life. You were always working at high pressure, and at the age of sixty you are a physical wreck, but your passion for every kind of activity is still unquenchable. You drag yourself up to your chair, leaning on your stick, you just manage to sit down, and now you are waiting for your grandchildren to whom you will be telling fairy stories, because these children are the only source of energy left to you.

Now, let us see what you will do. Good Lord, do you think you can express the nature of the feeling of waiting for someone by such physical actions? What does waiting for someone mean? To begin with, when waiting for someone you will be thinking what you are going to say to the person you are expecting to come when you meet him today. After a little time you begin to ask yourself anxiously, 'Have I made a mistake about the time?' That's right. Think your problem over again (in this case it is the fairy story you are going to tell your grandchildren) and try to remember some fresh detail. You have remembered something humorous, you are laughing, but there is still no indication of your feeling of uneasiness. But why are you suddenly turning this way and that? One of the conditions of the problem I had set you was that you were to represent a physical wreck of a man. Now instead of showing us the twists and turns of an unwieldy body, which you find it difficult to manage, show us the conflict between your weak and diseased body and your spirit which is still full of energy.

A quick glance. The way you lift up your eyes is not characteristic of an old man. Moving lips. And at the same time twisted fingers, bent legs, and a stiff back.

Only now does it occur to you that your watch has stopped

because you forgot to wind it up. You know that the children are punctual and could not be late. You put your watch to your ear. You don't trust your ear. You try to see whether your watch is wound up. It is ticking. Everything's in order. It is now that you should turn round for the first time. You are beginning to feel worried. What is the nature of your worry? Will the children come now? You are wondering why they are late. Are they ill? Have they had an accident on the way and are they hurt? Or has anyone frightened them away? You want to look at your watch again, but now your hands are trembling more than ever. You can't manage to put your hand in your watch-pocket to take out the watch, which a moment ago you had no difficulty at all in taking out. You drop your stick and your handkerchief. You have lost your head completely. Your thoughts and actions stumble over each other, and you give us the characteristic reflection of the nature of waiting: one problem and thought impatiently thrust aside, another seized in a hurry, then a return to the first problem, a transition to a third thought, and none of them is fully expressed by a precisely formulated 'I want to'.

One thing I believe stands out very clearly in all the innumerable examples we have considered in the course of our studies: the simpler the problem, the more difficult it is to express it in physical action. Why? Because in tense moments your nerves preserve the memory of the muscles much better.

The feeling of anguish at having lost someone in tragic circumstances is so great that you carry it about with you for years and years, if not your whole life.

The feeling of boundless joy and happiness when you were all at peace with yourself and the world and nothing existed for you except the great joy of your love is so overwhelming that you never forget it, even if you have only experienced it once in your life.

But the ordinary events of daily life you have to present on the stage never attract the *whole* of your attention. You have not acquired the habit of seeing the whole of the man before you and trying to understand him by concentrating the whole of your attention on him. And so we have once more come to our starting point—full and undivided attention.

Five Rehearsals of Massenet's Opera
Werther

I

Tomorrow we shall cast the new parts. Today let us talk about how, knowing already the meaning of the 'Stanislavsky system' and having been through a whole series of exercises, you are to make the whole of your apparatus ready for your initial analysis of your parts. It is important that you should be aware of nothing but your part when starting your creative work in it: you must be obsessed by it and be conscious that whatever you possess in you of value now exists only in it.

It is next that all your private life and its worries, that is to say everything personal, sink into the background, and there is formed round you a kind of empty circle which you can now fill with the help of your imagination, with the help of the magic word 'if', or in other words, with those new circumstances which your part offers you. Please note now at once that there is all the difference in the world between your creative imagination, that is to say, between the fruitful activity of your attention and the fruitless fantastic day-dreams which merely produce castles in the air and unrealisable dreams. The former, that is to say the creative imagination, is always ruled by logic and common sense. It is occupied with entirely concrete problems. The attention is concentrated and its circle is expanded with the help of 'if' always in strict accordance with your part.

The creative imagination of an actor must reach such force as to enable him to see with his inner eye the corresponding visual images. It is then that his creative imagination forms what we call the visual images of the inner eye.

A whole series of such uninterrupted visual images forms an unbroken line of illustrated and not plain given circumstances.

During every moment of his presence on the stage the actor must see either what is happening outside him on the stage or what is happening inside him, in his imagination, that is to say, his visual images which illustrate the given circumstances.

All these component parts form, either inside or outside, an

257

endless and uninterrupted series of visual images, a sort of reel of a film. While the actor's creative work goes on, it continues to unwind itself, reflecting the illustrated given circumstances of the play among which the actor—the performer of the part—lives on the stage.

During the creation of the film of visual images the following questions, besides 'if', are of importance: when, where, why, for what particular reason, and how. These help the actor to distinguish the contours of his new and hitherto unknown life, and introduce him into action, into the new and exciting inventions of his imagination. Now you have already forgotten all about your own person as Mr. So-and-so, and that is why you assimilate all the new circumstances of your part so easily and simply as to be unaware yourself that there is no more your part and 'I' but only 'part—I'.

All the exercises for the development of the imagination must show the actor *how* to create the material and the inner visual images, and not just how to day-dream 'in general'.

Let us draw this conclusion from all this: *each movement on the stage and each word must be the result of the true life of the imagination.*

And a second conclusion: one can do nothing on the stage mechanically, formally, and without bringing one's imagination into play. Such actions without the living force of imagination will never lead to truth, but only to automatism.

When the actor reaches the stage when life of his imagination is created in this way, nothing will interfere with him any longer. In this state it is quite impossible to separate your personal experience from your part, from the earth, from its truth and noblemindedness. It is by your nobility of mind that you cleanse all the passions of your part before presenting them on the stage.

But *what* passions are to be presented on the stage? All? No, not all, but only those you have selected as the organic parts of the life of your part and purged them of all naturalistic coarseness which is actually not needed either for your part or for the stage. Now you are no longer able to seek yourself in art, but only to seek art in yourself. You will give us on the stage that life of your part which you have found in yourself. And it is only now, having selected the organic parts of the life of your part, that you are able to put it together in one framework of your part, on which with the help of your imagination and your body freed from all strain you will create what we call the *through-action* of your part.

Always remember that the field of your activities is not the stage alone, and that your part has not come to an end with the fall of the final curtain. The actor must carry honour, nobility of mind, and beauty into life.

Another category of imagination is to keep your own person in mind all the time. The actor tries to invent as many given circumstances as possible in which he could give full play to his own egoistic fancies. And the more he tries to do it, thinking of making his part more interesting by his own inventions and in this way capturing the attention of the audience, the less interesting will his part become and the less likely is he to capture the attention of the audience. He will find himself again in the circle of instincts and exaggeration, and he will never discover the road to intuitive and subconscious creative work.

What is it we get here? It is not the person of the part that becomes the centre of attention, nor is it through *him* and *his* given circumstances that the actor sees the piece of earth, life and labour which he has to represent on the stage, but only his own 'I', 'I', 'I' into which he tries with all his might to squeeze in his part, as though it were a horse-collar. Here it is in vain that one looks for truth or logic. Everything such an actor does on the stage is merely the expression of his desire to be liked personally, to be successful, to exhibit himself before the audience.

And the meaning, the chief meaning, of any as well as this part, the *force* of the creative work by means of which the actor brings a new perception of beauty to the audience through his 'I—part' is utterly lost.

How is such a mistake to be rectified? We have already agreed that an actor's life on the stage finds expression through his creative imagination combined with his creative attention. To divert your attention from your personal 'I' and the audience as the main objects of your thoughts, you must concentrate your attention on what is taking place on the stage. The moment you get an absorbing object of attention, the auditorium as a distracting element will vanish. You must know how to fix your attention entirely on the stage, and you must learn both to see and look on the stage. You must know how to focus your attention on the nearest object, without allowing it to be distracted and wander off far away. A constantly flickering light becomes unbearable to human eyes. And the distracted attention of an actor is like a flickering light and is unbearable to the spectator. It does not gain the interest of the audience and merely creates a vacuum.

At first you must try to create for yourself the small circle of attention. It helps you, like a small spot of light, to give free play to your intimate feelings and makes you forget the auditorium. This state of mind is called, as we have agreed, public solitude. It is public because the public is with you, and it is solitude because you are separated from the public by the small circle of attention which you have created for yourself. In it you are able to shut yourself up in your solitude at a performance and in the presence of thousands of people.

The middle and large circle of attention demand even greater training. You must know how to restrict them, as though by an intangible wall on the stage, by a number of objects on which the actor must be able to keep his attention fixed. If you allow it to be dissipated, you must again gather it into the small circle. The more your attention becomes distracted in a moment of panic in the large circle, the tighter must be the middle and small circle inside it, that is to say, the greater must be your public solitude. These circles must as it were be carried inside you during the whole performance.

But however tightly you may shut yourself up in your public solitude and however lucidly your creative imagination may be working, there must be one more feature in your acting to assure the greatest possible success to the life of your part, namely stability.

We first create visual images of our inner life. These objects of your attention demand much more stability than external ones. Inner attention is as liable to be continuously diverted on the stage from the life of your part and get mixed up with your own personal life as outer attention. Here, too, as in the imagination, there is a constant struggle between the useful and the harmful.

Attention and objects in art must be extremely steady. Superficial attention is of no use whatever to the actor. The creative work of the stage demands the fullest possible concentration of the organism. And attention becomes creative only when it does not emanate from your cold and calculating mind, but when it is warmed by feeling. The actor's imagination arouses feeling, and feeling transforms attention into something cordial, or what is called in our psycho-technique, sensuous and not only intellectual.

In summing up our studies today, what conclusion can be drawn? If you have not created out of your workshop, that is out of your organism, the sort of lathe on which the greatest artist of all—nature—can work, then no exertions of yours will ever bring about a fusion between you and your audience. For you have not forgotten about yourself. And all those who came to you to find a rest in art and fill their heart with beauty have found neither art nor beauty in you.

The spectators have gone away empty-handed, collecting from you your personal vanity, of which they have enough without you.

I often hear you discussing my system, the so-called 'Stanislavsky system'.

You would be as justified to call a system any method of
study that provides the ways and means to real creative work if
onlythey are dealt with in a consistent manner. In my system we
apply ourselves to the study of the nature of the powers and
feelings which are inherent in man.

In what way can the actor's profession be said to be difficult?
What peculiarity does his profession possess that is characteristic
only of the arts in which the element of time plays an important
part?

The painter, the sculptor, and the scientist can observe the
result of their work. The scientist, let us say, observes the reaction
of the chemical substances and of the external life which surrounds him but which has nothing whatever to do with his work
and does not interfere with him. In his test-tube the substance he
has just discovered is bubbling, and while he is watching it, he
can read, think and talk about anything he likes. But an actor is
unthinkable as a human being cut off from the life of the stage
and from the people who are performing with him on the same
stage. The surrounding life *outside* the stage and the given and
conjured up circumstances of the play do not exist for him. His
test-tube is he himself. He cannot observe himself. He is only
wanted and valuable as an actor when life is seething in his
test-tube, life which he has quickened by his imagination with
the help of 'if'.

Imagine that you are Werther. You have to combine many
problems in one part. And if you cannot reduce to a system not
only your psychological problems, but also that shell through
which they have to be presented to the audience, that is, your
body and all your physical actions, you will never get a living
Werther, but the whole palette of your paints will be confused,
variegated, and—still monotonous.

Five Rehearsals of Werther

You know that Werther shoots himself at the end of the opera. Well, what does that mean? Does it mean that you have from the very beginning to paint him in the dark colours of agony and renunciation?

It is of the utmost importance that you should show the audience a man of the world who is full of life and is deeply in love. A man who coming out on the stage on a moonlit night arm in arm with the woman he loves, is *all* there. The whole universe to him is at that moment embodied in Charlotte.

Here the audience must already realise, that is, feel that you, Werther, suffer from no inner conflicts. Here it must see and perceive clearly that if scales are placed before you, Werther, and if in one scale is put the whole of the universe and in the other Charlotte, you will unhesitatingly choose the one in which is Charlotte. You, Werther, have no use for a universe in which she is not to be found, however many treasures other people might find in it in addition to love.

Do you really think it is possible to express so powerful a concentration of attention on love of the Charlotte given to you on the stage if you have not complete control over your body?

You have to communicate to the girl the great happiness you feel in her presence, the joy of touching her arm which lies in yours. You have to express by means of a series of simple but true physical actions the fact that you worship the ground she treads on. Your thought is as pure as that of those who worship the gods.

Your physical actions must be correspondingly concise, easy, true and simple. And you can't take two steps without stumbling. Your shoulders are raised up, your chest drawn in; your elbows are either thrust out or pressed tightly to your sides. In the old days they used to put corks in the armpits of the young ladies in public schools to make them press their elbows to their sides. But those times have gone and our conceptions of refinement have changed.

How rigid your neck is, as though you were afraid to turn round!

How can you possibly express in such a pent up, undeveloped and fettered body how your inner problem is emitting sparks inside you? How can you hope to fire us with it?

How have you to start work so as to be not X who is representing Werther, but Werther who at that moment is living in X's body?

You must walk on the stage with a quick, impatient step. Examine the long familiar house in which 'she' lives. Is everything in its old place? Has anything changed while you were away? So now you know. Well, but does 'she' still live here? I can't see any difference in the degree of your curiosity. Make this pose of yours produce the highest possible plastic effect so that I should believe that all your thoughts are centred *behind* that latticed window.

These are your first problems.

There follows your meeting with the children. To meet, raise and kiss a child. Are these not purely physical problems?

How strangely you lift up this child! Is he ill? He is neither ill nor is he a doll made out of sugar. He is smiling at you, stretching out his hands to you. Children are marvellous actors, and you should take a lesson from them.

Lift up this child; rock him; toss him up in the air. He is trying to please you, so you too try to please him; whisper in his ear that you have a lovely present for him. A whole number of simple but physically true actions has already created an interesting life for the spirit of your part. We are already with you.

But remember that there is no suggestion yet of a revolver or death. Why then do you assume such a tragic face? At the moment we must see an ordinary man who is fond of children. You feel particularly happy among these children because Charlotte loves them. That is why you are so attentive to them and why you love them twice as much.

Your love of Charlotte finds an object in the children. Again there appears a *new* physical problem: to examine this object thoroughly.

And next to it is the parallel spiritual problem: fondle the children because they are part of Charlotte herself. Give your imagination full rein. Look among them for the one Charlotte loves most, the one who is most like her, the one whose eyes are of the same colour as Charlotte's.

So far as you are concerned, 'she' is in everything. And so all your problems are threaded on one string. You have found a series of physical and spiritual problems which are fused together. The elementary physical action has produced the line of your attention, and this line of attention—love—will become the framework, the through-action of your whole part.

You have discovered this through-action not by your mind alone. Everything of which your 'I' is composed—your body, your thought and your heart—was working in unison and looking for this line along which your attention would be directed in your *entire* part.

But why do you lapse into sentimentality? Have you not noticed in your observations of everyday life that sentimental people are almost always cruel and sensual? Have you ever observed in Werther, throughout the entire part, any possibility of overdoing things? As it is he is overflowing with love and he needs no artificially contrived emphasis.

What you have to show is the *courage* of the man, the consistency of the actions of this character to whom life becomes meaningless if his beloved is, like Tatyana in *Eugene Onyegin* given to another. An ordinary man would go on living without 'her'. But Goethe has given you a man who does not know how to bend. And you must reveal this feature of Werther's character to the audience at your first entrance.

Now consider whether a man possessed of a love so tender, so pure and so noble as Werther's would ever stride along with the stiff legs of a soldier on parade? The soldiers in those days, you know, had splints tied to their legs to prevent them from bending them when marching.

You are young, and your legs and body are supple. You, too, will find it difficult to bend your legs when you are old, but even then they would not be as wooden as they are now as you walk across the stage.

Now you have a mincing gait just like Bobchinsky in Gogol's *Government Inspector*.

You can now see the importance of a man's gait on the stage from your own mistakes. Now I hope you will be convinced how important it is for you to take dancing lessons, do physical exercises, and develop the facility and precision of your movements.

Five Rehearsals of Werther

What sort of communication can you establish with your partners if all your thoughts are preoccupied with the desire to please me now with your movements? You must feel absolutely confident that 'if' you had been Werther, you would have walked like that.

And as soon as you start concentrating your thoughts on the objects and problems of Werther, and because of that, every way you walk will be acceptable, even if by itself it is not particularly good.

Gait on the stage is, generally, a very difficult thing. The character of a man's gait always reflects his own character. But it is difficult to change character, as such, while it is easy to change your gait, if you take good care of the physical development of the whole of your body.

Go over your thoughts and problems again and see if they are right. Look at the confusion you have got yourself into. No precision in your problems or your movements.

You, like any other living man on earth, can only have one problem on which to concentrate all your attention at any given moment. But you seem to have ten problems at the same time, and you behave as though you knew everything beforehand. You not only know what is going to happen in the second act, but also what will happen when Charlotte sings her pieces over you as you are dying. You even know beforehand how you will come to life again on the stage as soon as the curtain falls, how you will put your clothes straight, very satisfied that all is over and that the audience will be clapping like mad.

You are laughing? Well, let us see what your mistakes are. To begin with, what is the rhythm of your feeling like now? Everything is still very clear and simple in your life. You are happy because you are in love.

What are the problems of a man who is in love? To get ready for the meeting with his beloved. To dress up. Not to be late. Very well. You have met. What now? Look into her eyes. Try to find out what mood 'she' is in. Is she as full of happiness as you are?

You can colour all your problems externally and express them as you like and feel. What is upsetting you? Are you impatient? Are you at a loss? Or are you a pedant? A cold and sensible man?

Five Rehearsals of Werther

All right, I believe you. That was a man who is deeply in love. But there is no madness in the music. Poor Charlotte! You have nearly dislocated her arm just now. If you go on like this the poor girl will not survive the second act.

And I doubt whether you yourself will live as long as the fifth act. The powder magazine of your love is sure to explode long before that.

How are you to get into the right channel? What will help to get you there? Look what a lucky chap you are: Goethe has given you the words, Massenet has given you the rhythm—there is no need for you to devise anything of your own. All your problems depend on the data of your part; on the rhythm of the music. It tells you the sort of person you are and *how* you are in love. Only when you follow it will your problems be right.

You have nothing to be uncertain about. What does the music say now? This is no conflict with God. That conflict will come later. This is only happiness, rapture and union with nature. There is not the slightest suggestion of doubt.

But how can you hope to pick out the composer's rhythm if your attention is preoccupied with the problem—'Oh, I'm afraid to make a mistake!' or 'My voice seems to be a little hoarse'.

In this condition, entirely of your own making, you will never be the Werther you have created in your imagination, nor the one Massenet offers you.

What are you trying to learn now? To transfer to your heart a ready-made rhythm. From the rhythm which is given you, you ought to be able to guess how Massenet himself lived when he was composing the music for his heroes.

And how can you possibly enter into the life of your composer's rhythm, if it is all too clear that you are afraid of the high notes?

We cannot wait for you to become ideal singers. As you go on perfecting yourselves in your art, you will eventually become such singers. But now, while you are acting in the studio, carry on with the development of your parallel inner and outer actions. See that your correct physical actions help you to obtain the right feelings. Push off from them and your voices will respond to you.

Sound, however, does not depend on physical actions only.

The correct feelings create the right temperament and evoke the right sound.

Now you have stopped worrying about the sound as such. You are carried away by the meaning of the piece you are singing. All the tension of your body has disappeared. You are moving about effortlessly and naturally. And we no longer see you, but you—Werther, and once more we live with you.

You will acquire the habit of living in sounds on the stage only if you don't waste your words and sounds in idle talk during your vocal exercises.

When you are vocalising and trying to get some transitional notes, always try to associate some psychological problems with your singing, so as not to sing bare notes, but notes-thoughts.

The time when the public sought only entertainment in music has gone. In your vocalizations you must work exactly as a dramatic actor works.

You must render an account to yourself about every note you sing. What is it for? What does it express?

It is not the business of the student-actor to brag about his high notes or about his ability to hold them almost indefinitely, so as to make sure of the applause of the audience. You need not worry: you will never excel Caruso.

Let us hope that your laughter is a sign that you will learn to sing so that the whole man in you sings and not only your vocal organ. Vocal, sound producing, machines are of no use either to the public or to culture; what we want is living people, singing artists.

We were looking for the ruling idea of the opera and we decided to define it as a punishment for the crime against nature, a punishment for violating it and disobeying the law of love. Now that we know the ruling idea, how are we to prepare the parts? How are we to look for the through-action of the part?

If you put a special interpretation on each word and phrase so as to make it conform to the ruling idea, what is likely to happen? What we shall get again is artificiality, dummies on which you will be trying to force a straitjacket labelled 'doom'.

A doomed face. An exaggeratedly serious, self-restrained gait, as if personified doom were walking on the stage. A languid look from under lowered eyelids. And, beginning with the very first phrase, a voice with a tragic cast.

In short, the moment the curtain rises there comes from the stage a breath of graveyard gloom, and not of joy, peace and glowing warmth of the cosy little house of the judge.

Again we get the dismal feeling of dark colours.

Never, never forget that if you want to show a villain, look for goodness in him. You want to show the catastrophic end of two charming human beings because they did not listen to the voice of nature and did not obey the call of love.

You ought therefore to show us vividly those moments in their lives which were full of joy and happiness. Show us how, when and where they were really happy; happy and joyful because they lived in obedience to nature, and not against it.

You must first of all pick out all the organic feelings from your part. On them you must build the whole of your plan and the whole of the framework of your part, and only then can you proceed to introduce into it all the accidental given circumstances.

But when will the organic feelings become for you the framework of your part and not just absorbing given circumstances which your reason has depicted for you? They will become that when in your heart too they find an echo, that is, when they become the *rhythm* of your heart. For it is only then that you will convey in the sounds of your singing voice all the deep creative powers which have been awakened in *you*. Now you cannot any longer either change, or reduce, or hide them. They are given in your part. Your awakened temperament has picked them up there. And you have made them your own in the harmonious work of the whole of your organism.

These feelings will be appropriate not only to you, the pair of the composer's heroes. They will be the creative powers which will find an echo and arouse pity in the whole of the auditorium. Every spectator will feel them in himself.

If you have brought about this union between yourself and him, it does not matter to the spectator whether or not you look like Apollo or whether or not you have a Roman nose. What matters to him is that your—Werther's—face is glowing with happiness, that your movements are quick and dexterous, and that the whole atmosphere surrounding Charlotte breathes peace and purity. The whole cumulative effect of these qualities already *speaks* to the spectator. You are already drawing him into your circle of life on the stage, though he may not have as yet heard a single note from you.

At the same time, however wonderful your outer image may be—your costume, wig and the whole external background, the whole beauty the producer has brought out on the stage—it will merely underline your helplessness, if you come out empty on the stage.

What are you, Charlotte and Werther, doing just now? You are observing each other. You are trying to know each other inwardly and to feel your proximity to each other. But you are trying so hard that there is no communion for your life in your part, but your exertion itself becomes your problem. Do not exert yourself to do anything. Observe each other more closely. Give yourselves only one problem: 'to feel the happiness of our meeting'.

Try to penetrate into each other's hearts with, as it were, invisible feelers—with rays from your hearts—asking yourselves, 'Is he glad to see me? Is she glad to see me?'

You are both in the bloom of youth. There is no question here of the doubts that beset people in their thirties. You believe each other implicitly. Neither of your characters knows the meaning of hypocrisy.

The tragic denouement is caused just because people whose feeling know no conflict, staunch and honest people, will never agree to accept even a small compromise, let alone reconcile themselves to the idea that 'she to another has been given'.

Try to visualise not the external circumstances of a small German town, but its inner life. Those limitations of a conventional education which impose no hardships on average people, but which the great hearts of Charlotte and Werther could not accept.

Why have you, Charlotte and Werther, assumed such heroic poses just now, and why are your voices so powerful? Your heroic struggle, Werther, is still to come. And your line of heroic struggle, Charlotte, will come when you are reading Werther's letters; it will be then that you will put into your first words such an inflexion of sorrow, that your voice will convey so great a tragedy of your heart and your whole life as a woman, crushed by the social convention of your environment, that the audience will immediately prick up its ears and become aware of your tragedy.

For the time being, however, you are merely living in the accustomed circumstances of your day. Today your, Charlotte's, life is just like your life on any other day.

You walk out arm in arm with Werther into this lovely moon-lit night. The whole day you, Charlotte, have behaved just as usual. You carried out your accustomed duties, which were expressed in a series of physical actions. Well, show us now in simple physical actions how you have spent your day. Charlotte's ordinary day. Very good. I did not expect to be shown Charlotte's early morning, but I am glad to know how Charlotte washes herself and combs her hair. All right. So Charlotte's love of the children occupies one of the most prominent places in her daily life. Her self-denying care for them. Then comes her care for her father and for the house, but the children occupy the first place. Charlotte has no time to think of herself.

So you have yourself found and shown us two organic qualities of Charlotte. Her love and self-denial became clear to us all from a number of simple physical actions. Now it should not be difficult for you to add to Charlotte's ordinary day the unusual excitement of her dressing for the ball: your last admonitions to the children and your own flurry of excitement, the agitation of the young daughter of a judge caused by the expectation of an entertainment that does not occur too often in her life.

On coming out on the stage in your ball dress, you cannot entirely cut yourself off from the life you have lived before your appearance on the stage. Your excitement was awakened before you came on the stage, and you presented it to the audience not as your excitement from the beginning of the performance, but as the result of the life of your entire being. There must be no gap in your mind between the wings and the stage. You did not just 'stand in the wings' waiting and feeling nervous in expectation of the music for your entrance. Your attention, having created the circle of public solitude, has placed all your feelings and thoughts within the framework of the rhythm of the music and the circumstances given in your part. Look intently into your heart. What is happening inside it? If you are nervous not because this is the problem of your part, but because of stage-fright, your circle of attention is in a sorry state! You do, in fact, make it certain that your voice will sound cold when you begin to sing.

If you are not entirely in the power of your *thought* and if your heart, in reply, does not beat in rhythm with it, then neither you nor the audience will ever be able to grasp the true meaning of the problems of your part. And it goes without saying that you will not be able to charm anyone with your acting of the character of your part.

What is the best way of avoiding stage-fright? Narrow the circle of your attention. Concentrate as much as you possibly can on your very first words and actions. Forget entirely about the rest of your part. The whole of his part never exists for an actor at his first entrance. All that he is conscious of is only that one minute and only that one problem in it. When you are preparing your part, your consciousness is aware of the whole of the man of the part. And you yourself are entirely full of it. But when the part has been transformed into the man-part—the I-part—then the life of its separate pieces begins. For because the man lives, we perceive him only as he is 'now', and not as he was yesterday, or as he will be tomorrow, or in an hour.

So, please, present Charlotte's entrance and her meeting with Werther in the whole amplitude of the feeling of the girl whose day you have so excellently shown us a short while ago.

Wait a moment, Werther! I just can't understand anything! Are your, Werther's, problems the same as Charlotte's? And where did you find sentimentality in the music? How many times did we go through the exercises in courage, and here you are overacting again. Why do you walk as though you were carrying a cut-glass chandelier? Try to find in yourself the thought concerning everything highest and noblest. Then you will also find the gait which will be characterised by courage and not crudity; animation and not hurry; gladness and not sentimentality. Take for your starting point the very ordinary feeling of gladness but do not give it its theatrical form, but show it just as you would show it in your own life.

The secret of your imagination lies in your creative problems— it is only *your* secret. And just because it is yours, and has not been imposed on you from outside, just because you share the creative love of Goethe and Massenet, you can yourself be inspired by this love, overcome the theatrical routine, enter into the real life of the stage, and draw the spectators after you by the force of your inner experience.

IV

When passing from one phrase in your part to another, that is to say, when you realise and feel the living inner problem, can you as Werther stand as you are standing now?

Charlotte is recalling the death of her mother. And we can plainly read on your face that what you are thinking of is how to take your cue in accordance with the music. You are nervousness personified.

If you are not able to switch over your attention to sympathy with the woman you love and if you cannot put to yourself the problem, 'I want to keep up her spirits by my courage', or 'I want to dispel her sad thoughts', then change your problem.

Divert your attention from what is worrying you now to something that might happen in the future and put to yourself a problem which could *justify* your apprehension now. For instance, 'I am afraid she is *going* to burst into tears', if, that is, you are generally afraid of women's tears. Or 'I want to share her horror of death with her'.

The important thing is that you should not for one moment be without some problem in your part. Not a single word of yours, not one single moment of your silence, should be an empty gap in which your 'I want to' does not live as an action.

You are now listening to Charlotte's speech in silence. But the music goes on and it binds the two of you together. There can be no *dead* pause for you while you are silent because you are subordinated to the music as much as your singing partner and all the rest of the performers on the stage.

Thought-word-sound is the whole man.

I am now addressing you while the others are silent, but all of us, each in his own way, feel one and the same thing, namely, that you are cross with me.

What have you got to do now to make it possible for you to enter more easily into a calm creative state? You must not try to force your subconsciousness too hard. You will only succeed in frightening it. If it is rudely assaulted, it usually retires beyond your grasp. Try to arouse your creative imagination so as to make it more vivid. Concentrate in the narrow circle of your attention. Fortunately the attention of every man possesses several different planes, and each plane does not interfere with the other. Habits usually become automatic actions. In your attention, too, a great deal can be made automatic. Never forget that attention is your tool for obtaining your creative material. An actor must be attentive not only on the stage, but also in life. He must *look* not like an ordinary absent-minded man, but penetrate into the very heart of what he happens to be seeing and observing. Without it the entire creative method of an actor will be one-sided and alien to the truth of life.

An actor must be able to discover the state of mind of the person he is talking to by his face, look and the timbre of his voice. He must be able to enter into his position and hear *truly*.

To begin with, an actor must try to see the beautiful in men and not the bad in them. In trying to learn how to see the beautiful, you must start by examining the most beautiful thing there is, namely nature. But make sure that you are looking for the beautiful and not for the pretty, sentimental and sweet. And it is not the actor's reason that observes the beautiful, but he is *all* inspired by everything that is happening round him; he is swept away by life as a whole; he tries to imprint on his mind whatever he sees not as a statistician, but as an artist, not for jotting it down in his note-book, but in his heart. It is impossible to work in art in a detached way. What you want is warmth, that is to say, you want the kind of attention that can be given shape and form through your feelings.

If your imagination is sluggish, you must jog it on. Put to yourself the questions: who, what, where, why and for what reason whatever you see on the stage is happening. Your observations of life itself are of the utmost importance. For life is that emotional material from which there arises in the actor, 'the life of the human spirit of the part', that is to say, that which constitutes the *fundamental* aim of art.

Analyse your attention and imagination, Werther.

You have now concentrated your thought on a simple physical

action, while preparing yourself for your entrance. Very well, if that is so what is it you have got to discard? Is there anything you do not want now? Is there any unnecessary strain in your body? Check up and see. Personally, I have the impression that you have drawn yourself up as though you were an officer standing on parade with a bared sword.

No, that will not do, either. Now you seem to have just come out of your bath. Now all of you can see for yourselves quite plainly how difficult it is to cast off the bad habits which you have acquired. You are all either sitting hunched up or sprawling all over the place while I am sitting straight. Judging by my age, it would seem that the opposite should have been the case.

What is your conception of a pause on the stage? You have just finished your aria. You have carried out all the pieces of your part and its problems with the utmost conciseness. You *were* Werther. But where has he disappeared to now? I don't see Werther, but a man who is happy to have sung his aria satisfactorily without having been interrupted once. But the music goes on; the sounds are still resounding. We are all sitting here entranced by the life you have created for us. Life goes on, but you are standing as though everything had come to an end. Come to an end, mind you, because you are no longer uttering a sound.

You could only have arrived at such a state after your aria if you had carried out the different pieces of your part and your problems *mechanically* when working them out with me. Your dissociation from the music would have been impossible if the emission of the rays of your energy you had put into your man-part were still taking place. Thanks to the sum-total of the facts arising from your musical temperament, your ear and your voice, you possess a *special* ability which the people who are listening to you do not possess. You can *merge into the music* by means of your action and you can supply it yourself by means of your action, that is to say, your singing. You may not possess Caruso's or Patti's voice, but you can all the same force an audience to listen to you and share your life in music. Why? Because the whole image of your part lives for you now *only* through your music. Your musical ability as well as the timbre of your voice are your own unique gift which unites you with the auditorium.

But this peculiarity of yours will not always be a bait for the spectator. If you *drop out* of the life of your part during the pauses, if you sing out of tune, forcing the musical people in your audience to squirm as though in pain, and if you do not take your eyes off the conductor and make mistakes in the music, you will not gain the interest of any one in the auditorium.

You must know your part inside out. You must train your voice so that each musical phrase should *always* be associated with definite thoughts and feelings. This, however, does not mean swotting up your part so that you know it by heart and can, like a siskin, whistle one and the same tune at any moment. It only means that you are a precious musical instrument, and that your voice is the strings over which you can at the same time move not one, but three magic bows: mind, heart and body. If your physical actions are right and you live in full harmony of mind and heart, you will always be a truthful reflection of life on the stage. And all that *energy* which brings your bows into action and makes your strings resound, is not only the rhythm of your respiration. It is respiration plus heart, plus the feelers of your thought, plus your musical ability; but even that is not all, for there are still alive in you your sense of proportion, tact and good taste.

All these forces live, move about, and act *before* your strings produce a sound. And inasmuch as any of your bows is more energetically exerted, so there arise *different* shades and colours in your problems and sounds.

The whole of you sings. And if your heart beats in unison with your physical action and both are illuminated by your thought, your face cannot grow wooden just because you have finished your aria. And you cannot possibly stop listening to the life of those who are singing while you are silent.

V

Let us return to the pause on the stage. A pause on the stage is the highest point of stage art. During your exercises in establishing mutual communication between those of you who are acting on the stage, you have become accustomed to change the objects of your attention and transfer it effortlessly from one object to another, in accordance with the dictates of your imagination. You cannot possibly fidget about while you present your attention with the profound problem, 'I want to know in what sort of a mood Charlotte is now', or, 'I want to find out from her whether she has been thinking of me'. Or if your attention is fixed on the fact that it is Christmas now. And she had told you to come back at Christmas. Then your problem ought to be, 'I want to make sure whether she has been waiting for me as passionately as I for her'.

Whatever your problem may have been, if in your heart and mind the rhythm is beating, 'to see her quickly, to know quickly', then your feet, hands, neck, head and eyes will involuntarily respond to you, everything will rush forward. But there will be no sign of any fidgeting here. This is not at all the same thing as your excitement when you are afraid to miss your train and are hurriedly packing your trunks and rushing from one thing to another, picking up your things in a hurry and throwing them anyhow into your trunk. You are now all of you just one impulse. You are *entirely* preoccupied with the idea of rushing forward.

How then will you be acting physically? You cannot possibly 'act' an impulse. You are too well trained for that.

Your whole temperament is rushing forward. You have to keep yourself back so that it shall not appear to the people of that *time*, that *class*, among whom you, Werther, live, that you are an abnormal young man. What sort of people are they? They are highly respectable people, serious, brought up with the prejudiced notions of a small provincial German town. If they see you rushing along the street, they will certainly take you for a madman.

Your entrance was good. The feelings which you kept under control for such a long time on your way, break loose at once before even you have time to cross the threshold. You *tear* into the house. Very well. There is nothing wrong with that.

But, please! You seem to have entirely forgotten that you are a sensible man, however much in love you may be. The music does not justify your acting like a madman. It gives you the opportunity of controlling your feelings. We, the audience, must see clearly the *logic* of your thoughts, the logic of the whole of your psychological problem of this moment of your part which conforms entirely to the music.

We have already discussed together on one occasion the differences between the state of mind of a normal and an abnormal man. Normal life—the line of attention (dash) and the interval during which the object seen is perceived, that is to say, a certain pause (dot), or in other words, dash-dot, dash-dot and so on. In an abnormal man there are only dashes. It is raining outside, a cat sits on the stove, a band is playing in the courtyard, there are flowers on the window-sill, and so on. Everything is attention, attention, attention, without any pause for perceiving the thing seen. Is there any confusion in the music at the moment? No. It is absolutely restrained.

You want to show us now only *one* side of yourself, only your attention, and, moreover, the attention on which you are wholly concentrated during your own speech. But have you forgotten the importance of those dots, those pauses, which separate your attention? Is the concentration of your attention on *them* less important in the *general* life of your part? Is it less active during your silence than during the time when you are speaking?

What is of greater importance so far as the spectators is concerned? The moment when the actor is speaking or singing or that *inner* reaction that takes place before their eyes on the stage as a *result* of the words spoken by the actor? 'The latter, of course', you reply yourself.

Why then do almost all of you act on the stage contrary to what you have just been saying?

Let us analyse your actions, Werther. You have rushed into Charlotte's room. Very well, I have nothing against that. The moment of so high a tension could at any time take the form of such an ungovernable impetuosity of the whole of your organism. A heart in a storm! How is one to control one's feet, hands, or eyes in such a state? Your lips tremble, one can hardly hear your 'Yes, it's me!'

But let us go on. How do you behave after having seen and realised the frightened and confused state of the woman, of the Charlotte you are in love with and into whose house you have rushed so violently? You are an educated man, a man of the world, a man who is used to the society of ladies, that is to say, who possesses civility, courage and strength. And you can't manage a bow, a smile, a tender look for the woman you love? Is it natural to freeze like that at the door? If you had seen Charlotte lying dead in the room, I could have understood and justified your petrified pose. But now there is no reason for your petrified state. And how long do you intend standing there like that? A minute? Two minutes? Five minutes? Half an hour?

An actor is a man-part, that is to say, you-Werther are a living man. Could you possibly have lost the sense of the passing moment of the life of your part so completely as to discard entirely all the 'given circumstances' of the scene?

You rushed into the room and stopped dead. I can understand that. Charlotte looks disconcerted. I understand that, too. The storm of your two hearts has made you both forget the rules of behaviour of educated people. But the life of the stage goes on in rhythm with the beating of the hearts of all the living people on it. Where is the rhythm of this passing moment? Where are you to look for help? In the music. Listen to it and pick up its rhythm.

Seek in the music the new link with action. You have again to re-establish your unity with Charlotte because at this moment while standing motionless so long in contradiction to the music, you have dissociated yourself from your inner life with your partner. The pause has become not the continuation of your action, but an end in itself. You are entirely preoccupied with the thought of how to keep up this pause as an external effect. You, X, are interested in the picturesqueness of your pose, but you are not Werther. For so far as Werther is concerned, there could not be for him a single moment during which he would

at this time of inner storm have dissociated himself from Charlotte. Everything, all the objects that fill the room, once so
familiar and so dear to you, the harpsichord, the furniture, the
candle-sticks, the books, everything is Charlotte. And only
Charlotte.

Having found yourself in the once familiar and still dear surroundings, you, Werther, can now say to yourself, 'I am', that
is to say, you have already placed yourself in the very centre of
the conditions given you by your part. You live in the very
midst of the life created by your imagination. You begin to act
in your own name, in accordance with the dictates of your own
conscience and your feeling of apprehension. And you at once
pass from your first problem, 'I want to see her immediately',
to a new 'I want to'. This new 'I want to' arose quite normally,
because your, Werther's, life is moving on, and now it is already
different.

Now your consecutive problems are, 'I want to know what
place I occupy in her heart now', 'I want to convince myself that
there is still a chance of happiness for me', 'I want to believe
that there is no need for me to die'.

Charlotte's problems, complementary to yours, are, 'I want to
calm him'; 'I want to do my duty', 'I want to save myself and
conceal my agitation', 'I want our meeting to pass within the
limits of propriety', 'I want to drive away the terrible phantom
of death'.

As you see from the course of events in the opera, Charlotte's
thoughts are always occupied with Werther, in the same way as
Werther's thoughts are always fixed on Charlotte. She cannot
run away from them, in spite of her sense of duty which she
cannot shake off however hard she tries. And 'doom' lies in wait
for her as surely as it lies in wait for Werther.

Do not look for complicated problems. The more complicated
you make them, the more difficult you will find them to understand.

Present simply and concisely only one problem for each piece
of your part. 'I want to free myself from the horror of my
sorrow'. For it will be this desire to free yourself from your unbearable torments that will lead you to suicide in the end.

Divide up each piece of your part into a number of simple problems. Observe the sudden change in Charlotte, how her cheeks have lost colour, how her eyes have grown large. And where is the little mole on her face which you loved so much? Call to mind vividly some happy moment in your lives.

Nearer and nearer, as though through some veil, you begin to distinguish the features which were so dear to you formerly. Your thoughts and your attention grow sharper. You do not notice yourself how your memories—the memories which were so familiar to you in your past—have come to life. Now you are already standing beside the harpsichord; now you are holding your favourite book in your hands.

You lived every minute in the music, and it awakened in you the memories of your former happiness. You forgot about yourself as a personality. You are only Werther. You built the rhythm of your life in your part on the rhythm of the music. You are entranced by the memories of your past. And we no longer see before us the Werther who had rushed into Charlotte's house like an avalanche, but the pure love of two people, revived with renewed force, a noble love which has enticed us, the spectators too, into its orbit.

We, the audience, have no time now to distinguish what was more vivid: your pause or your words. But you can tell us yourself what was more important in the life of your part: your singing or your silence. You have not of course noticed either the words or the pauses as a self-sufficient force. The one as well as the other were in equal measure the expression of the life of your man-part.

Now, I think you see that it is impossible to 'act' a pause as it is impossible to 'act feeling'. So far as the life of the actor on the stage is concerned, there exists no pause that can be acted in a conventional way, that is to say, there exists no spiritual inaction.

If during someone's aria you on the stage are considering how to show your profile to the audience to the best advantage, or if you deliberately show your pretty foot because you know that it is your best asset, or if you are simply looking at the audience and thinking absent-mindedly what a mess your partner is making of his singing, we, the audience, immediately feel that you have dropped out of your part, which for an actor is equivalent to death on the stage.

Quite possibly your partner does sing badly today, but he is happy or unhappy in accordance with the demands of his part and there is such truth to life in the sounds of his voice that the audience does not even remember whether his voice is good or bad, or indeed, what sort of voice he has. The audience is carried away by the suffering or the happiness of the singer. It *lives*. While you, who have dropped out of your part and are criticising, are dead among the living crowd in the auditorium.

For the audience the actions on the stage have already become life. You yourself a minute ago helped to create this life and forced us to fall under its spell.

Who then has interrupted this life for us now? You have. You have broken the chain that unites the actors and the audience. How are you to correct your mistake? How are you to enter the life of the stage again and solder the broken chain together? This is as difficult for an actor to do as to revive his dead feelings. You have died as a man-part and are now living like any ordinary man. Hence, it is your job to start all over again. Once again create your circle of attention. Seek refuge in the small circle of public solitude. Narrow down your problem and your circle of attention as much as possible.

How can you do it?

Listen, listen with redoubled attention, to your partner's words. Look at what he is doing. And enter into *his* part entirely.

Now you have yourself realised from the example of your own absent-mindedness the utmost importance of the pause on the stage. You can't imagine how lucky you, opera singers, are. The music depicts for you all the contours of the movements and the stops of your parts. The statics and dynamics and their rhythm— all is given to you.

How much more difficult does the actor in a play find every- thing. He has to create everything for himself. He has to grasp the musical cadence of the poet's speech. He has to grasp it in a different way in each author, in accordance with his indivi- duality. He has to guess the rhythm of each word. He has to be composer, co-author, and performer rolled into one.

But for you all the limits of the given circumstances of your parts have been noted down and put into a ready-made rhythm. This is the same as presenting you with a house all ready to move into. All you have to do is to light it, warm it, and fill it with the charm and nobility of your heart in thought-word-sound.

Appendices

APPENDIX I

STAGE ETHICS

The question of stage ethics occupied Stanislavsky all his life. Already at the beginning of his career, during his first meeting with Nemirouich-Danchenko in June, 1897, when the main principles of the future Moscow Art Theatre had been formulated, they discussed theatrical ethics and included a number of 'aphorisms' about them in the agreement they signed after their eighteen-hour-talk. 'There are no small parts, there are only small actors', was one of these aphorisms. 'Every violation of the creative art of the theatre is a crime', was another. Much later in his life Stanislavsky was often heard to say that perhaps what the theatre needed most was a book on stage ethics, 'but', he usually added, 'I don't think I shall have time to write it'.

Stanislavsky never wrote the book, but he left a number of notes among his papers from which we can obtain a pretty clear idea of what he thought of this subject. Broadly speaking, Stanislavsky considers the problem of stage ethics from three angles: (1) the actor's behaviour in the theatre; (2) the actor's behaviour outside the theatre; and (3) the relations between the artistic and the administrative sides of a theatre.

The fact that the theatre so often forfeits its position as a temple of art, Stanislavsky thinks, is due chiefly to the actors themselves. For it is the actors who are in the majority of cases responsible for the introduction of every kind of abomination into the theatre, such as gossip, intrigues, slander, envy, and selfish ambitions. Stanislavsky, therefore, warns the actors that to wash their dirty linen in public is uncivilised, for it not only shows a singular lack of self-control and complete disrespect towards their surroundings, but is also a sign of egoism, general carelessness, and bad habits.

Stanislavsky, in fact, cannot find words strong enough to condemn unethical behaviour in the theatre, particularly as in the

287

theatre he has in mind everything depends on the collective work of the ensemble (he was always an outspoken opponent of the 'star' system), and those who interfere with it 'commit a crime not only against their colleagues, but also against the art which they serve'. Actors must therefore think more of others than of themselves, for only then is a wholesome atmosphere possible in the theatre, an atmosphere in which all bad feeling would disappear and all small worries be forgotten. Every actor would be glad to work under such conditions, and this readiness on his part to give his best to the stage is the best possible preparation of the ground for his creative state of mind when he starts working in earnest. Hence every actor, according to Stanislavsky, must observe the precept: 'Love art in yourself, and not yourself in art'.

It follows that the struggle for pre-eminence among actors and producers, jealousy of a successful fellow-actor, and rating of people according to the salaries or the parts they get, is a great evil. And no fine words, such as 'let the best man win', can disguise the fact that they are often used as an excuse for envy and intrigue which poison the atmosphere of the theatre.

Unfortunately, such unethical behaviour is rather common even among actors who have reached the top of the ladder in their profession. 'I myself', Stanislavsky writes, 'have heard two famous actresses addressing one another in the choicest Billingsgate not only behind the scenes, but also on the stage itself. I know of two well-known actors who refuse to make their entrances through the same door. I have been told of a famous actor who never talked to a famous actress at a rehearsal, but addressed his remarks to her always through the producer. "Tell her", the actor used to say, "that she's talking through her hat". And the actress, also speaking to the producer, replied, "Tell him he's a damn fool!" To such depths do actors descend if they do not get the better of their bad instincts. Let this be a warning and a lesson to every actor!'

How is discipline then to be enforced in the theatre? This is obviously a very important question, for nothing undermines discipline so much as the unethical behaviour of actors. To begin with, Stanislavsky points out that a healthy atmosphere in the theatre is only possible if the authority of the people who are in charge of it is generally recognised. 'If the director of a theatre does not enjoy proper authority', Stanislavsky writes, 'the work of the theatre will sooner or later come to a standstill'. On the other hand, the enforcement of formal discipline from above is certain to do untold harm. About this Stanislavsky had no doubts at all, and here, as in many other things, he merely followed the tradition established by the great Russian playwright Alexander Ostrovsky, who considered real stage discipline as vital to the success of a play. 'Without discipline there is no stage art', Ostrovsky used to say, which, he added, did not mean ordering the actors about, 'for no producer', Ostrovsky claimed, 'will ever get what is required from the actors, that is, talent and feeling, by ordering them about'. Such a crude conception of discipline, Ostrovsky thought, was only justifiable in the case of extras, for, as he put it, 'from a crowd only the outward manifestation of truth is required'. This was also Stanislavsky's opinion. The best way for those in authority in a theatre to enforce their will on the actors, Stanislavsky maintained, was by following the old precept, 'Physician, heal thyself', and trying to convince the actor by their own example. A healthy atmosphere in the theatre, then, can never, according to Stanislavsky, be created by rules and regulations, nor can it be imposed, as it were, 'wholesale'. Here only the personal 'touch' will be found to be of any practical use. Patience, self-control, firmness, and composure are the qualities a man who wishes to exercise any authority in the theatre must possess above all. In addition, he must have faith in people and trust them. He must believe that in his heart of hearts every man is striving to do good, and that once he has learned to distinguish between good and bad, he will always choose the first, because in the end good always gives more satisfaction than bad. Having, therefore, first approached every actor in the company and explained to him what is required of him and why it is required of him, the director or producer can then be as firm, exacting, and strict as he pleases. It would be a mistake, though, to force the pace; indeed, if a director of a theatre succeeds during the first year in forming a small group of five or six people who know what is required of them and are eager to carry it out, he will have gone a long way to obtain the kind of self-imposed discipline that is so necessary for the successful work of a theatre.

'There are many people in responsible positions in the theatre who are very sincere in their pursuit of the art of drama', Stanislavsky writes, 'but who are also very fervent adherents of the principle of "iron discipline" which is so characteristic of the commercial theatre. But how can such people who want to apply the ideas of discipline they derive from their office experience to actors, be expected to run a theatre if they have not the faintest idea of the great spiritual treasures true actors contribute to their work or of what a nerve-racking business an actor's work is! How can we get rid of these "business men" in the theatre? How are we to find people who understand and, above all, *feel* what the real work of an actor is and how has one to deal with him?'

As for crowd scenes, Stanislavsky, as already mentioned, is in complete agreement with Ostrovsky. 'Crowd scenes', he writes, 'demand quite exceptional discipline at rehearsals. They must be placed, as it were, under martial law. And no wonder. For a producer may sometimes have to deal with a crowd of several hundred people, and he could hardly be expected to do it without military discipline. If only one extra is late, or if he fails to follow the example of the actors and make a careful note of the producer's instructions, or if he talks when he should have listened, he may be responsible for all sorts of irritating delays involving the repetition of a whole rehearsal and unnecessary trouble for those who were doing their work conscientiously. Nor must it be forgotten that rehearsals of crowd scenes are extremely fatiguing both for producers and extras. That is why it is so desirable that such rehearsals should be both brief and productive. And this demands the strictest possible discipline. Therefore, as under martial law, every misdemeanour must be regarded as being a hundred times more reprehensible and must be punished accordingly. For if only a few people miss the rehearsal of a mutiny scene, where all the extras have to shout at the top of their voices and move about all the time, the whole scene can very easily be ruined. It is not so much the duty of the producer, however, as of the extras themselves to make sure that those members of a crowd scene whose discipline is slack are immediately called to account and taught to behave themselves'.

But the ethics of the stage cover a much wider field than that of fostering a sense of responsibility and a feeling of goodwill among the actors. An actor who in his anxiety to make a career for himself forgets his great mission as a creator and a preacher of the beautiful, Stanislavsky declares, is unworthy of it and degrades it. 'The stage', he writes in his journals, 'is a blank piece of paper and can serve both the high and the low ideals of humanity, according as to what is shown on it and who appears on it. Only think of the things that have been presented in front of the footlights! There were on the one hand the wonderful and unforgettable performances of Salvini, Yermolova, and Duse, and on the other the *café-chantant* with its indecencies, pornographic farces, and music-hall items, presenting a strange mixture of art and skill, trapeze acts, juggling, clowning, and low self-display. Where is one to draw the line between what is beautiful and what is hideous? Oscar Wilde was right in saying that an actor is either a high-priest or a clown. Actors ought therefore to search all their lives for the demarcation line between the good and the bad in our art. Not everything that glitters on the stage is gold. Many actors devote their lives to the service of the bad without realising it because they are unable to estimate correctly the influence of their acting on an audience. Indiscrimination and lack of principle in our art have brought about the decay of the theatre both in our country and abroad. It is only that that prevents the theatre from assuming the high position and acquiring the importance in social life to which it is entitled. I am saying this not because I am a puritan in our art. Heaven knows I am broadminded enough so far as the theatre is concerned. I like gaiety and a joke as well as any man'.

As for the actor's behaviour outside the theatre, it was Stanislavsky's opinion that he should 'unbutton himself' only in his intimate family circle. 'Owing to the very nature of our art', he writes, 'an actor is a member of a large and highly complex organisation, in whose name he daily appears before thousands of spectators. Millions of people read about his work and about the activities of the theatre in which he is employed. His name is so closely connected with that of his theatre that it is often impossible to separate them. Besides, both the artistic and the private life of an actor are inseparably associated in people's minds with his theatre. Hence, if an actor of the Maly Theatre, or the Moscow Art Theatre, or any other theatre has been guilty of any reprehensible act, then whatever excuses he makes or whatever explanations he publishes in the press, he will never be able to remove the stain or shadow he has thrown upon the good name of the theatre and its company. This obliges the actor to behave himself with dignity outside the walls of his theatre and protect its name not only on the stage, but also in his private life'.

There still remains the problem of a genius whose moral code leaves much to be desired, and Stanislavsky tries to find a solution for it by suggesting that the other members of the company in which the great man is acting should do their best to render his faults harmless. 'When such a dangerous microbe appears in the theatre,' he writes, 'all the other members of the company must be inoculated against it, so that the intrigues of the genius should not interfere with the general welfare of the theatre'. And in reply to the objection that in that case a theatrical company would have to consist entirely of saints, Stanislavsky contends that an actor cannot be expected to carry on a humdrum existence outside the theatre and then go on the stage and play the sublime characters of a Shakespeare. 'It is quite true', he writes, 'that there are many actors who have sold themselves to Mammon and are still able to thrill and enchant an audience. But these are geniuses who have sunk to the level of philistines, though their talent is so great that during their creative work they forget all the petty things of life. But, after all, not every actor can do this sort of thing and get away with it. A genius gets his inspiration 'from above' while the ordinary actor has to devote every moment of his life to obtain the same result. Besides, it is a mistake to attempt to follow the example of a genius who is quite a different sort of human being and does things in quite a different sort of way. Many fantastic stories are told about the dissipated lives of such geniuses, but when one examines the lives of actors like Shchepkin, Yermolova, Duse, and Salvini, and many others like them, one finds that they led quite different lives which could well be emulated by many of our own home-bred geniuses'.

And to prove his point, Stanislavsky recounts the following experience he had with one 'home-bred' genius:

'I cannot forget the bitter disappointment a famous actor made me feel when I was a young man. I shall not mention his name because I do not want to cast any slur on his memory. I had just seen him give an unforgettable performance, and so great was the impression it had made on me that I felt I simply had to talk it over with someone. So instead of going home, I went to a restaurant with a friend, and imagine our delight when in the midst of our discussion the great man himself came into the restaurant. We could not restrain ourselves and went up to him and told him how much we had admired his acting that night. The celebrity invited us to have dinner with him in a private room, where under our very eyes he proceeded to get blind drunk. The rottenness of his character came through the thin veneer of his reputation and took the form of the most horrible bragging, self-conceit, gossip, and intrigue. And to cap it all, he refused to pay for the drinks he himself had ordered. My friend and I had to economise a long time afterwards to defray the unexpected expense we had incurred. But we had the great privilege of taking our belching and blaspheming idol back to his hotel where they at first refused to let him in because of the disgusting state he was in'.

It would be a mistake, however, to imagine that the ethics of the stage applied only to actors and producers. Everyone engaged in the theatre, beginning with the commissionaire, the cloak-room attendant, the man in the box-office, and programme-seller, and ending with the men who are in charge of its administration, must realise that he is its servant and that he too contributes to its success. Anyone who in one way or another interferes with the smooth running of a theatre, Stanislavsky declares emphatically, must be regarded as its enemy. If the commissionaire, the cloakroom attendant, or the ticket-collector is disrespectful to the spectators and spoils their mood by his bad manners, he does harm to the cause of theatrical art in general. It the theatre is cold and dirty or if the performance starts late and is given without enthusiasm, it has a depressing effect on the playgoer with the result that the basic idea and feeling of the playwright as well as of the actors and producers do not reach him, which means that he has wasted his time in coming to the theatre and that the theatre has forfeited its position as an important social and artistic institution.

'While the playwright and the actor create the necessary mood on our side of the footlights', Stanislavsky writes, 'the administration of the theatre ought to create a corresponding mood for the playgoer in the auditorium and for the actors in the dressing-rooms. For it must not be forgotten that the spectator too takes an active part in the performance and that he too, like the actor, must be in the right mood to receive the basic idea of the playwright or composer and the impressions he wants to convey'.

Stanislavsky goes on to discuss the question of the antagonism between the artistic and the administrative sides of a theatre, 'a usual phenomenon in the life of a theatre', and demands that 'the office' should be put in its place. 'It is not the office', he writes, 'but the stage that gives life to art and the theatre; it is not the office but the stage that brings in the playgoing public and confers popularity and fame on the theatre; it is not the office but the stage that creates an impression on the spectators and is of immense educational value to society; it is not the office but the stage that brings in the money, etc. But', Stanislavsky continues, 'just try and tell this to an *entrepreneur* or a theatre manager or indeed any office employee and he will fly into a rage at such rank heresy: so firmly has the notion that the theatre's success depends solely on them and their administration taken root in their consciousness. It is they who decide whether to pay or not to pay, whether to put on one play or another; it is they who pass the estimates and decide what salaries to pay or what fines to impose; it is they who give fine receptions, who have luxurious offices, and who employ a huge staff which some-times eats up the greater part of a theatre's budget; it is they who are satisfied or dissatisfied with the success of a performance or of an actor, and it is they who distribute the complimentary tickets; it is they who walk importantly through the theatre and accept the humble greetings of the actors; it is they who are a terrible pest in the theatre and the oppresssors and destroyers of art. No words are strong enough', Stanislavsky declares, 'to express my detestation and loathing of these all too common types of office bosses of the theatre, these impudent exploiters of the work of the actors. Since time immemorial the office, taking advantage of the peculiarity of our nature, has been persecuting the actors. Always immersed in their creative dreams, over-worked, their nerves constantly on edge, highly sensitive, un-balanced, and easily depressed, the actors are often quite helpless outside the theatre. They seem to have been created to be ex-ploited, particularly as, giving everything they possess to the stage, they have no strength left for the defence of their human rights'.

It is the duty of the administration of a theatre, Stanislavsky maintains, to make the life of the actor in the theatre as pleasant as possible. That is the greatest contribution that the administra-tion can make to the creative business of the theatre. Order, quiet, and the absence of fuss in the dressing-rooms, for instance, exert a great influence on the formation of the creative state of the actor on the stage. 'It is in this sphere', Stanislavsky writes, 'that the people employed on the administrative side of a theatre are in close touch with the most intimate and important aspects of our creative life and can be of the greatest possible assistance to the actor. Indeed, good order means everything to the actor, for it helps him to concentrate on his work, and makes it possible for the spectator to get the best out of it, too. But if, on the con-trary, the atmosphere on the stage and in the auditorium irritates the actor and the spectator, if it interferes with them, gets on their nerves, and makes them angry, then the actor's creative work and its appreciation by the spectator become impossible. Worse still, sensing the disorder behind the scenes, the spectator becomes noisy, and begins talking and, especially, coughing during the performance, and there can be no greater calamity for an actor', Stanislavsky observes, 'than a coughing audience'.

'But to train the playgoer to behave in a disciplined way', Stanislavsky writes, 'to force him to be in his seat before the beginning of the performance, and to be attentive and make no

noise or cough during it, it is first of all necessary that the
theatre should have gained his respect and made him feel that
he has to behave decently. If the whole atmosphere of the theatre,
however, does not correspond to the high purpose of our art, then
the actor is faced with a task that is quite beyond his strength,
namely, the task of getting the better of the spectator and com-
pelling him to pay attention to what is happening on the stage'.

APPENDIX II

MELODRAMA:

A STANISLAVSKY IMPROVISATION

Every theatrical genre, including melodrama, exerted a peculiar fascination on Stanislavsky who was, above all, a great man of the theatre. His views on the nature of melodrama and on the way to play it have just been published in a book of reminiscences of Stanislavsky by N. Gorchakov, a producer of the Moscow Art Theatre. In 1927 Gorchakov was responsible for the production of an adaptation of an old French melodrama, *The Sisters Gerard*, under the supervision of Stanislavsky, and his account takes the form of a shorthand report with comments of one of the rehearsals at which Stanislavsky was present and during which he demonstrated the importance of improvisation in this type of play.

'Every stage genre', Stanislavsky is reported to have said during that rehearsal, 'demands a special approach by the producer to his work with the actors. To begin with, the producer must see that during the rehearsal of a melodrama both he and the actors are carried away by the strong situations in the play. On no account, for instance, must a rehearsal be stopped because an actor may have to be instructed how to play a certain scene. Special hours are to be set aside for such instruction. During the rehearsal itself, however, the producer must give the actor as much freedom as possible. He must set the actor interesting problems, and he must try to discover with him how a man lives and what he does in the extraordinary situations of a melodrama. Let the producer always look out for the life of the human spirit and help the actor to express it in simple but strong forms'.

In a melodrama, Stanislavsky points out, actors must be ready to believe absolutely everything. They must accept anything the writer has invented as having really happened. For it is only then

297

that the spectator will believe them. If, on the other hand, the actor is always, as it were, giving the audience a knowing look, if, that is, he wants it to be generally understood that neither his words nor his actions are to be taken seriously today because he is playing in a melodrama, but that it will be quite a different matter tomorrow when he will be appearing in a straight play, then the spectator will be bored whatever the horrors and however wonderful the stage effects.

Nor must the actor or producer overlook or underestimate the importance of humour in a melodrama, where an audience is very often expected to laugh at as well as to despise the villain and be horrified by his evil deeds. It is futhermore important that the first act of a melodrama should immediately create a feeling of suspense in the audience. A great actor appearing in a melodrama will always play a game of hide-and-seek with his subject: he tries to deceive the spectator as much as he can by *disguising* his true character. It is only his imitators among the less talented actors who prefer the more direct way of making the villain look villainous and his victim handsome and attractive. In melodrama great actors are also great masters of the art of inner dialogue. They can sit without moving a muscle or making a gesture, but the spectator can see that they are seething with excitement, and this excitement the great actor knows how to convey mainly through his eyes.

Indeed, it is only a great actor, Stanislavsky maintains, who is able to make a melodrama into a success. A second-rate actor cannot play in a melodrama, because in melodrama an actor has to improvise a great deal, and second-rate actors do not possess sufficiently vivid personalities to carry it off, nor do they possess the ability to add something essential to their parts. In the past, writers of melodrama always relied on the actor's talent to make their play come to life. Even the best of them were bad play-wrights and even worse psychologists, but they possessed a perfect sense of the theatre and they knew the secret of creating an impression on an audience. They were, in short, men of the theatre, and they wrote their plays for hundreds of thousands of spectators and not for a select band of aesthetes.

It is not true, Stanislavsky goes on to assert, that melodrama has always been given in bad theatres by bad actors. A famous melodrama is only created once. It is either born on the first night or dies on the first night and is never remembered again. That is why the birth of a melodrama always depends on the participation of great actors, and that is also the reason why its production is always so lavish. Indeed, the first night of a melodrama is a very expensive affair. If successful, a melodrama usually enjoys a very long run at the theatre where it was first put on. After that, however, all the theatres in the world copy the first production, and the actors in these theatres do their best to copy the actors of the original production from descriptions they have either heard or read. In fact, the whole production, planning, and sets of the play are faithful copies of the original production.

The actors must make their actions very interesting in a melodrama, Stanislavsky insists. 'That is why', he declares, 'I consider melodrama a very useful training ground for young actors; for it develops their faith in what they are doing, their naivety and the sincerity of their feelings, and it comples them to think out for themselves the different ways of making any action suggested by the author as interesting and as thrilling as possible. And to make an action interesting means not to make it as the spectator expects the actor to make it'.

Melodrama presents ordinary life in a highly concentrated form, omitting any unnecessary details and pauses. In watching a melodrama, the spectator must be convinced that whatever he is shown in the play has actually happened in life and not on the stage. That is why all stage conventions are contrary to the spirit of melodrama. And if the spectator can be made actually to believe that what is happening on the stage is happening in life a few paces away from him, he will be moved to an extent that is quite unusual in the theatre and will burst into laughter and tears. Laughter is quite a normal reaction of a spectator who has been deeply moved, provided, that is, it has been provoked by a character or a situation on the stage, and not by some crude gesture. As for stage effects in melodrama, the spectator, Stanislavsky observes, is only interested in them before and after the play. During the performance itself, however, they have to be so ideally fitted in and so well justified that the spectator should never notice them. Melodrama, in fact, is always illusory in the best sense of the word.

Melodrama becomes particularly popular, Stanislavsky remarked at the conclusion of the rehearsal, when the spectator is overflowing with noble sentiments which he has somehow or other to express. 'After the revolution', he added—and here, unconsciously perhaps, Stanislavsky seems to have hit the nail on the head so far as the character of Soviet drama in the first ten years after the revolution is concerned—'our people too are so full of noble aspirations and feelings that they want to see the same fine and strong feelings and noble actions on the stage'.

The need for improvisation in melodrama was demonstrated by Stanislavsky at the rehearsal of *The Sisters Gerard* in a short scene from the play which he first played with an actor who could not improvise and next with an old actor who was as good at the game as himself. (The play was put on by the Moscow Art Theatre during the 1927-28 season.)

The scene, which Stanlisavsky played first according to the script and then by improvisation, was one in which the villain, a disguised police agent by the name of Piccard, is trying to drop a sleeping powder into the glass of Uncle Martin, an old man who is waiting for the arrival of his two nieces, the heroines of the melodrama, from Normandy. In the first sketch Stanislavsky played the old man, and in the second the police agent. The scene is a cafe in Paris, and the name of the young actor playing against Stanislavsky in the first sketch was Verbitsky.

VERBIYSKY (*enters*): Well, grandpa, are you waiting for someone?

STANISLAVSKY: Eh? Oh—yes—yes. I'm waiting for someone.

VERBITSKY: I think I can hear the coach.

STANISLAVSKY: How do you know I'm waiting for the Normandy coach? (*Stanislavsky says this in a very suspicious voice, though there is no stage direction to that effect. The new 'colour' of adaptation creates a very interesting situation on the stage*).

VERBITSKY (*who did not expect this suspicious intonation, involuntarily replies in his own words*): Why, no. I—er—I'm just—er—guessing. People always wait for the coach here. As a matter of fact, I'm waiting for it, too. (*He then goes on according to the text.*) Won't you have a glass of cider with me?

STANISLAVSKY (*with the quite unexpected eagerness of a man who is fond of drinking*): Thank you, sir. I'd be glad to.

VERBITSKY: Two glasses of old cider, landlord! May I ask who you're waiting for? Is it for your wife? (*Produces the sleeping powder stealthily from his pocket*).

STANISLAVSKY (*again his suspicion aroused*): Yes, sir, my wife— my wife—perhaps someone else too.

The glasses of cider are placed on the table. Verbitsky is waiting for Stanislavsky to bend down to put straight the buckle of his shoe so that he should meanwhile put the sleeping powder in his glass. But Stanislavsky does not bend down, although the producer prompts him, 'Uncle Martin bends down to put straight the buckle of his shoe'.

VERBITSKY (*after an involuntary pause*): To your health, sir!

STANISLAVSKY: Thank you, sir, thank you. Oh, if only I'd been younger—stronger—

VERBITSKY (*looks embarrassed, the sleeping powder still in his hand, but he has to carry on with his dialogue*): What do you want to be stronger for? You're as fit as a fiddle.

STANISLAVSKY: Fit as a fiddle, am I? No, sir, I'm not the man I was. Feeling drowsy when it's much too soon to go to bed. Much too soon. Getting old, that's the truth of it. But I shan't go to sleep, sir. I shall not go to sleep!

Stanislavsky says it in so cheerful and confident a voice that it becomes quite clear that he does not dream of going to sleep as required by the play. There is no more dialogue left for Uncle Martin and Piccard, and the scene comes to an end.

VERBITSKY (*in his natural tone*): That's all!

STANISLAVSKY (*still acting the old man*): What's all?

VERBITSKY: I've no more dialogue. We've come to the end of the scene, sir.

STANISLAVSKY: But why didn't you drug me?

VERBITSKY: How could I if you didn't let me slip the powder into your glass?

STANISLAVSKY: But 'if' Uncle Martin had refused to drink his cider, what would Piccard have done?

VERBITSKY: I suppose he would have thought of something. Drugged him some other way.

STANISLAVSKY: Then why didn't you do it when you saw that I was not going to drink the cider?

VERBITSKY: But the script, sir, says 'He drugs him by slipping something in his glass'.

STANISLVASKY: That must have been what they did at the first performance. The text of a melodrama is usually a faithful reproduction of its first performance. You should never try to carry out the stage directions of a melodrama literally. That is, very unoriginal for a melodrama, in which, according to tradition, the actors are entirely at liberty to carry out all the physical actions in their own way, though always in accordance with the demands of the plot and the logic of the actions. Let's play this scene again.

Stanislavsky and Verbitsky play this scene again, and Verbitsky very cleverly slips the powder into Stanislavsky's glass, but at the last moment Stanislavsky unexpectedly pushes the glass off the table without drinking the cider.

VERBITSKY: But if Old Martin refuses to drink, we can't carry on with the play.

STANISLAVSKY: You think so? I'm afraid that means that your imagination is not working properly. All the stage direction says is 'Drugs him', but it does not really force us to drug him in a certain way, which means that Uncle Martin need not drink the cider if he doesn't want to. You see, Piccard should have prepared all sorts of alternative ways in which he could get rid of the old fellow.

VERBITSKY: Well, I really don't know what more I could have done.

STANISLAVSKY: All right, let me play the part of Piccard.

Stanislavsky asks Mikhailov, an old and experienced actor, to play the scene with him again. This time both of them are improvising the text. Stanislavsky begins and Mikhailov replies in the right 'tone'.

STANISLAVSKY: Nice evening—

MIKHAILOV: Yes, sir. Very nice evening, indeed.

STANISLAVSKY (*pretending to take out a snuffbox*): Will you take a pinch of snuff, sir? (*It is clear to the spectators, who know from the preceding scene that Piccard has been ordered by the Com-*

missioner of Police to get Uncle Martin out of the way, that the snuff had been drugged).

MIKHAILOV: No, thank you, sir. Don't take snuff.

STANISLAVSKY (*puts back snuffbox after pretending to take a pinch himself*): Would you care for a smoke?

MIKHAILOV: No, thank you. I don't smoke.

STANISLAVSKY (*aside*): Damn the old fool! I'll have to treat him to a glass of cider! (*Aloud*). Won't you have a drink with me, sir?

MIKHAILOV: Well, I don't mind if I do, though it doesn't seem right somehow, does it? I mean, accepting a drink from a stranger.

STANISLAVSKY: Landlord, two ciders! Are you waiting for someone?

MIKHAILOV: Me? No, not really. No one in particular, I mean. My two nieces may be arriving.

The landlord puts the two glasses of cider on the table. Just then Stanislavsky takes a silver coin out of his pocket and pretends to drop it accidentally on the floor. All the three of them naturally bend down to look for it. Suddenly Stanislavsky's hand raises itself slowly from the side of the table under which they are all looking for the coin, and this hand slips something from a piece of paper into Uncle Martin's glass. But the moment he sits up again, Mikhailov quite unexpectedly pulls a very suspicious face and stares in silence for a minute or two at the glasses of cider on the table.

MIKHAILOV: May I have your glass, sir? Your glass, please.

STANISLAVSKY (*is taken aback for a second, as no doubt even the real Piccard would have been taken aback by such a request*): What for?

MIKHAILOV: Oh, I'd just like to have a look at it, if you don't mind, sir.

STANISLAVSKY: I don't mind, I'm sure.

Mikhailov puts the two glasses side by side, gazes at them for a long time, and then says solemnly—

MIKHAILOV: My glass is fuller than yours, sir, and seeing that you're treating me, you really ought to have the fuller one. That's customary, sir.

STANISLAVSKY: I never heard of such a custom!

Appendix II: Melodrama

MIKHAILOV: If you won't accept my glass, sir, I'm not going to drink at all. (*He pushes the drugged glass of cider towards Stanislavsky*).

STANISLAVSKY (*aside*): Damn the old fool! Now he wants me to poison myself! (*Aloud*). Thank you, sir. To your health, sir! (*Suddenly begins to sneeze*).

MIKHAILOV (*sympathetically*): You haven't caught a cold, sir, have you?

STANISLAVSKY (*takes out a little bottle from his pocket and pours some of its contents on his handkerchief, taking good care that the spectators see him do it*): Afraid I have. A nasty cold. However, I have a good remedy for it. (*Still sneezing, puts bottle on table*).

MIKHAILOV: What is it? May I have a look?

STANISLAVSKY: Do! (*Still sneezing*). Excuse me, sir, I shall have to retire for a minute. (*Goes quickly behind Mikhailov's chair while Mikhailov is picking up the bottle, then suddenly presses 'drugged' handkerchief to Mikhailov's face, making a sign to the landord to come near*).

MIKHAILOV (*realising that the game is up, dozes off*): I don't want to sleep—I mustn't sleep—

STANISLAVSKY (*to landlord*): Take him to the other room! (*To Verbitsky*). Now you realise how you should have acted, don't you? (*To the other actors*). I hope you now understand the meaning of the logic of physical actions and its importance in melodrama.

Index

Index